Generational Shockwaves and the Implications for Higher Education

Generational Shockwaves and the Implications for Higher Education

Edited by

Donald E. Heller

Center for the Study of Higher Education, The Pennsylvania State University, USA

and

Madeleine B. d'Ambrosio

TIAA-CREF Institute, USA

In association with TIAA-CREF

Edward Elgar

Cheltenham, UK • Northampton, MA, USA

Published by
Edward Elgar Publishing Limited
The Lypiatts
15 Lansdown Road
Cheltenham
Glos GL50 2JA
UK

Edward Elgar Publishing, Inc.
William Pratt House
9 Dewey Court
Northampton
Massachusetts 01060
USA

A catalogue record for this book
is available from the British Library

Library of Congress Cataloguing in Publication Data

Generational shockwaves and the implications for higher education / edited by Donald E. Heller and Madeleine B. d'Ambrosio.
     p. cm.
   Includes bibliographical references and index.
   1. Education, Higher–United States. 2. Conflict of generations–United States. 3. Universities and colleges–United States–Sociological aspects. 4. Educational change–United States. I. Heller, Donald E. II. d'Ambrosio, Madeleine, 1950-
   LA227.4.G46 2008
   378.73–dc22

2008023129

Mixed Sources
Product group from well-managed
forests and other controlled sources
www.fsc.org Cert no. SA-COC-1565
FSC   © 1996 Forest Stewardship Council

ISBN 978 1 84844 049 4

Printed and bound in Great Britain by MPG Books Ltd, Bodmin, Cornwall

Contents

Figures

Tables

Contributors

Authors

F. King Alexander was named the 6th President of California State University, Long Beach, in November of 2005 after serving as the President of Murray State University in Kentucky from 2001–05. He is a well-respected national expert in domestic and international higher education finance and public policy. His research on university revenue and expenditure patterns has been featured in *The Economist, The New York Times, The Chronicle of Higher Education, The Boston Globe, The Australian, and The Christian Science Monitor*. Due to his expertise in these areas, Alexander was recently named as chairperson of one of the three national committees responsible for developing the Voluntary System of Accountability (VSA) advanced by the Spellings Commission for the Future of Higher Education. He also was recently selected by the Under Secretary for Higher Education as part of a national task force to develop recommendations to improve federal and state needs-based student aid policies. Prior to serving as president of two public universities, Alexander was a faculty member and director of the Higher Education Program at the University of Illinois at Urbana-Champaign from 1997–2001. He received his PhD from the University of Wisconsin-Madison in higher education finance and public policy, a Master of Science degree from Oxford University (England) in comparative education policy and his undergraduate degree in political science from St. Lawrence University in New York.

Herbert M. Allison, Jr. was Chairperson, President, and Chief Executive Officer of TIAA-CREF (Teachers Insurance and Annuity Association-College Retirement Equities Fund) from 2002 to 2008. He joined TIAA-CREF in 2002 after a 28-year career at Merrill Lynch & Co., Inc., where he last served as President and Chief Operating Officer until 1999. His professional career began with Merrill Lynch in 1971, serving as an associate in investment banking in New York and he also held posts in Paris, London, and Tehran. He became President and Chief Operating Officer and a member of the board in 1997. In 2000, Herbert accepted a leadership role in a start-up academic organization, the Alliance for Lifelong Learning, Inc., a joint venture by Oxford, Stanford, and Yale Universities. There, as President and Chief Executive Officer, he helped build an online learning forum for adults that provided the highest-quality college-level courses. Herbert is Chairperson of the Business-Higher Education Forum and serves on the Advisory Board of the Yale School of Management as well as the Advisory Council of the Stanford Graduate School of Business. He earned a BA in philosophy from Yale University. Following a four-year tour of duty in the US Navy, including service in Vietnam, he earned an MBA from Stanford University.

Carol A. Cartwright is Interim President of Bowling Green State University in Bowling Green, Ohio. Previously, she served as Kent State University's president for more than 15 years. She was the university's 10th president and the first woman president of a state university in Ohio. Prior to her career at Kent State, she was Vice Chancellor for Academic Affairs at the University of California at Davis and Dean for Undergraduate Programs and Vice Provost at The Pennsylvania State University. Kent State's eight campuses serve more than 33 000 students from throughout Ohio and the nation, and from 100 countries. One of the largest employers in Northeast Ohio, the university employs more than 4600 full and part-time faculty and staff. Carol has also held prominent leadership roles in higher education's most influential national organizations, chairing the board of directors of the American Association for Higher Education and serving on the boards of directors of the American Council on Education and the National Association of State Universities and Land Grant Colleges. She chaired the National Collegiate Athletic Association (NCAA) Executive Committee and served as a member of the NCAA's board of directors. She also served on the executive board of the National Council for Accreditation of Teacher Education, the Center for Research Libraries board of directors and the American Council on Education Commission on Women in Higher Education. She currently serves on the board of directors of the American Association of Colleges and Universities, the Knight Commission on Intercollegiate Athletics and the National Public Radio board of directors. She is also a member of the Wilson Council and chairs the Board's Fellowship Committee of the Woodrow Wilson International Center for Scholars. Carol earned Master's and doctoral degrees from the University of Pittsburgh and her Bachelor's degree from the University of Wisconsin at Whitewater.

Madeleine B. d'Ambrosio is Vice President and Executive Director of the TIAA-CREF Institute. She joined TIAA-CREF in 1975 as an Institutional Consultant. She spent nine years counseling colleges, universities, and other not-for-profit institutions on all aspects of their employee benefit programs. From 1984 until 1994 as Vice President, Institutional Counseling, she had management responsibilities for the design and administration of institutional benefit plans and the counseling and financial education of participants. During this time Madeleine introduced TIAA-CREF Financial Education Seminars, including a special financial education program for women. In 1994 she was named Vice President of Education and Financial Support Services responsible for training, financial guidance, and advice for participants, FINRA (Financial Industry Regulatory Authority) and SEC (US Securities and Exchange Commission) compliance, and further development of educational seminars on topics important to the financial well-being of individuals and families. In 1998 Madeleine was appointed the first Executive Director of the TIAA-CREF Institute. She received her BA degree from Manhattanville College and is a Certified Employee Benefit Specialist.

Ronald G. Ehrenberg is the Irving M. Ives Professor of Industrial and Labor Relations and Economics at Cornell University and a Stephen H. Weiss Presidential Fellow. He is Director of the Cornell Higher Education Research Institute and an elected member of the Cornell Board of Trustees. From 1995 to 1998 he served as Cornell's Vice President for Academic Programs, Planning and Budgeting. A noted labor economist and co-author of the leading textbook, *Modern Labor Economics: Theory and Public Policy* (10th edition, 2008), his recent research has focused on higher education issues. He is the editor of *American University: National Treasure or Endangered Species* (1997), the author of *Tuition Rising: Why College Costs So Much* (2000), the editor of *Governing Academia* (2004) and *What's Happening to Public Higher Education?* (2006), and the co-editor of *Science and the University* (2007), *Transformational Change in Higher Education: Positioning Colleges and University for future Success* (2007), and *Doctoral Education and the Faculty of the Future* (2008). Ehrenberg received a BA in mathematics from Harpur College (SUNY Binghamton) in 1966 and a PhD in economics from Northwestern University in 1970, and an honorary doctorate of science from the State University of New York in 2008. Dr Ehrenberg is a TIAA-CREF Institute Fellow.

Martin Finkelstein is Professor of Higher Education at Seton Hall University. He received his PhD from the State University of New York at Buffalo in 1978. Since then, he has taught at the University of Denver and Teacher's College, Columbia University and has served as a Visiting Scholar at the Claremont Graduate University and the Research Institute for Higher Education, Hiroshima University, Japan. Between 1989 and 1997, he served as the Executive Director of the New Jersey Institute for Collegiate Teaching and Learning. He is the author of *The American Academic Profession* (1988) and *The New Academic Generation* (with Robert Seal and Jack Schuster, 1998). His new book with Jack Schuster,

The American Faculty: The Restructuring of Academic Work and Careers, was published in early 2006.

Donald W. Harward served as President of Bates College from 1989 through June 2002. Before taking the office at Bates, Donald served as Vice President for Academic Affairs at The College of Wooster in Ohio; preceding his tenure there, he taught and served in the Department of Philosophy at the University of Delaware, and subsequently designed and led the university's Honors Program. He holds a PhD in philosophy from the University of Maryland, and has served as a senior advisor for the ACE Fellows Program and is a senior fellow with AAC&U (Association of American Colleges and Universities). He served as the consultant for the joint AAC&U and Campus Compact Project to establish a national Center for Liberal Education and Civic Engagement, and has, from its inception in 2003, served as the Director of the Bringing Theory to Practice Project— a national effort to understand and promote outcomes of liberal education, including those of student well-being and their civic development. The project is a partnership of the Charles Engelhard Foundation of New York City and the AAC&U, the largest and oldest professional association committed to liberal education.

Mark Heckler became the 18th president of Valparaiso University in July 2008, where he also holds a tenured appointment as Professor of Theatre. He was previously the Provost and Vice Chancellor for Academic and Student Affairs at the University of Colorado Denver. Mark arrived in Colorado in 1995 where he served as Director of the School of the Arts and Professor of Theatre, Film, and Television and later became founding Dean of the College of Arts and Media. Mark was Director of Theatre and Chair of the Department of Fine Arts at Siena College in Albany, NY, a post he held from 1979. As an actor, director, and designer for the stage, Mark has over 100 academic and professional productions to his credit, including performances throughout the United States, Europe, and the Middle East. Active for over a decade in international education, Mark has been heavily involved in innovative educational and research partnerships in China, Russia, Africa and the European Union.

Donald E. Heller is Professor of Education and Senior Scientist, and Director of the Center for the Study of Higher Education, at The Pennsylvania State University. He teaches and conducts research on higher education economics, public policy, and finance, with a primary focus on issues of college access and choice for low-income and minority students. He is the editor of the books *State Postsecondary Education Research: New Methods to Inform Policy and Practice* (with K. Shaw, 2007), *Condition of*

Access: Higher Education for Lower Income Students (2002), and *The States and Public Higher Education Policy: Affordability, Access, and Accountability* (2000). Donald has testified in front of Congressional committees, state legislatures, and in federal court cases as an expert witness. He earned an EdD in higher education from the Harvard Graduate School of Education, and holds an EdM in administration, planning, and social policy from Harvard and a BA in economics and political science from Tufts University. Before his academic career, he spent a decade as an information technology manager at the Massachusetts Institute of Technology. Donald received the 2002 Promising Scholar/Early Career Achievement Award from the Association for the Study of Higher Education, a scholarly society with over 1500 members dedicated to higher education as a field of study. He was also the recipient in 2001 of the Robert P. Huff Golden Quill Award from the National Association of Student Financial Aid Administrators, for his contributions to the literature on student financial aid. Dr Heller is a TIAA-CREF Institute Fellow.

Neil Howe is a historian, economist, and demographer who writes and speaks frequently on generational change in American history and on long-term fiscal policy. He is co-founder of LifeCourse Associates, a marketing, HR, and strategic planning consultancy serving corporate, government, and non-profit clients. He has co-authored many books with William Strauss, including *Generations* (1991), *13th Gen* (1993), *The Fourth Turning* (1997), and *Millennials Rising* (2000). His other co-authored books include *On Borrowed Time* (1988). He is also a senior associate at the Center for Strategic and International Studies, where he helps lead the CSIS "Global Aging Initiative," and a senior advisor to the Concord Coalition. He holds graduate degrees in history and economics from Yale University.

D. Bruce Johnstone is Distinguished Service Professor of Higher and Comparative Education Emeritus at the State University of New York at Buffalo. Before he retired in July 2006, he specialized in higher education finance, governance, and policy formation, and in international comparative higher education. He was Director of the Center for Comparative and Global Studies in Education. He continues to direct the International Comparative Higher Education Finance and Accessibility Project, a multi-year examination into the worldwide shift of higher education costs from governments and taxpayers to parents and students, as well as to write, lecture, and consult in international higher education finance. In a 25-year administrative career, Johnstone has held posts of Vice President for Administration at the University of Pennsylvania, President of the State University College of Buffalo, and Chancellor of the State University of New York System, the latter from 1988 through 1994. He holds a BA in economics from Harvard, an MAT from Harvard's Graduate School of Education, and a PhD in higher education from the University of Minnesota. He has honorary doctorates from California State University San Diego, Towson State University, and D'Youville College. Dr Johnstone is a TIAA-CREF Institute Fellow.

Rebecca Klein-Collins is the Director of Research for the Council for Adult and Experiential Learning. Her research projects have included analyzing state adult learning data and policies, identifying the exemplary workforce development practices of employers, assessing the impact of employer-funded tuition programs on employee retention, and describing innovative, system-transforming practices in workforce development. She has a Bachelor's degree from Grinnell College and Master's degrees from Indiana University and the University of Chicago, Harris School of Public Policy.

Valerie Martin Conley is Associate Professor of Higher Education and Director of the Center for Higher Education, Ohio University. She specializes in quantitative applications for educational policy and research drawing upon her experience as a consultant to the US Department of Education's National Center for Education Statistics (NCES). Valerie teaches courses on institutional research, assessment, management of higher education, and policy. In June 2007, she received the Ohio University Outstanding Graduate Faculty Award. Valerie's work has been published by the US Department of Education, *Research in Higher Education*, and *Academe*. She co-edited (with David Leslie) *New Ways to Phase into Retirement: Options for Faculty and Institutions* (2006) and she regularly writes on retirement and benefits for the National Education Association's *Higher Education Almanac*. Her 2008 chapter was titled *Retirement and Benefits: Shifting Responsibilities*. A former institutional researcher, she is currently serving on the board of directors for the Association for Institutional Research (AIR) and chairs the association's Higher Education Data Policy Committee. She received her PhD (2002) in educational leadership and policy studies from Virginia Tech (Blacksburg, VA) and her MA (1990) and BA (1987) in sociology from the University of Virginia (Charlottesville, VA). Dr Conley is a TIAA-CREF Institute Fellow.

Virginia Michelich is the Vice President for Academic and Student Affairs at Georgia Perimeter College (GPC), a multi-campus institution with five campuses located in the metro-Atlanta area. As the Chief Academic and Student Affairs Officer of the College, Virginia is responsible for ensuring excellence in the breadth and quality of academic programs and student affairs services.

She is the college's liaison to the Board of Regents of the University System of Georgia for both academic and student affairs. Virginia holds the rank of Professor of Biology and has served the college as a faculty member and department chairperson of science. She earned a BA in microbiology from the University of Missouri and a PhD in microbiology from the University of Minnesota. Virginia served as an instructor for the Medical College of Georgia prior to teaching at GPC. She has received the Regents' Distinguished Professor of Teaching and Learning and the Faculty Recognition Award from the Consortium for Community College Development. In 1999, she was awarded a Board of Regents' Teaching and Learning grant to develop technology-infused and online courses.

Reena Nadler is the program director of LifeCourse Associates, a marketing, HR, and strategic planning consultancy founded by best-selling authors and generational experts William Strauss and Neil Howe. She works with the authors to give corporate, government, and non-profit clients powerful insights into who today's generation are, how they interact with each other, and how they will shape our national future. Most recently, she helped write the newly released second edition of *Millennials Go to College* (2007), about today's rising generation of young people and how they are transforming higher education. She is currently working on two more books, *Millennials in K-12 Schools* and *Millennials in the Workplace*. Reena has collaborated with Howe and Strauss on articles appearing in a variety of publications, most recently the *Harvard Business Review*. A graduate of Swarthmore College and a first-wave Millennial herself, she brings a first-hand perspective to the authors' work on today's youth generation.

Kenneth E. Redd is a Senior Fellow at the Institute for Higher Education, University of Georgia, and also serves as Director of Research and Policy Analysis for the Council of Graduate Schools (CGS). In his positions Ken provides research and data analysis on graduate school financial aid, enrollments, degrees conferred, and international admissions, applications, and enrollments. Prior to joining CGS, Ken served as Director of Research and Policy Analysis for the National Association of Student Financial Aid Administrators, and also served in various research and policy analysis positions for other organizations. Ken is the author or co-author of numerous research reports, book chapters, and journal articles on a wide variety of issues in higher education. He also serves on the board of directors for the Sallie Mae Fund, on the advisory panel for the National Postsecondary Student Aid Study and the Baccalaureate and Beyond Longitudinal Study. Ken holds a Master's degree in public affairs from the University of Minnesota, and a Bachelor's degree in English and political science from Tufts University.

Phyllis Snyder is Vice President of the Council for Adult and Experiential Learning. She has consulted with organizations to increase the quality and availability of learning opportunities for their workforce during the last 13 years. With funding from the US Department of Labor, she has designed a Nursing Career Lattice program using the apprenticeship model that has been implemented in nine states. She has studied the implications of the aging workforce on business and has developed programs to help address the transition to an encore career. She is a graduate of Smith College and holds Master's degrees in education from Harvard University and in city planning from the University of Pennsylvania.

Karen Steinberg joined the Council for Adult and Experiential Learning (CAEL) as its first Executive Vice President in 2002. Prior to joining CAEL, Karen was the Senior Vice Chancellor for Administration and Finance, United States Open University (USOU), a nationally accredited, not-for-profit, online university established in 1998 by the British Open University to serve adult students. From 1985 through 1999, Karen was Senior Deputy to the Chancellor with the University and Community College System of Nevada. She holds a BA degree in English from California State University at Chico and a Master's degree in public administration and public policy from the University of Nevada, Reno.

William Strauss, who passed away in December 2007, was a speaker, writer, historian, playwright, theater director, and performer. He was an authority on generational change in American history and the co-founder of LifeCourse Associates, a marketing, HR, and strategic planning consultancy serving corporate, government, and non-profit clients. He co-authored many books with Neil Howe, including *Generations* (1991), *13th Gen* (1993), *The Fourth Turning* (1997), and *Millennials Rising* (2000). He was the co-founder and director of the Capitol Steps satirical troupe, for which he performed up until his death, and wrote three musicals and two plays. In 1999, William co-founded the Cappies, now an international high school "Critics and Awards" program, and in 2006 and 2007 he advised the creative student teams that wrote the musicals *Edit: Undo* and *Senioritis*. William held graduate degrees from Harvard Law School and the Kennedy School of Government.

Teresa A. Sullivan became Provost and Executive Vice President for Academic Affairs at the University of Michigan on 1 June 2006. She is also Professor of Sociology in the College of Literature, Science, and the Arts. Prior to joining the University of Michigan, Teresa was Executive Vice Chancellor for Academic Affairs for the University of Texas System, a position she held from 2002 until May 2006. In that role, she was the Chief

Academic Officer for the nine academic campuses within the University of Texas System. Her responsibilities included developing tuition-setting procedures, initiating and supporting educational and research collaborations among the various campuses, and developing external collaborations. Teresa first joined the University of Texas at Austin in 1975 as an instructor and then Assistant Professor in the Department of Sociology. From 1977–81, she was a faculty member at the University of Chicago. Teresa returned to Texas in 1981 as a faculty member in the Sociology Department. In 1986 she was named to the Law School faculty as well. Teresa also held several administrative positions at Texas including: Vice President and Graduate Dean (1995–2002), Vice Provost (1994–95), Chair of the Department of Sociology (1990–92), and Director of Women's Studies (1985–87). A graduate of James Madison College at Michigan State University, Teresa received her doctoral degree in sociology from the University of Chicago. She is a TIAA-CREF Institute Fellow.

Cathy A. Trower is Research Associate at Harvard University, Graduate School of Education. Her current project, entitled the "Collaborative on Academic Careers in Higher Education," has as a primary purpose making the academy a more attractive and equitable place for new teacher-scholars by giving voice to pre-tenure faculty about the quality of their work life and their level of satisfaction with the workplace including climate, clarity of tenure, and promotion processes and criteria, professional development opportunities, and the equity of policies and practices. A secondary purpose of the project is to increase the recruitment, retention, status, success, and satisfaction of faculty of color and white women. Cathy has studied faculty employment issues, policy, and practices for the past 14 years during which she produced an edited volume, numerous book chapters, articles, and case studies. Cathy has made dozens of presentations over the past several years on tenure policies and practices, faculty recruitment strategies, and the issues of women and minority faculty. Previously, Cathy served as a senior-level administrator of business degree programs at Johns Hopkins University with responsibility for corporate and community alliances. She has an MBA and a BBA from the University of Iowa and earned a PhD in higher education administration at the University of Maryland, College Park. Dr Trower is a TIAA-CREF Institute Fellow.

Conference panelists and moderators

F. King Alexander (see list of authors)
Herbert M. Allison, Jr. (see list of authors)
Andrew K. Benton, President, Pepperdine University
Janet Bickel, Principal, Janet Bickel & Associates

Father Lawrence Biondi, President, Saint Louis University
Linda Bunnell, Chancellor, University of Wisconsin, Stevens Point
Carol A. Cartwright (see list of authors)
Madeleine B. d'Ambrosio (see list of authors)
Ronald G. Ehrenberg (see list of authors)
Joan Girgus, Professor of Psychology and Special Assistant to the Dean of the Faculty, Princeton University
Robert Glidden, President Emeritus, Ohio University
Richard Guarasci, President, Wagner College
Donald W. Harward (see list of authors)
Mark Heckler (see list of authors)
Julie K. Little, Associate Director, EDUCAUSE
John Lombardi, President, Louisiana State University System
Virginia Michelich (see list of authors)
Steven G. Poskanzer, President, SUNY New Paltz
Kenneth P. Ruscio, President, Washington and Lee University
Lou Anna K. Simon, President, Michigan State University
Debra W. Stewart, President, Council of Graduate Schools
William Strauss (see list of authors)
Teresa A. Sullivan (see list of authors)
Jerry Sue Thornton, President, Cuyahoga Community College
Lee T. Todd, President, University of Kentucky
Nancy Uscher, Provost, California Institute of the Arts
Michael K. Young, President, The University of Utah

Foreword

Herbert M. Allison, Jr.

TIAA-CREF (Teachers Insurance and Annuity Association-College Retirement Equities Fund) is pleased to partner with the higher education community by offering forums such as the TIAA-CREF Institute National Higher Education Leadership Conference where leaders can share their perspectives on critical issues that affect the academic community. In November 2007, the Institute hosted university presidents, chancellors, and other senior officials at the "Generational Shockwaves: Implications for Higher Education" conference. The sessions addressed the growing challenge of managing faculty, staff and students from different generations, often with very different perspectives and priorities—and how this ever-widening generational gap is impacting their institutions.

Over the course of the event, conversations focused on three key generations of students and employees—the Baby Boomers, Generation X, and the Millennials—and their influence on both the pedagogical and operational aspects of higher education. Colleges and universities are compelled—by the realities of addressing aging faculty, retaining talented professors and researchers, and attracting new ones—to accommodate the particular goals and circumstances of each generation while adhering to the missions and values of their institutions. It is our collective responsibility and challenge to fulfill the expectations of today's college and university students and faculty, while preparing to meet the needs of generations to come. As all of us rethink strategies for effective institutional evolution, we must consider how to meet the often divergent needs of these groups.

This book includes chapters authored by prominent thought leaders who have synthesized the themes and discussions of the conference and also further elaborated on issues and challenges raised. Additionally, it represents the contributions of the more than 100 higher education thought leaders who attended. All of us at TIAA-CREF are appreciative of their efforts.

TIAA-CREF's historic mission remains constant: to aid and strengthen institutions of higher education by offering strategic expertise focused on the specific needs of colleges and universities and by seeking to provide lifelong financial security through our comprehensive financial services capabilities and advisory services. As competition for faculty and students increases, and institutions adjust to meet those evolving needs, TIAA-CREF is committed to being their trusted partner.

NOTE

TIAA-CREF Individual & Institutional Services, LLC and Teachers Personal Investors Services, Inc., members FINRA (Financial Industry Regulatory Authority), distribute securities products. Advisory services are provided by Advice and Planning Services, a division of TIAA-CREF Individual & Institutional Services, LLC, a registered investment advisor.

C40914

Introduction

Donald E. Heller

The forces of demographics have brought our nation to a critical point. The Baby Boom Generation, which has so influenced the country since the first Boomers were born as World War II was coming to a close, is beginning to near retirement. Kathleen Casey-Kirschling had the distinction of being the first Baby Boomer to file for Social Security benefits on 15 October 2007, an act one newspaper noted as being "one giant leap for her Baby Boom generation—and a symbolic jump toward the retirement system's looming bankruptcy" (Wolf, 2007, 1A).

American colleges and universities as we know them today have been greatly influenced by the Baby Boomers. The great growth of higher education in the 1960s, which saw the creation of new community colleges and the expansion of public four-year institutions, was in large part driven by the demands for postsecondary training by Baby Boomers. Many of these college students moved on to become the core of the faculty teaching and conducting research in these institutions today. And like Ms. Casey-Kirschling, they too will soon be facing decisions about retirement.

But Baby Boomers are not the only generation of Americans who have, and are, influencing colleges and universities across the country. The two subsequent generations, Generation X and the Millennials, as they have been named, have also helped to shape these institutions. Members of Generation X, which followed the Baby Boomers and were born largely in the 1960s and 1970s, placed new demands on college faculty when they entered postsecondary education. Many of these students have become the younger cohort of faculty who are today helping to teach the Millennial Generation of students, those born since 1980. Millennial students, with their focus on multitasking and integration of technology into all aspects of their lives, have helped to shape the way that education is delivered. In some cases, this means replacing a mode of instruction that has largely dominated for centuries, the notion of the "sage on the stage," or the lone faculty member standing up in front of a group of students.

The TIAA-CREF Institute 2007 National Higher Education Leadership Conference addressed these issues in a symposium titled, "Generational Shockwaves: Implications for Higher Education." The conference drew over 100 college presidents, faculty, and administrators to New York City on 1 and 2 November 2007 to hear a variety of speakers discuss these issues. The dialogue revolved around the impact of these three generations currently populating campuses: Baby Boomers, Generation X, and Millennials.

This book presents the findings from that conference, summarizing the presentations made by the college leaders who spoke there, as well as contributions from other leaders and scholars who have researched the impact of these generations on American higher education. The book opens (Chapter 1) with an overview of how different generations have impacted the country in general, and higher education in particular, during the 20th century and the early part of the 21st century. Neil Howe, the late William Strauss, and Reena Nadler describe each of the generations and how they have helped to shape—and have been shaped by—colleges and universities across the country.

D. Bruce Johnstone, the former Chancellor of the State University of New York System and President of the State University College of Buffalo, presents in Chapter 2 the perspective of a college leader on how the new generations of students are causing colleges to examine who they are and how they serve these students. He examines how what are often described as change-resistant institutions are able to transform themselves to meet these new demands. Following this examination of the impact of Millennial students, Ronald Ehrenberg turns in Chapter 3 to the impact of Generation X on colleges. He summarizes the discussions of a panel he moderated at the conference, which focused on how Generation X—largely represented on campus today by the younger cohort of faculty—has influenced the work environment for these young professors.

The impact of Generation X faculty is discussed further in Chapter 4 by Cathy A. Trower, a researcher at the Harvard Graduate School of Education. She presents the work she has done on the demands for a changing workplace presented by this generation of faculty members. Unlike the previous generation, these new faculty have very different expectations for balancing work and family life, and Trower describes how universities are responding to these demands.

The next two chapters (5 and 6) focus on the Millennial Generation, who in large part make up the student body on most college campuses today. Donald W. Harward, former President of Bates College, summarizes in Chapter 5 the presentations from a panel on Millennial students that he moderated at the conference. Much of the discussion at this session revolved around the relationships between Millennials and their parents, as well as how Millennials use technology in their daily lives, and the requirements these relationships place on colleges and universities today. In Chapter 6, Kenneth E. Redd, Director of Research and Policy Analysis for the Council of Graduate Schools, describes how universities need to adapt in the race for recruiting and retaining Millennial students on their campuses. As he describes it, the Millennial Generation has "rising diversity, aspirations, and wealth" in comparison to earlier cohorts of students. These changes, along with the other characteristics of Millennial students noted by other authors in this volume, have forced higher education institutions to adopt new enrollment management strategies and techniques.

From the subject of recruiting and retaining students in Chapter 6, Chapter 7, by Martin Finkelstein, focuses on recruiting and retaining the next generation of college faculty. Finkelstein, a long-time scholar of the American professoriate currently at Seton Hall University, begins by providing a brief history of how different generations of faculty have worked on our campuses. He then builds on Trower's contribution by documenting how colleges and universities have adapted how they construct faculty employment arrangements. These changes have been driven, he notes, not just by the demands of the new generation of faculty members, but also by outside pressures facing colleges and universities.

In Chapter 8, Carol A. Cartwright summarizes the conference panel on the Baby Boom Generation and its impact on higher education. As noted earlier, Baby Boomers helped to drive the expansion of the postsecondary sector during the second half of the 20th century, and make up the core of the faculty (and administration) today. The presenters at this session, all college presidents, described how their campuses have evolved under the influence of Baby Boomers, and how they are likely to change in the coming years as more Boomers move into retirement.

Chapter 9, by Karen Steinberg, Phyllis Snyder, and Rebecca Klein-Collins of the Council for Adult and Experiential Learning, moves beyond the gates of academe to examine how the broader implications of the retirement of the Baby Boom Generation are likely to affect higher education. They note that many Boomers, in contrast to earlier generations, expect to be much more active during retirement and thus, will be looking to colleges and universities to provide them with lifelong learning. This will present both opportunities and challenges for these institutions.

Valerie Martin Conley, a higher education scholar at Ohio University, next (Chapter 10) addresses the fiscal and legal issues institutions and their employees will be facing as Baby Boomers move into retirement. Since Congress legislated the elimination of mandatory retirement for faculty approximately 15 years ago, the courts have put certain constraints on what colleges and universities can do with respect toward encouraging faculty members and other employees to retire. This chapter addresses some of these constraints, along with the financial concerns faced both by the institutions and their employees.

The TIAA-CREF Conference included three breakout sessions, where the participants had an opportunity to discuss in a smaller group setting these generational issues. In Chapter 11, Mark Heckler of Valparaiso University, Virginia Michelich of Georgia Perimeter College, and Teresa A. Sullivan of the University of Michigan summarize the discussions in these breakout groups. The participants had a wide range of views about different generations of faculty and students, and how their institutions were responding to and were shaped by each.

In the concluding chapter of the book, Chapter 12, F. King Alexander, President of California State University, Long Beach, discusses some troubling trends in the higher education policy arena that threaten college access for future generations of college students. Alexander outlines the forces that are moving the nation in this direction, and provides recommendations for ways in which the country can recommit to the goal of promoting access for under-represented populations of students.

A note about generational definitions: you will observe that the authors of this volume use varying year boundaries in their classification of Baby Boomers, Generation X, and Millennials. This is not unusual, as there is no standard definition of each agreed upon by researchers, journalists, and even demographers. For example, while William Strauss and Neil Howe (1991) define the Baby Boom Generation as those Americans born between 1943 and 1960, the United States Census Bureau (2001) uses 1946 and 1964 as the boundary years. Similarly, Strauss and Howe categorize Generation X as those born between 1961 and 1981, while the Census Bureau (Crowley, 2003) uses 1968 and 1979. As one article noted, "Generations have a natural fluidity—it can be hard to say where one group ends and the next begins. . . . If you aim for precision in defining a generation, you can end up being imprecise" (Bader, 2008, p. 3). Because of these differences, the chapters in this volume use varying definitions of each group, and these definitions are noted throughout.

REFERENCES

Bader, J.L. (2008), "In the eye of the beholder: when a boom begins," *The New York Times*, 17 February, 3.

Crowley, M. (2003), "Generation X speaks out on civic engagement and the decennial census: an ethnographic approach," June, Washington, DC: United States Census Bureau.

Strauss, W. and N. Howe (1991), *Generations: The History of America's Future, 1584 to 2069*, New York: William Morrow.

United States Census Bureau (2001), *Age: 2000, Census 2000 Brief* (C2KBR/01-12) October, Washington, DC: USCB.

Wolf, R. (2007) "Social Security hits first wave of boomers; drain on the system picks up in Jan., when millions born in '46 start taking benefits," *USA Today*, 9 October, 1A.

1. Generations of Americans: a big picture look at the future of higher education

Neil Howe, William Strauss, and Reena Nadler

"I Am a Student! Do Not Fold, Spindle, or Mutilate!" read the signs of picketers outside Berkeley's Sproul Hall in 1964, mocking the computer-punchcard treatment the university was supposedly giving them. Through the postwar years, Americans had grown used to talking about a conformist Silent Generation of college students. Now, a new generation was arriving, the Boomer children raised in the aftermath of World War II. These megaphone-toting, confrontational students launched a "Consciousness Revolution" to demand that their war-hero elders live up to higher moral standards.

Twenty years later, US campuses experienced another surprising shift. The *Wall Street Journal* noted in the late 1980s, "It is college presidents, deans, and faculties—not students—who are the zealots and chief enforcers of Political Correctness" ("Politically correct," 1990). The new batch of students, born during the Consciousness Revolution—children of rising divorce, latchkeys, and ad hoc day care—showed much less ideological passion. These Gen Xers left the moralizing to older people as they brought a new pragmatism to the nation's campuses.

Today—40 years later—graying college leaders on the verge of retirement continue to carry the ideological torch, crusading for various causes in ways that often irritate their younger Generation X faculty. Meanwhile, newly arriving undergraduates are showing yet another generational personality. Born after the Consciousness Revolution, this rising Millennial Generation is generally upbeat, team-oriented, close to their parents, and confident about their future. Unlike Boomers, they do not want to "teach the world to sing."[1] Unlike Xers, they would rather plan ahead than "just do it."

How do we explain the changes in 20-year-olds from self-absorbed moralizers in the 1960s to busy and risk-averse achievers today? To understand such dramatic shifts, we must recognize that these very different groups of young people are from distinct generations. The moral megaphones have remained in the hands of aging Boomers, while the two generations of youth who came after have developed their own very different personas. To learn what makes these three (or indeed any) generations different, we need to ask how they were raised as children, what public events they witnessed in adolescence, and what social mission elders gave them as they came of age.

Understanding the personas of today's generations can inspire powerful insights into what motivates them as consumers and workers. For example, today's 60-year-olds have a very different set of attitudes and priorities overall than 60-year-olds did 20 years ago, and as younger generations pass through this age bracket in the decades ahead, their attitudes and priorities will shift yet again. Most companies and institutions desperately seek clues about future swings in a particular age group—but most fail to understand that the key to predicting these swings is to look at the next generation due to "age into" that target zone.

THE GENERATIONAL CONSTELLATION

During the Middle Ages, travelers reported an unusual custom among villagers in central France. Whenever an event of local importance occurred, the elders boxed the ears of a young child to make sure he or she remembered that day—and event—all his or her life.

Like those medieval French villagers, each of us carries deeply felt associations with what has happened at various points in our lives. Public events like Pearl Harbor, the Kennedy and King assassinations, the *Challenger* explosion, and 9/11 burn so deeply into our consciousness that it is impossible to forget what we were doing at the time. As we grow older, we realize that the sum total of such events has in many ways made us who we are. Exactly *how* these major events shaped us has much to do with how old we were when they happened.

This is what constitutes a generation: historical events shape peer groups, and shape them differently depending on the phase of life they occupy. Then, as each generation ages into the next phase of life—from youth to young adulthood to midlife to elderhood—its attitudes and behaviors mature and develop, producing new currents in the public mood. People, in other words, do not "belong" to their age bracket. A woman who is 45 is not on common ground with 45-year-old women across the ages. Rather, she belongs to a generation that happens to be passing through an age bracket—a generation united by memories, language, habits, beliefs, and life lessons.

Nineteen generations have lived on American soil since the 1620s. Each is a series of consecutive birth years, spanning roughly 20 years, whose members grew up and came of age during the same defining historical era, and, as a consequence, exhibit distinct beliefs and behavior.

Let's take a closer look at the six generations that are alive today, their life stories, and their collective personas. For those generations whose presence will still be vital 20 years from now, we will also examine how they are likely to develop in the years ahead as they enter the next phase of life.

The GI Generation (GI is a term describing members of the US armed forces, and is thought to stand for "government issue.")

Born 1901–24, now aged 84–107, the GI Generation grew up after the "Great Awakening" of the late 19th century. They enjoyed a "good kid" reputation as the beneficiaries of new playgrounds, scouting clubs, vitamins, and child-labor restrictions. They came of age with the sharpest rise in school achievement ever recorded. Parents, educators, and leaders were determined to protect this generation from the corrupting social forces of the 1920s, and to foster a new wave of youth civic engagement through the crisis years of the 1930s. As young adults, GIs were the first Miss Americas and All-American athletes. Their various uniformed corps (Civilian Conservation Corps, Work Projects Administration) patiently endured the Depression, after which they conquered more oceans and continents than any other fighting generation in world history. In midlife they were subsidized by the GI Bill and built up the postwar economic system, facilitating upward mobility, erecting suburbs, inventing vaccines, plugging missile gaps, and launching moon rockets. Their gaps in family wealth and income were relatively small.

The GIs reveled in the strength of the family as a stable institution, but no generation in the history of polling got along worse with its children. They were greatly invested in civic life, institutions, and community, and focused more on actions and behavior than on values and beliefs. Their unprecedented grip on the presidency (1961 through 1992) began with the New Frontier, Great Society, and Model Cities, but wore down through Vietnam, Watergate, Iran-Contra, and budget deficits. This generation also formed a cadre of top-quality female educators at a time when women were blocked from many other careers.

The first American elders to call themselves "senior citizens," GIs have continued to preside over institutional structures late into elderhood, but have kept little influence over culture and values. Having lifted America from the Depression to economic prosperity, they later developed a powerful new senior lobby, safeguarded their "entitlements," and gathered a hefty array of senior benefits. The new senior subsidies (including a newly powerful Social Security) allowed this generation to vacate the workplace, voluntarily, as the youngest retirees in US history. Millions of retiring GIs separated into seniors-only communities, often far from their adult children, where they settled into a cheerful, vigorous leisure world. Reflecting their upbeat new emphasis on active aging, *Modern Maturity* magazine refused to accept ads that suggested physical decline. Those who are still alive today are mostly in dependent care.

The Silent Generation

Born 1925–42, now aged 66–83, the Silent Generation grew up as the seen-but-not-heard "Li'l Rascals" of the Great Depression and Shirley Temples of World War II. They were the least immigrant generation in American history. They came of age just too late to be war heroes and just too early to be youthful free spirits. Instead, they became, like James Dean, "rebels without a cause," part of a "lonely crowd" of risk-averse technicians in an era in which conformity seemed to be a sure ticket to success. A vast new gap emerged between women's and men's education as this generation became the youngest mothers and fathers in American history, joining older GIs in gleaming new suburbs. They rode the wave of institutional civic life and conventional culture established by GIs as gray-flannel *How to Succeed in Business Without Really Trying*[2] corporate careerists.

Come the 1960s, the Silents stopped taking their cues from up the age ladder, and instead started looking down—following the lead of Bob Dylan ("Ah, but I was so much older then, I'm younger than that now"[3]). They became America's leading civil rights activists, rock 'n' rollers, antiwar leaders, feminists, public interest lawyers, and mentors for young firebrands. They were America's moms and dads during the divorce epidemic. They rose to political power after Watergate, with their Congressional leadership marked by a push toward institutional complexity and vast expansion in legal process. To date, they are the first generation never to produce a US president (John McCain, born in 1936 would be their first if he gets elected in the 2008 election), and the first never to produce a Chief Justice of the Supreme Court of the United States.

As educators, the Silents set the tone for the nation's schools during the 1970s and 1980s—a time of experimentation. Of all of today's generations, they seem the most tolerant of diverse points of view, and also the most disappointed by the venom of culture wars polarization. They were very influential on campuses during the 1990s, and remain important today as trustees and senior faculty of many universities. As graying leaders, they have focused on discussion, inclusion, and process, but not on decisive action.

Having benefited from the collective upward mobility of the GI economic machine, the Silents are spending elderhood with a hip style and unprecedented affluence. Where retirement once meant a vanilla-flavored GI public reward, the Silents see it as full of options as they yearn to stay involved with what everyone else is doing. Seniors-only communities are losing popularity as Silent tastemakers prefer townhomes within reach of restaurants, theaters, and sports arenas populated by younger people. Long a generation of reliable donors, they have become renowned senior philanthropists, providing unprecedented support to fine arts and sophisticated cultural institutions. Many are finding their links with grandchildren weakened by their own (and their children's) divorces, but are now working to rebuild broken family relationships. In the decades to come, the Silents will enter late elderhood, and other than the occasional octogenarian advisor, into increasing dependence and disengagement from public life.

The Boom Generation

Born 1943–60, now aged 48–65, the Boom Generation grew up as indulged youth during the post-World War II era of community-spirited progress. Parents, educators, and leaders were determined to raise young people who would never follow a Hitler, Stalin, or Orwellian "Big Brother." As kids, Boomers were the proud creation of postwar optimism, Dr. Spock rationalism, and *Father Knows Best*[4] family order. Coming of age, they loudly proclaimed their rejection of the secular blueprints of their parents. They scorned institutions, civic participation, and team-playing while pushing toward inner-life, self-perfection, and personal meaning. There was quite a bit of screaming—on the streets, in dorms, and in families. Crime rates, substance abuse, and sexual risk-taking all surged, while academic achievement and SAT scores[5] started to fall. The Consciousness Revolution climaxed with Vietnam War protests, the "summer of love" (1967), Chicago Democratic Convention (1968), Woodstock (1969), and Kent State (1970).

In the 1970s, Boomer women began challenging the "glass ceiling" in the workplace. Both genders began designating themselves the arbiters of the nation's values, crowding into such "culture" or "mind" careers as teaching, religion, journalism, law, marketing, and the arts. During the 1980s, Boomers were the "yuppie" individualists in an era of deregulation, tax cuts, and entrepreneurial business. During the 1990s, they trumpeted a "culture war," touted a divisive "politics of meaning," and waged scorched-earth political battles. Their two presidents (Bill Clinton and George W. Bush) each attracted powerful enmities among their peers. As family heads, Boomers have developed very close individual relationships with their children, to the point of hovering. From first-to-last cohort, they have been a generation of declining economic prosperity. On the brink of old age, their economic outcomes are vastly divergent. Many have vast wealth, but many more have little-to-no net worth.

Boomer teachers have dominated America's K–12[6] and college class-rooms for the past two decades—and they often still consider their peers at colleges and universities a key part of how their generation has made, and is continuing to make, its unique mark on the world. They are now at their peak of influence in universities, the US Congress, and the White House. What are they doing with this authority? The same generation that once demanded "unconditional amnesty," pass-fail courses, and a "don't fold, spindle, or mutilate" anti-computer ethos is now imposing zero tolerance, more homework, and a wide array of tests on their own children.

What comes next: the aging of Boomers

As Boomers reach the traditional age of retirement, many will remain involved in the working world. The very word *retirement* will acquire a neg-ative meaning, connoting indolence and mindless consumption. The new goal will not be to retire, but to replenish or reflect—if not simply to keep working. With this anti-retirement ethic, Boomers will in part be making a virtue out of necessity: compared with the Silent Generation, Boomers (especially late-wave Boomers) have experienced less real income growth, have less saved, and expect to rely less on public programs like Social Security.

As they are increasingly unable to steer fiscal benefits in their direction, the "money can't buy me love"[7] generation will once again gear their energy towards otherworldly purposes, solidifying a lifetime of leadership over culture and values. "Cultural tourism" and wilderness outings will continue to age with Boomers, many of whom will keep fit by overnighting at monas-teries, visiting old wineries, exploring biodiverse beaches, and gazing on pristine mountains. Many will eschew high-tech hospital care for holistic care and spiritual healing (some hospitals are already opening new "alter-native medicine" wings). Unlike elder GIs, they will avoid large-scale pre-planned communities and keep their children and families around them. Many will remain at the head of multigenerational households, or simply age in place in a new trend experts are identifying as "Naturally Occurring Retirement Communities."

Generation X

Born 1961–81, now aged 27–47, generation X grew up during the Consciousness Revolution, an era when the welfare of children was not a top societal priority. From their 1960s' childhood to their 1980s' time on campus, they learned young that they were largely on their own—and could not count on any institution, including schools, to watch out for their best interests. While Gen Xers were in grade school, the adult world was rocked by the sexual revolution, divorce epidemic, and shift from a G to an R rating[8] in the popular culture. As women entered the workplace before child care was widely available, many Gen Xers endured a latchkey childhood. Teacher pay declined dramatically in inflation-adjusted dollars, the teaching of "the basics" was de-emphasized, and in-school supervision was curtailed. Even as this generation's school achievement leveled out, *A Nation At Risk* report accused them of being "a rising tide of mediocrity" (National Commission on Excellence in Education, 1983, p. 1). Come the 1980s, their new cultural statements—hip-hop, grunge, heavy metal, alt-rock—revealed a hardened edge. In the late 1980s, the crime rate surged.

In jobs, Gen Xers embraced risk and prefered free agency over loyal corporatism. Through the 1990s, they faced a *Reality Bites*[9] economy of declining young-adult living standards. They responded by becoming the greatest entrepreneurial generation in US history, and their technological savvy has helped America prosper in the new era of globalization. They have also emerged as the most immigrant generation born in the 20th century. As young adults having to navigate a sexual battlefield of AIDS and blighted courtship rituals, they dated cautiously and married late. Many have now begun to reconstruct the institutional strength of family that they missed in their own childhood. Determined to avoid the mistakes they believe the Silent Generation parents and educators made when they were growing up, they are protective of their children and family time and cynical about schools and other public institutions. Politically, they lean toward non-affiliation and tend to see volunteering as more effective than voting. They have been very slow to come to public office, though a new breed of Gen-X-style leaders (including Barack Obama) has now begun capturing the public imagination.

Gen Xers have generally viewed education as a less prestigious career path than have previous generations, and are less likely to view their peers who entered teaching as the best of their generation. Though they believe strongly in lifelong learning, many also believe that the traditional college is only one of a multitude of settings in which people can educate themselves. As PTA members, as voters, and—increasingly—as state, local, and national officials, Generation X has provided the most vocal constituency for educational reforms that set standards, require transparency, impose accountability, and allow parents to remove their children from institutions that appear to be failing.

What comes next: the midlife of Gen Xers

Gen Xers will retain their reputation for alienation, cynicism, and hard-scrabble resilience into midlife—but having had so many choices and taken so many risks in their youth, they will feel like Generation Exhausted. For their Silent parents, the "midlife crisis" meant breaking out of early conformity and taking more risks—but Gen Xers entering midlife will veer in the opposite direction, searching for greater security in their families, jobs, and communities.[10] They will begin to push down the divorce rate and will be extremely protective of their children. In personal finances, this generation will fare even worse than Boomers did at like age. While the media will be saturated with tales of wealthy celebrities, the core image of a middle-aged worker will be that of a job-hopper who's doing alright but losing ground.

As they fill the ranks of midlife consumers, Gen Xers will continue to evaluate products in terms of their efficiency, convenience, and "mass customization." Even as mature workers, they will want to negotiate their own deals, to seek out wide-ranging incentives, and to shift employers at a moment's notice. Top Gen X managers will excel at quick decisions, streamlining the middle ranks, and downsizing bureaucracy. This generation's aversion to large-scale, institutional politics will continue, but could gradually subside as they pass through midlife. Gen X political leaders will seek out pragmatic, no nonsense solutions, with far less discussion and argument—and far more action—than Boomers have done.

The Millennial Generation

Those born since 1982, now up to age 26, the Millennials came along at a time when attitudes about children began shifting toward a greater emphasis on protection and structure—in families, schools, and communities. Gen Xers became known as a "baby bust" generation, the small demographic product of an America that had simply lost interest in kids. Millennials are often called a "baby boomlet" generation, the large demographic product of a birth-rate reversal. In stark contrast to Gen Xers, they have arrived in an era of glorified family values.

These "babies on board" have been regarded as special since birth, and have been more obsessed-over at every age than the Gen Xers ever were. In the early 1980s, the Hollywood portrayal of kids did a sudden about-face, from demon-seed children to cuddly babies. The budding Lamaze[11] movement spearheaded the new popularity of "attachment parenting." Soon after these new trophy kids began entering kindergarten, the President declared—and the public loudly agreed—that school reform should be a top national goal. The "Goals 2000" movement demanded improved student behavior and achievement from the high school Class of 2000. Educators spoke of standards, cooperative learning, and "No Child Left Behind." Meanwhile, the proliferation of child-safety products and regulations paved the way for a "zero tolerance" approach to hazards and misconduct in the classroom.

Millennials have become a generation of improving trends, with consistent decreases in high-risk behaviors. Rates of tobacco and alcohol use, violent crime, pregnancy, and suicide rates are all way down among today's teenagers, while SAT and ACT[12] scores have been rising. As their first cohorts graduate into the workplace, record numbers are gravitating toward large institutions and government agencies, seeking teamwork, protection against risk, and solid work–life balance. The youth culture is becoming less edgy, with a new focus on upbeat messages and big brands, and more conventional, with a resurgence of "oldies" and "remakes." Millennials are far more likely than Boomers or Xers to feel close to their parents, agree with their values, and rely on their support and guidance.

What comes next: the adulthood of Millennials

This generation will prove false the supposition (promoted by the experience of Boomers and Xers) that each generation of young adults is more alienated and risk-prone than the last. They will develop new community norms centered on rules, standards, and personal responsibility, making young-adult domains more mannerly, structured, and civic-spirited. As they move through their twenties, Millennials will already be accustomed to meeting and exceeding adult expectations. Many older adults will be pleased with how the young are doing, while others may misinterpret their confidence and ambition as self-centeredness. Millennials' close family relationships will continue as they move into young adulthood: they will live longer at home, follow parents' guidance on careers, and ground their own young nuclear families in extended family networks.

Many will face financial challenges as they enter the workplace, with student loans skyrocketing and entry-level pay remaining flat. Non-cash benefits will grow, from health insurance to pension plans, as young workers place a higher premium on job-security and guarantees. Employers will find it easier to cultivate long-term loyalty and career predictability in a generation with unusually long time horizons. As more Millennials reach voting age, they will become a political powerhouse, confounding pundits with huge youth-voter turnouts. Just as the political agenda of the 1990s centered around children, the political agenda of the next two decades will center around the needs of young adults.

The Homeland Generation

The Homeland Generation are probably arriving now in America's nurseries. These will be the babies born roughly through the mid-2020s. Their highly protective nurturing style will be substantially set by Gen Xers, but half of their parents will be Millennials. While it is still too early to set their first birth year, this will become clear in time.

FROM BOOM TO X: THE PARENT TRANSITION IN HIGHER EDUCATION

The personas of each of today's living generations come together in schools, workplaces, and institutions, significantly affecting their direction and environment. As each generation ages into the next phase of life in the years ahead, some generations will lose influence while others take on increasing responsibilities. This will prompt a number of important institutional shifts—shifts that are broadly foreseeable, given the different collective personas and life histories of each generation.

Higher education is on the brink of experiencing one such major generational transition: the transition from Boomer to Gen X college parents. Gen X parents will bring a range of new tactics to college parenting that could affect university life at many levels. When Boomer parents came to campus, a new light of public attention was cast on the collegiate experience. As Gen X parents arrive, that light will become glaringly bright, more probing, less supportive—and, to some eyes, less welcome. As the parental transition takes place, the world of higher education could experience institutional shifts unlike any seen in living memory.

At any time, people across a wide range of ages have key roles in campus life—from 17-year-old prospective students on up. Administrators and their staffs range in age from their twenties through their fifties. Faculty members tend to be a little older, trustees older still. Parents generally range from their forties to their sixties, but their ages tend to cluster more. Major changes can occur in higher education whenever a new generation ages into one of these institutional roles.

Based on calculations from US Census data, we estimate that the median birth year of the parents of first-year college students is now 1960—the final birth year of Boomers.[13] Starting in 2009, Gen Xers will become the majority of first-year parents. Between now and 2012, they will come to dominate the ranks of all collegiate parents. In time, they are likely to transform everything from the way classes are taught to the way college presidents think about the value of higher education.

Colleges may not feel the change right away, but sometime within the next ten years, probably in the early 2010s decade, the transition from Boomer to Gen X parents will reach a tipping point. The entire flavor of parent–college relationships will then take on a Gen X quality that will be very different from what colleges now see with Boomer parents. From then on, Generation X will dominate the national discussion about higher education.

As parents of collegians, Gen Xers will differ from Boomers in ways that are broadly foreseeable, given these generations' very different collective personas—and how differently they tend to recall their own educational experiences. Boomers passed through college during the 1960s and 1970s, the height of the Consciousness Revolution, when campuses were at the center of a swirl of counter-cultural change. Many Boomers today recall their college years as the apotheosis of their lives, their years of collective catharsis, their linkage to the larger events of their time—much as the land and sea battles of World War II had been for so many of their parents. Boomers have generally wanted to replicate this positive generational experience for their own children (albeit with less risk-taking).

By contrast, the first Gen Xers entered college and the labor force just as the "Reagan Revolution" swept over America, bringing deregulation, skimpier safety nets, and a new enthusiasm for markets, entrepreneurship, and personal risk-taking. Gen X attitudes toward their college experience were therefore shaped by a pragmatism and survivalism that few Boomers ever felt. Whereas Boomers had reveled in the whole college "experience," Gen Xers instead engaged in an energetic search for the right combination of courses, degrees, skills, and contacts that would give them a material edge. As parents, Gen Xers have tended to want to protect their own children from the academic deficiencies and family problems they recall from their own youth.

K–12 schools have already experienced much of the transition from Boomer to Gen X parents—with fairly dramatic repercussions. Over the past ten years, Gen X parents have demanded standards for schools, teachers, and students, data to measure the achievement of those standards, and transparency, giving them full and immediate access to all data. They have wanted accountability, for any schools and teachers that fail to achieve the promised results, along with bottom-line cash value, the confidence that, in the end, what was provided was worth all the investment of time and money. Above all, they have wanted as much choice as possible—for themselves, not their children. Gen X parents will soon expect the same of colleges.

As Gen Xers replace Boomers in the ranks of collegiate parents over the next decade, the "No Child Left Behind" parents of the K–12 world will become the "not with my child you don't" parents of higher education. Where Boomers have been interested in the public purpose of a college, in creating a more civic-minded society of educated people, Gen X moms and dads tend to be more interested in its private purpose, in how higher education creates concrete opportunities for their own children. According to the Datatel 2006 College Parent Survey, Gen Xers are more openly protective of their college-aged children than are Boomers, and are more likely to intervene directly if their children experience difficulties with anything from housing to attendance to substance abuse (LifeCourse Associates and Crux Research, 2007).

Boomer parents generally assume that the rewards of higher education are vast but impossible to measure—but Gen X parents will be more likely to assume that anything immeasurable is untrustworthy. They want proof that the money a student will spend and the debt a student will incur constitute a solid investment in that student's future. If one college charges a student $30 000 per year and another charges $20 000 per year, a Gen X parent may ask what that extra $10 000 is actually buying. The following quip attributed to Education Secretary, Margaret Spellings (herself a late-wave Boomer, born in 1957) speaks to many Gen X parents: "In God we trust. All others bring data" (US Department of Education, 2005).

In their children's college education, as with other expensive purchases, Gen Xers want a fair and open transaction, with complete and accurate information, cash value, and unconstrained consumer choice. As K–12 schools have already seen, these parents want administrators to run their schools like marketplace businesses—while they as parents have the freedom of marketplace consumers.

In their usual approach to the marketplace, Gen X consumers are menu-driven. They tend to compartmentalize, viewing every transaction as a series of discrete and categorical choices. Not many Gen X consumers want to buy a CD anymore when they can buy precisely the songs they want on iTunes and not pay for unnecessary extras. Similarly, Gen X parents are likely to wonder why they should purchase a whole college package that comes with a slew of expensive extras, which they may view as neither necessary nor useful to their particular child. Instead, they will tend to split the college experience into its major components and pick and choose exactly what they want for their children. Every component will need to measure up. If any one does not, Gen X parents will be inclined to go elsewhere for that piece of the product.

Gen X parents will likely identify three components: *brand*, the reputation or name recognition associated with a degree from a certain college; *experience*, the non-academic life enrichment provided by a college; and *learning*, the academic component of college, the knowledge taught in class.

These parents will want to know what each of these three components—brand, experience, and learning—will be worth to their child. They may want to purchase one or two of them, but not the others that they deem unnecessary, unsatisfactory, or not cost-effective. Can a student transfer from a community college and get a brand-name degree for less money? Can a student who spends most off-hours working at a job avoid paying student activity fees?

As consumers, these new college parents will be increasingly empowered by their peers, who will fill the ranks of administrators, business executives, entrepreneurs, and political leaders. As midlife Gen X parents call for cost-effective college learning, midlife Gen X entrepreneurs will find new ways to offer this learning outside of the traditional college setting—through for-profit institutes, in-house corporate training, distance learning, foreign colleges, and military service, among other possibilities. Gen Xers in public office may facilitate this trend by broadening the qualifications for professional and academic certification, while demanding data-driven standards for higher education institutions.

The transition from Boomer to Gen X parents will likely affect people at all levels of university life, from students up to college presidents and board members. Whereas Boomer parents (along with older generations) considered a tenured faculty to be a permanent fixture of the academic chain of being, Gen X parents will be more willing to question why they are not subject to the same bottom-line incentives and market forces that most Gen Xers face daily in their own jobs. They will raise new questions about how tenured faculty, presidents, and deans are paid, what proportion of the budget goes toward their retirement and benefits, and what value they actually bring to students.

FORECASTING THROUGH GENERATIONS

In every field and industry, forecasters make the flawed assumption that the future will be a straight line extrapolation of the recent past. They predict that the next set of people in each phase of life will behave like a more extreme version of the current occupants. Sometimes they are right for years on end—until a new generation comes along and fundamentally changes the way we think about people that age.

Recall how mistaken forecasts can be when they miss the arrival of a new generation. By the early 1960s, for example, Americans had grown used to talking about a "Silent Generation" of college students. As experts looked ahead to the onrushing bulge of children known as the "Baby Boom" who were about to arrive at college, they foresaw a new corps of technocratic corporatists, a Silent Generation to the next degree, even more pliable and conformist than the gray-flannel "lonely crowd" right before them. "Employers are going to love this generation," the Chancellor of the University of California-Berkeley, Clark Kerr, declared in 1959. "They are going to be easy to handle. There aren't going to be any riots" (Salter, 1973, p. 330).

Events, to say the least, turned out otherwise. Remarkably, none of the biggest-name social scientists—not even Erik Erikson or Margaret Mead— saw a hint of the youth explosion that was about to shake America.

Understanding the personas of today's generations makes it possible to anticipate such non-linear changes, those bends in the road that so often confound everyone from educators to businesses to pundits. The attitudes and behavior of every age group undergo constant flux. From one decade to the next, youth can turn from do-wop to acid rock to rap; midlifers from gray-flannel to midlife crisis to spiritualism; elders from reclusive apathy to senior-citizen entitlement to other-directed compassion. To see how any age bracket is likely to transform in the decades ahead, don't look at the set of people who currently occupy that bracket—look down the age ladder at the next generation due to pass through it.

This generational perspective can lend order, meaning, and predictability to personal interactions, institutional shifts, and national trends. In business, government, education, and other areas, those who can anticipate the changes on our horizon will be those who understand generations.

NOTES

1. "I'd like to teach the world to sing (in perfect harmony)" was a pop song and advertising jingle for Coca-Cola in a TV Commercial in 1971.
2. *How to Succeed in Business without Really Trying* was a musical launched on Broadway in 1961, based on a book by Shepherd Mead, of 1952.
3. From "My Back Pages," by Bob Dylan, written 1964.
4. Popular radio and television sitcom from the 1950s and 1960s portraying an idealized vision of American middle-class life.
5. Scholastic Aptitude (or Assessment) Test. While there is evidence that the decline in SAT scores during this period was due in part to the expansion of the pool of test-takers, our research on this point leads us to conclude that the SAT decline was also a reflection on learning and achievement.
6. Kindergarten to twelfth grade. The sum of primary and secondary education in the United States.
7. "(Money) Can't Buy Me Love," was a song composed by Paul McCartney in 1964.
8. The Motion Picture Association of America's film-rating system: G = general audiences, all ages admitted; R = restricted, people under 17 not admitted without parental guidance.
9. Film from 1994 about Generation X graduates facing life after college.
10. Every generation is parented by the two generations that precede it: the first half of Generation X was parented by the Silent Generation and the second half by Boomers.

However, the older generation of parents tends to influence the nurturing style of the whole generation. The Silent Generation was Generation X's dominant parent generation, the parents of the first-wave Gen Xers who set the cultural tone for their younger peers.

11. Childbirth technique developed in the 1940s by French obstetrician Dr. Fernand Lamaze, which gained popularity in the US after Marjorie Karmel wrote *Thank you, Dr. Lamaze* in 1959.

12. College admission test in the US.

13. According to US Census data, around 1990, the median age of a mother at the birth of her child was 27 and the median age of the father was 29. We estimate that the median age of a mother or father at the birth of their *college-bound* child was about two years older than the median for the entire population (calculated from the later median child-bearing age of parents with increasing levels of education and the share of current college students who have college-educated parents). We therefore estimate that around 1990 the median age of a mother at the birth of her college-bound child was 29 and the median age of a father was 31. To estimate the median age of a parent of traditional first-year college students, add 18 to 30 and you get 48—a little less for a mother, a little more for a father. Subtract 48 from the calendar year, and you get the median birth year of a first-year college parent.

REFERENCES

LifeCourse Associates and Crux Research (2007), *Millennials Go to College: Surveys and Analysis*, Great Falls, VA: LifeCourse Associates and Crux Research.

National Commission on Excellence in Education (1983), *A Nation at Risk: The Imperative for Educational Reform*, Washington, DC: NCEE.

"Politically correct" (1990). *Wall Street Journal*, 26 November, A1.

Salter, B. (1973), "Explanations of student unrest: an exercise in devaluation," *The British Journal of Sociology*, **24**(3), 329–40.

US Department of Education (2005), "To raise achievement of students with disabilities, greater flexibility available for states, schools: proposed regulations to be published in Federal Register" (press release), Washington, DC: US Department of Education.

2.   Perspectives from the presidency

D. Bruce Johnstone

Know your students. Another of higher education's many aphorisms and platitudes—which of course does not make it incorrect or unimportant. But why, or to what end, should we in higher education seek to better understand our students? To increase our respective market shares? Or to cater better to *their* tastes and needs (perhaps as opposed to what *we* believe they should be taught)? Or to teach them whatever they are to be taught more effectively?

But which students? The ones we are now attracting and who are selecting our institutions? Or the ones we wish we could attract away from other, more selective institutions? Or the students who are currently not attending anywhere—to their and to society's presumed detriment—whom we (or at least some of us) would attract, enroll, and serve to a greater extent than we now do?

Such questions lay at the heart of the TIAA-CREF Institute's 2007 National Higher Education Leadership Conference, entitled "Generational Shockwaves: Implications for Higher Education," held in New York City in November 2007. As a new member of the Institute and as a presumed leader (former college president and system chancellor) and also as a recently retired professor and scholar of higher education (specializing in finance, governance, and policy in domestic and international contexts), I was asked to be a participant. However, as I was unable to attend due to a previous unbreakable commitment, I was asked instead to contribute a chapter to the conference volume based on reading a transcript of the opening roundtable panel and supplemented by my own musings on the topic, especially on the usefulness of the *generational* perspective, as attributed to the opening keynote speaker, William Strauss, co-author of *Millennials Rising: The Next Great Generation.*[1]

This perspective views today's entering students as the Millennials, born after 1980—in contrast to yesterday's students, the Generation Xers, born between 1965 and 1980, and their more distant predecessors, the Baby Boomers, born from the end of World War II through 1964, or the Silent Generation—that is, older folks born before the entry of the United States into World War II. (In the interest of scholarly transparency, I am a young Silent, born in early 1941.)

My license from the conference organizers, then, was to consider this generational nomenclature, admittedly without the benefit of hearing either William Strauss's keynote speech or the opening plenary roundtable, but having read Howe and Strauss and other proponents of the generational perspective as well as the transcript of the opening panel (and having lots of opinions on higher education that I am always more than willing to share with anyone who will listen).

Aphorisms and platitudes come easy in higher education. The reason, perhaps, is because most of us truly believe that the college or university is a very special place and that there is something noble about teaching and writing and pushing forward the elusive frontiers of knowledge. Leadership in the academy is an especially heady calling, whether from the vantage point of professor, dean of a faculty, vice president for student affairs, director of the library, president of a college or university, or any of the many other positions from which higher education can be influenced. We take these leadership roles very seriously, as though not only the beliefs, values, and skills of our students, but also the competitiveness of our economy, the stability of our democracy, and the harmony and justice of our society depend on the job we do.

Furthermore—and very contrary to much of the conventional criticism of the academy, which alleges a complacency, an excessive self-satisfaction, and a resistance to all change—we are in fact very self-critical and perpetually seeking (or so we say) to change ourselves: indeed, to reform. We readily proclaim the need to recruit more effectively, admit more sensitively, teach more effectively, and better serve the community around us.

These aspirations, however genuine, are not always consistent. We *say* we need to admit more ethnic minorities and first-generation students—but we also want more of the very brightest (on standard measures such as average SAT scores) and also more of the most interesting (as in the high school senior who spent the previous summer on an archeological dig in Guatemala). We *say* we need to steer more students in the direction of science, technology, engineering, and mathematics—but we also proclaim the need to do a better job educating the "whole person" as well as to teach the liberal arts better . . . and along the way to develop better our students' social values and leadership skills for the needs of contemporary society. And our faculty need to publish more and bring in more grants so the institution can rise in scholarly reputation and therefore in someone's *league table*—even as we wish for them to pay more attention to the craft of teaching.

The legitimate multiplicity of our goals and the difficulty of their measurement impart a certain looseness to these agendas and a déjà vu to most of our reforms. There is a disquieting disconnect between what those of us in leadership positions profess to be our reform agenda and the actual decisions that are presumably within our grasp but that seem never to be made—or never made to stick. We (ignoring for now just who "we" is) continue to teach pretty much the same courses and look for pretty much the same accumulation of general education credits, distribution requirements, and courses in the major as we did 10 or 20 or 30 years ago.

Every bit as disquieting as the reforms that do not seem ever to *take* are the reforms that do take but do not last, or that are on the verge of implementation when we realize we tried that change in the mid-1980s (and perhaps before in the early 1970s) but had to modify it because, well, there were unintended consequences and unforeseen costs . . . and then our dynamic change agent left for another institution (or failed to get tenure) . . . and then the students seemed to lose interest. This is not meant to take anything away from the kinds of exciting changes reported in the Leadership Conference's opening roundtable by University of Kentucky President, Lee Todd, or Wagner College President, Richard Guarasci, or Cuyahoga Community College President, Jerry Sue Thornton. Their examples of dynamic leadership and exciting campuses are vivid demonstrations of my point: that colleges and universities are neither complacent nor unchanging. That most of these programs and activities (like similar examples from many other campuses) are neither new nor exactly revolutionary does not detract from their appropriateness or their value to these campuses.

Admittedly, leaders in business and industry see our kind of change as slow and insufficiently dramatic. And it is true that colleges and universities do not generally sell out to leveraged buyout offers, or remove a program from production the moment its demand weakens, or pull up stakes and move to a lower-wage, less regulated venue just south of the Mexican border—as so many dynamic corporations do. Yet colleges and universities seem to change when they need to (or when society truly needs them to). Consider all of the formerly private, Roman Catholic, liberal arts colleges for women that are still private, but are now largely secular, coeducational colleges featuring higher education for business and the health professions. And consider the race, class, and gender profiles of the entering classes of most of the most selective colleges and universities that bear so little resemblance to those of 20 years ago. Or consider the elite research university departments and faculties at the cutting edge of the most radical scientific changes, such as in the fields of molecular and sub-cellular biology and genetics, where the scholarly agendas and research techniques bear little resemblance to those of a mere decade ago.

It is also true that some higher educational change comes slowly. Colleges and universities that have the luxury to do so (mainly in the form of substantial endowments and deep applicant pools) may question and often resist the latest trends in collegiate curricula, marketing, or student lifestyles. While needing at least to keep alert to changing students and markets, such colleges and universities, in effect, slow down and smooth out the pace of change in higher education. In so doing, they honor another noble function of the academy, which is to preserve and defend culture and to uphold more rigorous standards for what in the larger society can so easily be lost to trendy whims. In short, colleges and universities do change—mainly when they have to, and even then not easily. And some of the change, when observed from a distance (both in space and in time), can appear circular. However, the underlying dynamics and the continuous quest for excellence of the academy, even when seemingly circular, and even when contested, are still there—and some of us would have it no other way.

But what does this have to do with *knowing our students* and with what was asserted by the opening keynote speaker, William Strauss, and reinforced by roundtable participant and State University of New York-New Paltz President, Steven Poskanzer, to be an entirely new generation, dubbed "the Millennials"? Poskanzer provided an excellent overview of Millennial students, describing the SUNY New Paltz students as:

- more diverse—as in more under-represented minorities, more international, and more female students than ever before;
- more atomistic—with smaller and less intersecting circles of friends and less interest in campus-wide events and activities or occasions through which to make new friends;
- more adept with and dependent upon technology, reinforcing this atomism in what Poskanzer called their "electronic cocoons";
- different in the way they learn: more visual and interactive and therefore less textual and passive, with shorter attention spans and less willingness to engage intellectually, especially when such engagement is difficult or is apt to be challenged;
- more practical and more oriented to careers and making money, and commensurately less motivated by that which is *merely* intellectual or ideological;
- but at the same time, more community-minded and giving.

Other speakers in the opening roundtable provided their perceptions of the differences among the generations of students and faculty currently populating the nation's higher education institutions. Janet Bickel, who describes herself as a career and leadership development coach, noted that while Generation X students tended to have parents who were absent, Generation Y feels more protected and pressured by their parents. Generation Y is characterized by multitasking even faster than its predecessor, something those of us who teach college students today have undoubtedly noticed.

Lee Todd, President of the University of Kentucky, discussed how his institution has responded to the pressures of meeting the needs of the Millennial Generation. He characterized Millennial students as being very civic- and community-oriented. He also described how the parents of today's students are much more involved in their children's education than were previous generations, noting that "I can't even imagine my parents sending the president of the university an e-mail or calling them, but I get them all the time now, about parking tickets or anything you can think of."

Richard Guarasci, President of Wagner College, on Staten Island in New York City, presented his perspective on Millennial students, a group he characterized as having "seven traits: special, sheltered, confident, team-oriented, conventional, pressured, and achieving." Guarasci described the efforts Wagner has undertaken to meet the educational needs of this new group of students, what he labeled "Millennial pedagogy." At Wagner, this includes active techniques such as experiential learning, learning communities, internships, student/peer learning groups, and senior theses. Many of Wagner's efforts are aimed at breaking down the larger college into smaller entities for students.

Jerry Sue Thornton, President of Cuyahoga Community College in Ohio, described the challenges of serving largely a non-traditional student population that is characterized by having a wide range of ages, having diverse educational goals and interests (from vocational to baccalaureate transfer), and being largely part-time with much instruction occurring on weekends and in the evenings. Because of the wide age range of students served by her institution, it must meet the needs of not just Millennial students, but earlier generations also. She spoke, for example, about the impact of technology on each generation, noting that "Millennials are actually expecting the digital divide, Generation Xers are tolerating it, and Baby Boomers in some way wish it would go away."

The generational perspective, according to Strauss (the conference keynote speaker) contends not only that today's students are different from yesterday's (as the students of any period have always been from the students of an earlier period), but that the differences today—at least those differences that are alleged to matter the most and/or seem to be understood the least by colleges and universities—are a function of real historical events that have shaped the way young people behave and what they believe in ways different from and more profound than would been anticipated from the mere passage of time or the day-to-day occurrences of growing up. So the young of today—born after 1982—are more affluent, sheltered, confident, conventional, team-oriented, pressured, achieving, healthier, and technologically aware than the preceding generation, which has been dubbed Generation X. And therefore we in positions of higher educational leadership need to adjust to this greater diversity, greater technological sophistication, greater self-confidence, and the like in ways that are more profound and presumably require greater leadership than might have been the case with our predecessors in most years past.

But the generational labels also seem a bit too easy: almost pat. Could we not find another label as well for those born after 1992 . . . or those coming of age with the first invasion of Iraq . . . or with the second invasion of Iraq . . . or those born during the so-called (and also too facile) dot.com era . . . or those born between just about any two notable historical events that arguably had some impact on American lifestyles, especially of the young?

And some of the alleged Millennial characteristics have been around for some significant portion of entering college classes for decades. Take, for example, the association of the Millennials with greater diversity. True, there is a dominant rhetorical theme of diversity as a social and political agenda, by which is generally meant the need for and/or desirability of increasing diversity in today's entering college classes. But the word diversity applied to higher education has been largely co-opted (for important and essentially right reasons) by those with a clear agenda of giving those who have not been historically (or even presently) privileged greater access to higher education and thereby to the jobs, the status, the incomes, and the positions of power to which higher education or the lack thereof has been thought to be either a facilitator or a barrier. In this way, the supposed diversity that is claimed to be a characteristic of the Millennials refers in large part to the continuing social and political agenda that has been with us not for just the decade that our entering students have been referred to by that label, but for at least 30 years. And by some measures—for example, the percentage of black males entering a college or university—diversity has been steady or even waning, and certainly not notably increasing.

Furthermore, there are lots of other diversities, many of which may be associated with social class, ethnicity, and gender, but which can also be quite independent of one another. To begin with, there have always (that is, at least in the past century or so) been seemingly profound differences within a population of college students regardless of the selectivity or narrowness of the social, or financial, or ethnic, or gendered strata from which this cohort is drawn. From literature, conventional wisdom, remembered experiences, and scholarly studies, there have been, for example, conformists and non-conformists, intellectuals and grinds, socials and political activists, artists and the upwardly mobile, and other admittedly unscientific but recognizable dichotomizations of attributes. Such differences—at least in their extremes—are probably associated with differing needs, goals, and learning styles of which student affairs staff, and perhaps faculty, should be aware and possibly responsive to. But "probably," "perhaps," and "possibly" in the preceding assertion reveal the ambivalence with which I would be prepared to alter curricula or standards or teaching methods according to such characteristics.

More important to our consideration of the generational labels, such typologies, while notably unscientific and some would claim too facilely crafted, are almost certainly as applicable (or not) today applied to the so-called Millennials, as they were 40 years ago to the Baby Boomers or 60 years ago to the Silents. We might need to add some typologies for today's students, capturing the extremes of musical tastes, for example, or video game predilections. But do we add useful insights to our higher educational leadership roles by more layers of labels?

To further complicate getting to know today's students, there is another source of increasing diversity (although no longer so new or sudden) as United States higher education expands in its gross participation rate, bringing an inevitable widening or stretching of the extent of academic preparedness and intellectual interests of entering students. There is always, by definition, a potential participation margin composed of those who do not enter—presumably for lack of academic interest, or ability, or finances, or role models, or combinations of the above—but who are on the participation edge and who would enter if participation rates were to increase for any reason. When the participation rate does increase, these are the students who now try college who some years prior would not have entered at all. As the participation rate steadily increases, this margin inevitably enters with, on average, less accumulated knowledge, fewer academic skills, and less interest in the kinds of intellectual engagements that have traditionally been associated with college courses and the associated demands of reading, writing, research, and completing assignments. And a cohort limited to the top 10 percent of 18-year-olds on any standard measure of academic preparedness (regardless of how accurate the measure) will be fundamentally different from a cohort of the top 50 percent—again, regardless of whether these two hypothetical cohorts are from last year or from 20 years ago, and quite in addition to whatever increasing diversity there may be as a result of more non-traditional age students, more students of color, or females.

Similarly—and a third dimension of diversity—there will be a broadening of ages in the undergraduate classroom. This broadening is a function of the increasing ease of return, the increasing need for additional education as the good jobs for high school graduates disappear, and as increasing affluence makes a return to higher education more possible for more middle-aged and older adults who did not finish. Seventeen- and 18-year-olds differ from 27- and 28-year-olds, and they always have. They differ in substantial measure because of developmental differences—for example, in physical, social, sexual, and other maturational characteristics—quite apart from any systematic differences between today's 17- and 18-year-olds and the 17- and 18-year-olds of 20 years ago. In other words, the young have always been different from the middle-aged and the elderly, and the need for understanding the special needs of an older generation, or for understanding the impact on the college experience for the entire student body as the result of an older generation, is probably nowhere near as great today with the Millennials as it was when this phenomenon first occurred in those heady early years of the post-World War II, GI Bill era when the underlying student body was still composed mainly of members of the Silent Generation.

In short, there are at least these three dimensions of increasing difference, or increasing diversity, among college students, the first of which (that is, the typologies of learners) has arguably always existed, and the second and third of which (the expansion of the participation rate for the 17- to 20-year-old cohort and the extension of the college-going cohort to adults) are a function of the expansion of the higher educational franchise, as it were, that has been going on for at least 50 years (and that has actually slowed down in recent years). My point is less to question the accuracy of the current fad of generational labeling as it is to question the usefulness of the characterizations of Millennials to our tasks of resolving the financial, managerial, curricular, and pedagogical issues presumably requiring our leadership.

Nevertheless, whether the first Millennials appeared in 1999 or in 1997, or whether Millennial is still the most useful label to apply to the first-year class that will enter in the fall of 2008, are in a larger sense questions beside the point. What was stressed in the 2007 TIAA-CREF Institute Leadership Conference is that our students are ever more diverse: in ethnicity, first language, age, accumulated knowledge, and reasons for being our students in the first place. They almost certainly read even less, at least on average, than the students of a decade or two or three ago. They are far more computer-literate—and this literacy extends to everything in the new digital age. They are entering a world of employment possibilities that is ever more uncertain, requiring from us (whether or not they know this) a higher education that is both demanding and broadening. And they are entering a world where the position of the United States is less secure, both in the literal sense of less safe from adversaries as well as in the less dramatic but more profound sense of less able to control world events.

I do not believe that this requires dramatically different or even necessarily stronger leadership than did the challenges to higher educational leaders at any other time in the past century. Leadership has always been vital and always been challenging. The students are different—but they always have been. And we must strive to know them better—as we have always had to do—with whatever tools and nomenclatures and labels that help us understand them, because their and our futures are at least partly in our hands. And we must remain vigilant, as always, lest we get so consumed by the financial and managerial (and sometimes political) tasks before us that we lose sight of our proper objectives, which have always had to do with learning and scholarship—and only secondarily with market share, average entering SAT scores, or the compatibility of roommates.

NOTE

1. Howe, Neil and William Strauss (2000), *Millennials Rising: The Next Great Generation*, New York: Vintage Books. Sadly, Strauss passed away six weeks after the conference.

3. Generation X: redefining the norms of the academy

Ronald G. Ehrenberg

INTRODUCTION

The members of Generation X are the young faculty members of today and the immediate future. The panelists at this session of the conference were asked to discuss the effects of this generation on academic norms and institutional governance and the types of new models that may be emerging for academia as a result of them. More specifically, they were asked if the attitudes and loyalties of these young faculty members really do differ from that of the Baby Boom Generation, how their attitudes and behavior affect graduate programs, what academic institutions will need to do to attract the next generation of faculty members, and how they will influence governance in academia. And given the growing number of two-career families and single parent families, will changes in the tenure system take place?

The panel, which it was my pleasure to moderate, consisted of four distinguished academic leaders. Linda Bunnell has been the Chancellor of the University of Wisconsin, Stevens Point since 2004. Prior to assuming that position, she was a Senior Vice President at the College Board, the Chancellor of the University of Colorado at Colorado Springs, Vice Chancellor of Academic Affairs for the Minnesota State System, and a consultant to higher education and non-profit organizations.

Joan Girgus has been a Professor of Psychology at Princeton University for 30 years. She has served Princeton in a variety of administrative positions, including Dean of the College, Chair of the Psychology Department, and (currently) Special Assistant to the Dean of the Faculty. In the latter role, she was one of the people responsible for Princeton's policies and programs that seek to make graduate education and faculty life more "family-friendly." She is well-known in the higher education community for her extensive national leadership activities, including her work with the Knight Higher Education Collaborative and her leadership in the Pew Higher Education Roundtable program.

John Lombardi became the President of the Louisiana State University System in September 2007. Prior to his appointment, he served as Chancellor of the University of Massachusetts at Amherst, President of the University of Florida, Provost at the Johns Hopkins University, and Dean of Arts and Sciences at Indiana University. He is co-editor of the Center for Measuring University Performance and writes a regular column for InsideHighered.com.

The final panelist, Kenneth Ruscio, became the President of Washington and Lee University in March 2006. An alumnus of Washington and Lee, he is a distinguished scholar in the study of democratic theory and public policy. Previously he served as Dean of the Jepson School of Leadership Studies at the University of Richmond and in various administrative positions at Washington and Lee.

THE PARTICIPANTS' REMARKS

Linda Bunnell led off the panel and stressed the importance of creating institutions in which Generation Xers can thrive. She began by cautioning that many of the characteristics attributed to this generation are also characteristics that have often been attributed to faculty more generally. These include that they identify with their disciplines, rather than with their institutions or even their departments; that they value only those things that help them to succeed; that they are resistant to authority and behave like individual contractors; and that they challenge each other's thinking.

On the other hand, as she works to adapt her leadership style and her leadership team to work with this generation, she is aware of many other important aspects that they possess. They are good leaders with a strong sense of competency, they spend a lot of time acquiring information on their own and are very savvy technologically, they are drawn to teams of their own choosing, and they are very creative and find routines repetitive and distasteful. Two key words that describe them are "balance" and "family" and she noted what a contrast this was to the start of her and other Baby Boomer careers when family responsibilities had to be kept in the background and were not allowed to intrude upon one's professional work.

The University of Wisconsin, Stevens Point (UWSP) is a large comprehensive institution located in a beautiful scenic area of the state. It grew rapidly after World War II and the social norms of the faculty at UWSP were established by that generation of faculty. These include dedication to students, formality, dignity, high expectations for students, and civility towards each other and towards administrators. However, due to retirement and growth, almost 40 percent of the faculty now are Generation Xers. To understand better the policies needed to help UWSP prosper in such an environment, in 2004 UWSP participated in the UCLA Higher Education Research Institute survey of faculty.

The results of that survey were quite striking to Linda Bunnell and they suggested that Generation Xers at UWSP differ from their older colleagues in a number of ways. Among the key findings were that the former were more stressed about household responsibilities and finances, as well as professional matters. While some of these differences may relate to their different stage of the life cycle, almost 40 percent of them reported that they had received at least one job offer during the last two years and roughly an equal percentage reported that they were thinking about leaving academia. Both of these percentages were considered much higher than is desirable and suggest real issues of commitment to their institution and to academia more generally.

As a result, UWSP has responded with a variety of efforts. It has developed an outstanding orientation program and a mentoring program for new faculty. It is bringing in speakers to talk about stress management and balancing work and family matters. It has adopted family-friendly policies, including time off for birth, adoption, and family illness, hosted family events on campus, provided child care on campus (starting as early as age one), and provided assistance to spouses seeking employment.

Given the numbers of people contemplating employment elsewhere, UWSP allows faculty to try out academic positions elsewhere, rather than requiring them to resign; the hope is that some will realize that the "grass is not greener" elsewhere. It also allows a transition to part-time employment for faculty who want to pursue non-academic options locally.

Finally, it is very strategic in its recruitment of new faculty. It has a program to attract back to campus graduates of UWSP who have gone on to graduate study elsewhere; these individuals come to faculty positions with more institutional loyalty than the typical new faculty hire. It also makes special efforts to attract faculty with interests in the area's beautiful outdoor environment and in hunting and fishing; such faculty are also more likely to remain at the institution than faculty who long for an urban environment.

Joan Girgus's discussion focused on the importance of rebalancing the work–family-life relationship. She pointed out that Generation Xers in academia are ethnically and racially much more diverse than their Baby Boomer counterparts. Echoing Linda Bunnell's description, they are self-reliant, value diversity, desire work–life balance, are technologically savvy, and are attached to their work but not necessarily to their employers.

Two defining events happened right before Generation Xers were born and while they were very young: the civil rights movement and the women's

liberation movement. As a result of these events, they are the first generation that has always believed that both men and women will be in the labor
force and that careers and families will proceed at the same time. Thus, they
are deeply concerned about work–life balance issues. And given the substantial increase in the share of college and university faculty that is female,
these issues have become increasingly important for academia to address.

When addressing these issues, Girgus stressed that a number of key
points must be kept in mind. First, consideration of work–life balance
issues should begin while potential future faculty members are in graduate
school and continue throughout faculty careers and into retirement.
Second, work–life balance for Generation Xers matters as much for men as
it does for women. Third, a multiplicity of services and programs must be
provided because different individuals will have different needs; one size
does not fit all.

Academic institutions have always been concerned about family life
issues. However, in an earlier generation, when most faculty members were
males and their spouses had the primary child care responsibilities, the
needs of faculty in this area were much smaller. Policies such as tuition
remission and family health insurance coverage were about all that were
needed. However, a much wider range of policies are needed today.

Princeton University has been in the forefront of the development of
family-friendly policies at major research universities and Joan Girgus summarized some of the policies now in place at Princeton. These include
maternity and paternity leave, automatic one-year extensions of the tenure
clocks for assistant professors for each child that is born, workload relief
for the primary caregiver in a family, back-up care programs (both for children and other family members), dependant care travel funds, employee
child care assistance programs, expanded on-campus child care facilities,
employee assistance programs that provide counseling on a wide variety of
issues (including finding a child care provider or a day care center for elder
care), and partner placement assistance. And, she stressed that in each case
these policies either also cover graduate students and postdoctoral research
associates, or there are parallel policies that cover these groups. In each
case, the policies are designed to facilitate the covered individuals doing
their academic work.

However, in spite of Princeton's great efforts, Girgus feels there is still
more that can be done. She thinks that maternity/paternity leaves might be
made longer than Princeton's policies currently provide. She believes that
adoption assistance programs, such as the one that UWSP has, are necessary. And more generally, she believes that universities need to think
seriously about redesigning their employment structures to allow for long-
term, part-time tenured faculty employment so that individuals can more

easily combine parenting and work. She also discussed the importance of academia thinking more seriously about what she calls "off ramps and on ramps." An example of the latter type of policy, which she did not mention, is a policy that the University of California System has that provides post-doctoral appointments to PhDs who have been out of academia for a number of years raising their families, to allow them to retool and become competitive again for faculty appointments.[1]

John Lombardi is well known for saying exactly what is on his mind and his comments at the conference were exactly in this vein. He questioned the usefulness of using the generational perspective around which the whole conference was organized. Moreover, he argued that given the heterogeneity of higher education institutions it is somewhat foolish to talk about the policies "higher education" should put in place in response to generational issues. Different institutions have different resource bases; some are much more heavily tuition-dependent than others and thus have to be much more sensitive to how the policies they adopt affect their tuition-paying customers. Many do not have the option of passing the expenses that family policies may entail on to their students.

As the president of a major public higher education system, he is very sensitive to how public institutions allocate resources. He pointed to the development of honors colleges at public universities as a possible misallocation of public resources. These colleges are designed to improve the academic profile of the entering class by attracting students with high test scores, who tend to come from higher-income families. Given that more resources are spent educating these students than an institution's other students who have not been admitted to the honors colleges and who tend to come from lower-income families, he asked whether this allocation of resources is socially responsible.

Turning to for-profit higher education institutions, he pointed out that their goal is to produce higher education at a low cost so that they can earn a profit, so they do not invest in the type of amenities that most higher education institutions invest in and they relentlessly hold costs down by controlling faculty costs. He mused that if we as a society were interested in holding down the costs of higher education, we might emulate more what is going on in for-profit higher education rather than having discussions like the one the panel was having about the actions that might be undertaken to make faculty members happy and more productive.

Put simply, his point was that all of the programs designed to make the academy a more desirable place to work for Generation Xers cost money, and someone has to pay for those programs. At rich private institutions like Princeton, it may be possible to finance these costs out of endowment income, but most public and private higher education institutions are heavily dependent on tuition and thus anything that adds to costs will necessarily result in higher tuition levels. Moreover, when budget crises come, and we look for places to cut, he worries that these programs will not even be considered for cuts; instead we will be forced to cut the core academic operations of our institutions.

Why don't discussions such as the panel's focus on how to reduce the costs of higher education? Lombardi asserted that colleges and universities are engaged in a "dog eat dog" competition to be the most prestigious institutions they can and as a result, all the pressure they face is to spend more, not less. So they keep piling on amenities to attract students, finance research facilities to attract faculty, spend fortunes on large athletic programs (which often have little to do with the academic mission of the university but which alumni and state legislatures like) and increasingly use grant aid to attract top students. They want to be the most prestigious that they can because this enables them to attract the very best students and faculty and to produce high-quality teaching and research.

Kenneth Ruscio's remarks were based upon his perspective as a political scientist and as president of a national liberal arts college that has a strong sense of tradition, a strong sense of norms, a strong sense of community, and a commitment to liberal arts education. Rather than addressing the types of policies needed to attract and retain Generation Xers as the other panelists did, his remarks focused on how this generation is influencing governance in higher education.

Ruscio pointed out that Generation Xers came of age during a time of mistrust and that, as Kennedy School of Government professor, Robert Putnam, has pointed out, a declining sense of community and commitment to common values. While this leads to a declining sense of trust in individual leaders and thus makes leadership in higher education more difficult, it is also associated with increasing trust by them in the process by which decisions are made, as things such as tenure and promotion processes, are subject to much more codification than in the past. He finds, from his experiences first as a dean and then as a president, that this is exactly what Generation Xers want. They want to know what the quantitative standards will be for both research and teaching that will determine whether they get tenure. He asserted that process is increasingly becoming the source of justice in their views and thus faculty and administrative decision-makers increasingly become hesitant about making substantive judgments; rather they seek to follow the prescribed process as closely as possible.

Curriculum reform is another example. It is increasingly difficult in his view to get individual faculty members and departments to think about what the broad purpose of the curriculum is; instead the focus is on how any change will affect each department and even each individual faculty member. So bargaining and negotiations have replaced persuasion and the search for a common view or set of values in curriculum decisions.

Thus, even at a small liberal arts college such as his own, he feels that the changing generational norms have substantially affected academia. Academic discourse is less about discovering common purposes and more about negotiating differences between individuals and units. Trust in process has become as important as trust in subjective judgments. Leadership is increasingly about developing acceptable formats for negotiating conflicts as well as about gaining consensus on purpose. The challenge for small liberal arts colleges that are accustomed to high levels of consensus and a strong sense of community is to incorporate more formal procedures without losing a sense of common purpose.

AUDIENCE DISCUSSION AND MODERATOR'S THOUGHTS

During the discussion period, Joan Girgus was asked how tenure committees at Princeton react to individuals who have had their tenure clock delayed because of child birth. Would an assistant professor who had two children during the probationary years and was considered for tenure during her eighth year be held to the same standard as assistant professors without children who were considered for tenure during their sixth year? Girgus stressed that tenure committees are instructed that the "bar" for tenure should not be changed, but admitted that it is hard to know for sure how they are reacting. Princeton has urged tenure committees to evaluate the quality of a person's work and its impact on the field rather than simply counting publications in some quantitative and mechanical fashion. It hopes this will help keep the tenure "bar" unchanged.

As moderator, I perhaps should have pointed out after this question that Princeton is in a rather unique position; it is one of our nation's truly most selective academic institutions, in terms of its undergraduate student body, its graduate student body, and the academic stature of its faculty members. As such, its faculty may be much more willing and able to make qualitative judgments about their colleagues' professional accomplishments than the faculty at other institutions. This stands in stark contrast to Kenneth Ruscio's description of how tenure and promotion decisions are becoming more codified and numbers-driven at other institutions. So picking up on one of John Lombardi's points, the impact of Generation Xers on our academic institutions may well depend upon the characteristics of an institution;

where an institution is in the selectivity hierarchy clearly matters. So too does the nature of the institution. A selective national liberal arts college, such as Washington and Lee, has to evaluate in a very qualitative way teaching and advising as well as research (teaching and advising matter at research universities but are not given as much weight as research). So in some respects, the subjective judgments that must be made at national liberal arts colleges during the tenure process are much more multidimensional, which leads to greater attention to process at these institutions.

An institution's financial resources also clearly matter, as John Lombardi stressed in his remarks. During the discussion period, I noted that my institution, Cornell University, which is one of the wealthiest institutions in the nation, has an endowment per student that is less than one-eighth the size of Princeton's endowment per student. Thus, it is impossible for Cornell to afford to do all of the things that Princeton is doing in terms of family policies, just as it is impossible for Cornell to pay faculty salaries as high as Princeton, to have class sizes as small as Princeton's, and to have financial aid packages as generous as Princeton's. Institutions that are more poorly endowed than Cornell obviously face even more stringent financial constraints.

Another audience member noted the growing trend in higher education toward the use of part-time and full-time non-tenure track faculty members. He wondered if efforts to provide enhanced family policies for tenure track faculty members will be financed by a reduction in the number of full-time tenure track faculty and an increased growth in the number of contingent (non-tenure track) faculty. He noted that the tendency to use non-tenure track faculty was not the result of a generational change, but rather of the economic conditions facing higher education. However, the response of institutions to the generational change may hasten the rate of growth of contingent faculty.

John Lombardi responded that the different segments of the higher education market will respond differently to changes in economic conditions just as they will respond differently to the generational changes. He expects more institutions to offer forms of rolling five-year contracts in which some faculty will get paid well for specific responsibilities (teaching or research) and if they do well, institutions will have to compete with higher salaries to compensate them for the risk of not having tenure. To date, institutions do not do this, the highest-paid faculty members are the ones who have tenure or are on the tenure track. Such forms of contracts would give institutions more flexibility in meeting changes in demand for different disciplines and changes in economic conditions.

Still another audience member questioned how the emphasis on work–life issues plays out with single faculty members. She worried that this emphasis may discourage single individuals (defined as people without partners) from entering academia because they will feel that they are not getting their "fair share" of the resources.

Joan Girgus responded that this does not appear to be an issue at Princeton. However, she acknowledged that this may be because Princeton has enough resources to provide whatever it takes to recruit, nurture, and retain the very best faculty members, regardless of family status. Whether lesser-endowed institutions will face the problem the audience member raised is an open question. Kenneth Ruscio noted that this issue fits neatly into his framework of academic institutions increasingly having to negotiate between the interests of different groups. And John Lombardi noted that this issue is not anything new; historically, academic institutions have devoted more resources per faculty member for family health insurance than they have for single health insurance coverage and some institutions have provided children's college tuition benefits, which increases the cost of faculty with children relative to the cost of single and married faculty without children.

CONCLUDING REMARKS

One comes away from the panel and the discussion that followed with a sense that Generation X has impacted both the way that colleges and universities are governed and the policies that they pursue. However, there are a number of important points that must be kept in mind.

First, virtually all of the changes that the panelists talked about are going on outside of academia as well as within. Our society has become much more litigious and therefore policies and procedures for hiring and discharge have been codified throughout the economy. The growing share of females in the labor force, among college graduates, and among advanced degree-holders (law, medicine, business, and PhDs) has led corporations to worry about family policies and promotion policies at least as much as colleges and universities do. The ability of faculty in public (but not private) higher education to form unions and bargain collectively goes back to the growth of state statutes governing public sector collective bargaining; these began in the late 1960s. These changes all started well in advance of the time Generation Xers approached academia and so to attribute these changes to their characteristics alone seems inappropriate. In many respects, they are a result of the Baby Boomer Generation.

Second, as John Lombardi stressed, higher education is not a homogeneous set of institutions. We are very heterogeneous in terms of the academic programs we offer, the selectivity spheres in which we compete, the degrees that we offer, and the resources that we have at our disposal. So the responses of institutions to Generation X are likely to vary widely across institutions.

In recent years there has been a dramatic widening in the distribution of resources across private higher education institutions; the rich have gotten richer, which mirrors what is going on in the economy as a whole. Financial problems faced by state governments have also resulted in a dramatic decline in the resources that public higher education institutions have available relative to their private sector counterparts, with the decline being the greatest for the non-flagship public institutions. As a result, faculty salaries have fallen in public higher education relative to private higher education and, within both sectors, average salaries have become more diverse across academic institutions. As such, the ability of academic institutions to adopt family-friendly policies is going to vary widely across institutions. Institutions that have no money to send faculty to professional meetings will not be able to provide funds for child care for faculty attending those meetings as Princeton did. Institutions that barely have enough funds to offer graduate student stipends that are half those at the richest private universities will not be able to offer maternity leave for graduate students as Princeton did.

Of course, it is worth emphasizing that family policies, which may have costs in the short run, also yield benefits to institutions and in the long run may actually reduce costs. Linda Bunnell's discussion of the policies UWSP has adopted made clear that a major driver of these policies is to enhance faculty retention, which often helps reduce costs. UWSP is not a wealthy institution but it understood that it needed to implement these policies for financial reasons. So while we should take John Lombardi's caution about academia's need to rein in costs very seriously, sometimes new programs that introduce additional costs can actually save institutions money.

Colleges and universities make decisions all the time about how to allocate their resources. Historically, they have not included many work–life benefits in the mix. Increasingly, corporations have come to see such benefits as essential to their ability to attract and retain the most talented and loyal workforce. Much of corporate America no longer sees these benefits as "add-ons" but rather has come to see them as essential characteristics of the working environment. Higher education institutions need to consider seriously whether they need to follow this lead if they want to attract the strongest undergraduate and graduate students to faculty careers. As Joan Girgus has stressed, instituting even one or two family-friendly policies or programs can make a substantial difference. Not only will they provide help in specific situations, they will also send a strong signal about what an institution values.

NOTE

1. For more details on this and other policies that are part of the University of California's "Faculty Friendly Edge," see http://ucfamilyedge.berkeley.edu.

4. Young faculty and their impact on academe

Cathy A. Trower

Every generation blames the one before. And all of their frustrations come beating on your door. (Song lyrics "The Living Years," 1988 Mike & The Mechanics)

Each generation imagines itself to be more intelligent than the one that went before it, and wiser than the one that comes after it. (George Orwell, author)

Each generation must recreate liberty for its own times. (Florence E. Allen, Federal Judge)

Each new generation is a fresh invasion of savages. (Hervey Allen, poet)[*]

Whichever quote you prefer, there's plenty here to make us stop and think about the generations: blame, imagined superiority, recreation of liberty, and savagery! This is juicy stuff and it is not just fodder for good songs and great quotes; these themes are playing themselves out right now in the hallowed halls of academe. Because I agree with C. Stone Brown (2005) who wrote, "it's counterproductive to judge generational differences as a right way or a wrong way of doing tasks or learning, because there are differences in how generations feel about work, learn new tasks, and process information" (p. 30), the purpose of this chapter is threefold, to: (1) highlight the values that shaped the policies and practices composed by the Lost Generation (born 1883–1900), which worked well for the GI (1901–24), Silent (1925–42) and Baby Boom (1943–60) Generations, which do not work so well for the 13th Generation (referred to throughout this chapter as Generation X or Gen X (1961–81[1])); (2) discuss the tension points that result; and (3) suggest what higher education institutions might do to attract and retain Gen X faculty.

DIFFERENT ASSUMPTIVE WORLDS AND CORE VALUES

The assumptive world of those seated around tables at convenings of the American Association of University Professors (AAUP) and the Association of American Colleges (now the Association of American Colleges and Universities) beginning in 1934 as they crafted the "1940 Statement of Principles on Academic Freedom and Tenure" (a restatement of principles set forth in 1925) was vastly different from that facing the current generation of young scholars. Let's imagine that illustrious group. My mind's eye pictures the average age of the group to be 50 (born in 1884—part of the Lost Generation) and the predominant skin color to be white and the sex to be male. I have not been able to ascertain whether there were any women or persons of color at these meetings, but I do not think it is a stretch to assume none at all—or at least very few—so as to render their voices largely insignificant. The people around those tables are dead now, yet their legacy lives on in the form of tenure and promotion policies and practices largely unchanged[2] from that era (Trower, 2000). The Lost Generation grew up amidst urban blight, unregulated drug use, child sweat shops, and massive immigration (Strauss and Howe, 1997). Some values we see reflected in the AAUP statements of this era are academic freedom, job security after a "reasonable" probationary period, autonomy, stability, seniority, and continuity. The policies were designed to provide faculty members with due process in order to protect them against capricious acts by management.

Regardless of who actually wrote the original AAUP-endorsed language used in many policy statements governing the work life of faculty today, one thing is true—those policies have served faculty and the academy well over the years, in part because:

> Since World War II, each generation has assumed two things about the younger generations entering the workplace: 1) Senior generations assume that the younger generations will measure success the same way they themselves have. 2) Senior generations also believe that younger workers should pay their dues, following the same paths to achieve the same levels of success. (Marston, 2007, p. 3)

Embedded in these statements are assumptions about measurement of success, dues payment, and achievement. It seems folly to assume that any of these notions would be the same for every generation and, indeed, we are finding out that they are not—not in the slightest.

Values of the GI and Silent Generations

With such defining events as World War I and II, the Great Depression, the Korean War, and the GI Bill, the GI and Silent Generations grew up in an age of scarcity; they learned to do without as they saved for a "rainy day" and learned to "waste not, want not." Sacrifice was an expectation, as were hard work, conformity, patience/delayed gratification, adherence to rules, and duty before pleasure (Zemke et al., 2000, p. 30). Those born between 1901 and 1942 found that individual goals must often be sublimated to group goals; faith in institutions was required to win wars, and loyalty ensued. Since over 50 percent of these men were veterans, their experiences taught them that using a top-down approach was the most efficient way to get things done (Lancaster and Stillman, 2002, p. 19). The work ethic of these individuals is marked by dependability, loyalty, and a "stay until the job is done" attitude. Work life and family life were separate and distinct (Zemke et al., 2000, p. 51). Married men of these generations were likely to have a stay-at-home wife who looked after all things domestic, including the children—academics were no exception.

Values of the Baby Boom Generation

Almost the opposite of those who came in the two prior generations, Boomers grew up in positive, wealthy, and optimistic times. This was the first generation in which child rearing was a hobby and a pleasure and not an economic necessity and a biological inevitability (Zemke et al., 2000, p. 64). This generation values teamwork and competition, personal gratification, health and wellness, youth, work, and involvement (ibid., p. 68). Rather than following the rules (as their fathers did), Boomers manipulated the rules to meet their own needs as they redefined the workplace and the home alike. Ever-striving workaholics, Boomers have been accused of having "no life beyond work." For them, getting the job done means putting in long, visible hours (Marston, 2007, p. 58). Accused of hedonism and materialism, this generation made sacrifices of home life stability to get ahead in the workplace; divorce became commonplace as men and women sought to get ahead, with or without a family. Yuppies (young urban professionals), yumpies (young upwardly mobile professionals), dinks (double income, no kids), and divorcees characterize the Baby Boom Generation.

Values of Generation X

This generation is marked by skepticism and self-reliance in part because nearly 50 percent of their parents' marriages ended in divorce. In addition, this is the first generation of kids in the bounds of the two-income family (Zemke et al., 2000, p. 98). They value diversity, technoliteracy, fun, informality, pragmatism, and balance. They are seeking a sense of family that is different from the Boomers; both Gen X parents want to play a close role in raising the children. A very important, relatively new trend is the return of the stay-at-home mom and the three-child household; in less than a decade, the number of women staying at home and caring for their children has increased by nearly 13 percent. Two-thirds of all working mothers between the ages of 25 and 35 work part-time (Marston, 2007, p. 170). Unlike their parents' "live to work" mentality, Gen Xers "work to live"; thus, they have very different expectations of and demands for the workplace. Importantly, "Many Generation Xers also witnessed their parents reap downsizing in exchange for their loyalty to an organization. So Generation Xers first loyalty tends to be to themselves rather than to any institution" (Bickel and Brown, 2005, p. 206).

My understanding of the primary works cited here (Zemke et al., 2000; Lancaster and Stillman, 2002; Marston, 2007), and the values outlined above, is summarized in Table 4.1.

RESULTING CHALLENGES AND TENSION POINTS

Given the information presented above, it is not surprising that certain challenges and tensions arise in the workplace. Contextualizing to academe, it is likely that the majority of the senior faculty are from the Silent or Boom Generations; most of the administrators are Boomers and some are Gen Xers; and most of the junior faculty are Gen Xers. Thus, let's look down that fourth column in Table 4.1 and examine the impact of young faculty on academic institutions.

Skepticism, Self-command, and Flat Structures

"Breathes there a cohort with a soul more dark or with such an edgy skepticism about them?" (Zemke et al., 2000, p. 21). As a group, Gen Xers are nothing if not skeptical, as they grew up when every major American institution—religion, the presidency, the military, corporate America—was called into question (Lancaster and Stillman, 2002). "It's rare to find a Gen Xer who isn't dissatisfied with something, although it's hard to pinpoint exactly what the dissatisfaction is about" (Marston, 2007, p. 60). In academe, this skepticism can translate into deep anxiety about the tenure process, its fairness, whether it is possible to achieve it, whether the game is worth the candle, and whether it will even be offered at institutions in the future.

Table 4.1 The generations at work

	GI and Silent Generations	Baby Boomer Generation	Generation X
Key descriptor	Loyal	Optimistic	Skeptical
Notion of command	Chain of command	Change of command	Self-command
View on hierarchy	Prefer military model; top-down hierarchy	Comfortable with top-down hierarchy	Prefer flat organization structures
What they're building	A legacy	A stellar, upward career	A portable career
Job changing	Carries a stigma Stay for a lifetime	Puts one behind Stay if moving up	Is necessary Follow heart
Motivator(s)	A job well done	Money, title, recognition, promotion	Freedom, fun, fulfillment; time
Workplace flexibility	Who will do the work?	The nerve of those Xers—they want it all!	I'll go where I can find the lifestyle I want
Working long hours	Required; prudent	Will get you ahead; money; bonuses	Get a life!
Productivity	Inputs and outputs matter	Input matters most	Output is all that matters
Give me more	Essentials	Money	Time
Performance reviews	If no one is yelling, all is well	Once a year; well-documented	Sorry to interrupt again, how am I doing?
Work–family	Work matters most; stay-at-home wife	Work matters most; dual career or divorced	Family matters as much; dual career
Career paths	Slow and steady Seniority Stability	Ladder Upward mobility	Lattice Plateaus are fine Creative journeys
Career pace	Prove yourself with loyalty Pay your dues	Prove yourself with long hours Pay your dues	I want to know all my options now

> • *Tenure is like the Social Security System—I doubt it will be available by the time I get there.*[3]

In some cases, junior faculty are skeptical about their senior colleagues and the advice they're being given:

> • *Sometimes I think senior faculty are a bit self-serving in their advice. You wonder if you're somehow being manipulated in a bad way— sometimes knowingly and sometimes not. I'm in a very competitive field and I wonder if the senior faculty in my department want the credit and so misguide me.*

Junior faculty, like their senior colleagues, are attracted to academe in part for the promise of autonomy—to follow their research wherever it may lead, unfettered by outside interference from other faculty or from administrators. Further, many Gen Xers prefer to work in cross-disciplinary teams that do not require or even lend themselves well to hierarchical command:

> • *Point me in the right direction; give me a few signposts along the way, and let me go. I don't want anyone telling me what to do, when to be in my office, or the best way to conduct my research or teach my classes.*

Many Gen X faculty do not fully subscribe to the notion of top-down hierarchies that have prevailed in academe for decades. "For Gen Xers, company hierarchy is a barrier to the discovery process" (Marston, 2007, p. 118). In part because of their inherent skepticism and resulting mistrust of management, and in part because of their strong desire for self-command, many Gen X faculty prefer flat structure with minimal red-tape. One of the primary complaints we hear from tenure-track faculty on surveys and in interviews and focus groups is how they detest the paperwork and slowness that result from the large, bureaucratic structures of academe:

> • *This appointment would be perfect—I love my colleagues, the research, and my students—but for the fact that I spend inordinate amounts of time doing paperwork to satisfy the bureaucracy that is this university. That is not why I got into academe and it makes the private sector look very appealing.*

A Portable Career and Changing Jobs

Unlike their Silent and Boomer seniors, Gen Xers express far less interest in staying at one institution for their entire careers:

In interviews, Xers tell us they can't stand the thought of reaching a dead end. Their greatest fear is that they will become stagnant. The rate of change they've seen during their lifetimes and the cynical sense that everything is temporary play into their distrust of career permanence. (Lancaster and Stillman, 2002, pp. 58–9)

It is still unknown what impact this will ultimately have on academe and even tenure. The University of California, Davis, School of Medicine noted, "we may have lost some of our junior faculty because we did not recognize that many tend to see themselves as 'free agents' who are not reluctant to move for a perceived better offer" (Howell, et al., 2005, p. 529).

The academy has certainly seen increasing numbers of young faculty members choosing to work part-time and on non-tenure-track lines. They are cautious about where they take their first academic appointment, worried about how it will somehow place them on a certain track that they are not yet sure they want:

- *I worry that if I don't take my first job at a research university instead of at a liberal arts college, I will be tracked as uninterested in research and that is simply not the case. I have a great offer from a really spectacular liberal arts college, but I have been advised against taking it for this very reason.*

- *I'm much less concerned about where I start than where I'll eventually go because I have no intention of staying at one place. You have to stay flexible and move on when it's time.*

Again, unlike their senior colleagues, for whom tenure means security and permanence, many Gen Xers expect to change jobs (maybe more than once) even after achieving tenure. Twelve percent of the nearly 6000 junior faculty members who responded to a COACHE survey question asking how long they intend to stay at their present institution, assuming they achieve tenure there, reported "less than five years." A variety of reasons offer insight into young faculty including the most predominant—better geographic location (22 percent); better fit/climate/culture (15 percent); family/spouse issues (14 percent); professional advancement (11 percent); better compensation (11 percent); and to work at a better department or institution (11 percent).

Motivators, Workplace Flexibility, and Productivity

Less concerned than their predecessors with job security and staying at one place for an entire career, Gen Xers find motivation in jobs that are fun.

Rather than seeking monetary rewards at the expense of personal time and a home life, this generation wants freedom (now, not when they retire) and finds time a big motivator. "Employers can expect that . . . Generation X will continue to put a high priority on control of their own time. This point is scarcely negotiable. Gen Xers have no intention of becoming the workaholics their parents were" (Marston, 2007, p. 171).

A flexible workplace where they can find balance between work and home is not just a value of Gen X faculty, it is an expectation. As one of my administrator colleagues said, "Gen Xers do not suffer silently. They tell me what they want in no uncertain terms. And a flexible workplace is one of those things they demand—one of the reasons they were attracted to academe."

Gen Xers think mostly in terms of output rather than number of hours on the job—they say, "If I can produce all this in half the time, why should I hang around the office?" This can cause tension with their elders who feel they had to "pay their dues" and with administrators demanding a certain number of office hours each week. Given technology, most faculty can, and many do, work long hours and are accessible day and night on e-mail.

Let's face it, these younger workers have an attitude toward work that is as different from that of previous generations as anything we've seen before. . . . Flexible hours, an informal work environment, and just the right amount of supervision are great places to start. . . . If you're searching for the Generation X work ethic, don't look through the traditional lens. You won't find it. If you want to tap into it, give them a lot of freedom regarding how the work gets done. (Zemke et al., 2000, pp. 111–12):

- *I think some of the senior faculty and administrators put way too much emphasis on face-time and not enough on output. I don't need to work from 9 to 5, or be in my office at certain times everyday to be productive. In fact, I can produce much more when I can do it during my peak hours, which happen to be very late at night.*

- *The most important commodity is time. The tenure track requires that you be an expert researcher and an excellent teacher while overseeing the work of graduate students and advising undergraduates, all the while showing up for faculty meetings to show you're a good citizen. The one thing we all need more of is time, and since that's a finite thing, we need the flexibility necessary to make it all work out.*

- *We all work hard, but it's not a cookie cutter, assembly line approach. I detest all the counting that occurs—like how many hours were you in the lab? How many in your office? Why weren't you at the faculty meeting? How many articles in peer-reviewed journals? It should be about quality not quantity.*

Performance Reviews

One of the greatest conundrums surrounding Gen Xers is that they desire autonomy and constant and immediate performance feedback at the same time. And as we all know, feedback is not something we do particularly well in the academy. All too often, the message is, "We'll know it when we see it!" and that is disheartening to Gen Xers who most likely harbor some skepticism about those above them, mentioned earlier. Baby Boomers were content with, and even seemed to like, well-documented feedback once a year when called for by human resources. This not only means that Gen Xers will want a thorough third-year review (which most institutions have now instituted), but also well-documented annual (or even semi-annual) feedback from their department chairperson.

Another major difference between Gen Xers and their senior colleagues in terms of feedback is the directness of desired communication in both directions. "Traditionalists and Boomers . . . are often shocked by the younger generations' frank and direct style of feedback" (Howell et al., 2005, p. 528). Marston (2007) noted, "Boomers and Matures—the senior management—are often reluctant to give clear, direct, specific instruction about what they want an employee or subordinate to do; perhaps it seems too blunt and rude to them to give a direct order" (p. 124) and thus, Gen Xers hear the directives of superiors as suggestions. "Generation X . . . want and need clear, concise, and direct communication. They want to be directed in their jobs. There should be no hidden messages or 'They should know what I mean' type of communications" (p. 125). This is one reason why junior and senior faculty all too often clash about the requirements for tenure—the young faculty member is thinking, "Why don't they just tell me what they want and I'll do it" and the older faculty member is thinking, "Why should we have to spell this out? Don't they learn this in graduate school? No one told *me* exactly what to do and I survived."

Work–Family Balance

There may be no larger gap between generations than this one. Gen Xers are unwilling to sacrifice balance and a personal life for work. They are adamantly against doing what they saw their parents do—give up on a home life to get ahead at work. This issue is not one of gender—young men are as likely as young women to seek time off work to spend with family, as more and more partnerships are truly that; women expect that their partners will give equal time to domestic responsibilities, including childrearing.

Several recent studies have shown the generational shift toward men desiring more time with family, being more involved with child care, and spending more time on household activities. A study by the Radcliffe Public Policy Center reported that:

> Having a job schedule that allows for family time is more important to young men than money, power, or prestige. . . . Eighty-two percent of men aged 20–39 put family time at the top of their list, keeping pace with 85 percent of women in those age groups. Breaking ranks with their fathers and grandfathers on the important issue of work–family integration, 71 percent of men 21–39 [sic] said they would give up some of their pay for more time with their families. . . . While women's struggle to balance work and family has been a focus of much study, Center researchers discovered that family time is as important to young men as women. In fact, survey data show that young men in their 20's are seven percent more likely than young women to give up pay for more time with their families. (Radcliffe Public Policy Center, 2000)

Another study by the Family and Work Institute (Lang and Risman, 2007) showed that:

> Significantly, younger fathers spend more time with their children than older fathers do. When the Families & Work Institute compared the work-day hours Gen-X and Boomer fathers spend caring for and doing things with their children in 2002, they found that Gen-X fathers spend more than an additional hour every day than did Baby Boom generation dads. After controlling for the possible effect of the children's age, the same difference remained. The Baby Boom generation of men was the first that had to deal with a new kind of family life, where women demanded more equality at home and at work. Generation X men may not talk as much about changing family roles as the Baby Boomers, but in practice they are breaking new ground in co-parenting their children.

Indeed, one of the consistently lowest scores on the COACHE survey of junior faculty is satisfaction with the ability to balance professional time and personal/family responsibilities (overall mean = 2.79 on a 1.00 to 5.00 point scale); female junior faculty rate balance significantly lower than their male counterparts (2.57 vs. 2.96). Two other low scores concern agreement that one's institution does what it can to make child-bearing (overall mean = 2.85) and childrearing (2.69) and the tenure track compatible. Again, females rate these factors significantly lower than males.

An open-ended COACHE survey question requests that junior faculty write the number one thing that they personally feel their institution could do to improve the workplace—12 percent listed issues surrounding work–family balance, spousal hiring, child care, and personal leave.

Career Paths and Pace

As mentioned previously, paying one's dues is not really part of the Gen X mentality. They expect to hit the ground running, know where they're running, and to get there in record time. They have little tolerance for bureaucracies, politics, or game-playing. "Generation Xers are demanding that organizations speed up the duration of career paths. While Boomers generally assumed they'd spend one to five years in a position before being promoted, Xers want to know where they're going to be next month" (Lancaster and Stillman, 2002, p. 63). Gen Xers "enter the workplace seeking self-fulfillment from the get-go and aren't interested in paying their dues for unknown periods of time" (Marston, 2007, p. 10).

In addition to a faster pace, Gen Xers want multiple paths—not just one. Both of these notions clearly run counter to the pace and path of academe:

- *Even the name—tenure track—is unappealing to me. They might as well call it the tenure rut because that's what it feels like. There is one way to get there and that is the way the senior faculty say, regardless of what makes sense in today's environment.*

- *Whoever decided that six years on the tenure track makes sense for everybody? That seems odd to me. Some people are ready sooner and some need more time; it's the quality of the work not the speed by which it is accomplished.*

The workplace *ladder* of the Boomer Generation is of less interest to Gen Xers than a workplace *lattice*:

> We need to replace the corporate ladder with a corporate lattice—a term implying a more adaptive framework which allows individuals to move in many different directions, not just upward or downward. . . . This plateauing is part of a bigger phenomenon in the workforce—one that also includes people putting higher priorities on activities outside their jobs, from family to volunteer work to hobbies. (Knowledge@Wharton, 2006)

Bickel and Brown (2005) reported that "Individuals with multilayered commitments will not build careers in the linear fashion. . . . Career trajectories are now more likely to undulate and include more plateaus and spirals" (p. 208). The authors suggest that this phenomenon is quite natural given that people live longer and young people may have many careers over several decades:

> it encourages new ways of thinking about health, balance, and energy management. Naturally . . . young people question the requirement to push so very hard early in their careers at the expense of nutrition, exercise, family, and other interests. Rather than "slacking off," Generation Xers may actually be extending their productive personal lives . . . By adhering to an inflexible career trajectory that requires the greatest time commitment in the same years that young families need the most attention, academic medicine forces unnecessary "either/or" choices between work and family. (Ibid., pp. 208–9)

IMPLICATIONS FOR POLICY AND PRACTICE

The 14 areas that differentiate generations in the workplace (presented in Table 4.1), while certainly not exhaustive, provide an excellent place to start as we rethink faculty appointment policies and practices for Gen Xers and the generations to follow them. The prior discussion leads to six areas where academic institutions might focus their attention as they reform faculty employment policies:

- clarity;
- collegiality;
- equity;
- flexibility;
- interdisciplinarity;
- productivity;

Clarity
Because Gen Xers may be skeptical, prefer self-command and frequent performance feedback, clarity is essential to workplace satisfaction and successful recruitment and retention. This generation does not want to "figure it out" or play politics to succeed. They want clarity in all personnel policies and practices. They are willing to work hard as long as they understand the parameters of the game and know as precisely as possible on what criteria their performance will be judged. Traditionally, in academe, promotion and tenure processes have been anything but transparent, and, in fact, described by young scholars as "archery in the dark":

- Be transparent. Of tenure process, criteria, standards, and body of evidence clarity, junior faculty are least satisfied with standards. COACHE institutions that score well in terms of tenure clarity are the ones that are transparent about the performance threshold—the expectations for scholarship, teaching, service, campus citizenship, and colleagueship are discussed. The best results occur when chairpersons take time with junior faculty, at the outset, to explain departmental expectations and ensure that the faculty member is fully informed about what he/she might need and that it's okay to ask questions.

- Be frequent. Connect junior faculty with mentors and create a culture where conversations about progress are frequent.
- Document progress. Annual performance feedback from the chair should be documented in writing. A thorough third-year review should be conducted during which junior faculty are told precisely what they are doing that is on target and what needs to be improved should also be put in writing.
- Provide training for department chairpersons. Not all chairpersons are effective communicators, especially when it comes to providing cross-generational feedback. A little training can go a long way.
- Illuminate the path to success and provide milestones. Remember, Gen Xers do not like surprises or delayed gratification.
- Be participative. Allow the junior faculty member to have a say in performance outcomes and goals—be clear about what needs to get done, but allow some choice about how.

Collegiality

Marston (2007) reminds us that "Gen X works out of loyalty to people, not to the company, but only when their supervisors are superb communicators and know their employees well" (p. 115). This speaks to the importance of clarity (above) and mentoring. Gen Xers have been compared with wolves—they want to be part of the pack; some lone wolves exist, yes, but for the most part Xers want to run with a group of talented colleagues. They expect to be connected to that pack in person and in cyberspace. A sense of community is extremely important to Gen X and they are less likely than older generations to seek only community membership in a single discipline or department:

- Pay attention to colleagueship. COACHE results show that departmental climate, created by colleagues, is the most important factor affecting global satisfaction.
- Pay attention to fit. Of all the climate measures in the COACHE survey, how well one feels they fit in their department has the biggest impact on global satisfaction. Junior faculty members feel as though they fit when: (1) they feel welcomed, (2) their ideas and research

are valued, (3) they are expected (and are given resources) to succeed/achieve tenure, (4) they have a voice in departmental decisions, (5) they have champions who are vested in their success, and (6) senior faculty do not stand on ceremony or tradition. Gen X faculty want to be seen as equal participants in a collaborative effort. For them, collaboration trumps competition almost every time.

- Connect faculty across campus up, across, and down; hierarchy is not as important as it is to prior generations. Provide opportunities for junior faculty to socialize and conduct research with colleagues and students across campus.
- Be sure that technology is current. Gen Xers are much more likely to use instant messaging and e-mail to communicate with colleagues so it is imperative that technology is up to date.

Equity

Gen X faculty members expect equity, which translates into demands for transparency (discussed in the clarity section). In addition to clarity about the expectations for tenure and promotion, they expect equitable workloads, including number of students and courses/new preparations and service requirements. As mentioned previously, Gen Xers will not be shy about speaking up regarding perceived workplace inequities. As tempting as it might be for older faculty to lament that younger faculty members are "whiners" and not willing to play by the old rules, such temptation should be resisted. Because Gen Xers are less worried about job security than career security, they will leave situations where they feel they are being treated inequitably. Further, if we are honest with ourselves, we will readily see that expectations for research funding, publications, teaching, and service have increased over the years and during a time when research funding is increasingly more difficult to attain and numerous publication outlets have increasingly longer lead-times:

- Pay attention to course and advisee load as well as committee service for junior faculty. Some departments provide tenure-track faculty with course reduction and relief from service commitments during the probationary years; this should be consistent across all faculty in a department.
- Be aware of unintended inequities and right them. Sometimes, in our eagerness to ensure diversity, we over-burden women and minorities with committee assignments. Pay particular attention to such "cultural taxation."
- Allow junior faculty the freedom to say "No" without fear of reprisal. It is important to create a climate where Gen X faculty

are empowered to decline "opportunities" to participate in all
events.

- Be aware of equity in terms of office and lab space as well as access
to teaching assistants and research/graduate assistants.
- Be consistent. Do not give everything to the best negotiators and
nothing to those who don't ask. Numerous studies have shown that
women are less likely than men to negotiate and when they do, it is
often held against them (but expected of men).

Flexibility

"Having it all" for Gen Xers means having balance between work and
home life. This generation does not want to be just like their workaholic
parents; therefore, they demand a flexible enough environment to find that
balance—willing to work at home, but also needing sometimes to bring
home into work. As stated, this generation will work hard but wants to
decide where, how, and when. The notion of a 9 to 5 workplace is no longer
entirely appropriate, especially with so many members of dual career
families:

- Provide flex time, modified duties, and job sharing arrangements.
Increasingly, universities are adding a variety of options for staff—
why not for faculty? Gen Xers will certainly appreciate the option,
whether or not they opt in.
- Assist young faculty in finding balance. Employee Assistance
Programs (EAPs) have been utilized for the past few decades, but
recently their focus has shifted to accommodate new generations of
workers with different values and lifestyles. Institutions are also
offering wellness and work–life balance programs, and concierge
services.
- Allow less-than-full-time tenure tracks. While an attractive concept,
part-time tenure tracks are not yet commonplace and are not without problems (Williams, 2004; Bombardieri, 2005), but should be
explored. The University of Washington allows two options: a permanent part-time tenure-track and a temporary part-time option
that combines partial leave with an extension of the tenure clock
(Quinn, Lange, and Olswang, 2004).
- Provide off-ramps and ramps back on. Hewlett and Luce (2005)
remind us that getting off a career track is relatively easy, but getting
back on is enormously challenging. As a result, many talented
women who wish to step off a track temporarily, to have children,
never get back on. In academe, on-ramps mean keeping women net-
worked, connected, and their lab running while they're out on leave.

- Allow choice in career paths. Not uncommon in medical schools, the University of California, Davis, College of Medicine offers five different tracks including three that are hypothesis-based research-intensive, of which only one is tenure track, and two non-tenure clinical tracks, with one requiring creative work (Howell et al., 2005, p. 530).
- Vary departmental meeting times, but avoid meetings before 8:00 a.m. and after 5:00 p.m.—times when people with children will most likely need to attend to activities outside of work. Consider teleconferencing as an alternative to in-person meetings.
- Utilize technology to increase flexibility. This will allow Gen Xers to choose when, where, and how to work, and ultimately keep them happier.

Interdisciplinarity

Many Gen Xers were socialized in graduate school to cross discipline lines and consider research at the intersections of fields. They took courses across discipline lines and may have enjoyed working with colleagues in other departments, schools, and even institutions. Indeed, many of today's problems and issues demand interdisciplinary solutions and Gen Xers are not only interested in, but are also especially well-poised, to do this work:

- Hire onto interdisciplinary lines. Provide paths to tenure and promotion by honoring and rewarding this work.
- Provide support for collaboration across disciplines including mentors, internal grants, and assistance with interdisciplinary grant-writing.

Productivity

Making an impact, and doing so relatively quickly, is important to many Gen Xers. Call it a short attention span if you like, these scholars multitask and seek instant gratification like nobody's business:

- Ensure that all required forms of faculty work count toward tenure and promotion. Gen X faculty express frustration that they are required to perform in multiple areas but everyone knows that published research is all that really counts. If academic institutions are to get the most from young faculty, and honor their multifaceted missions, it is crucial to give credit for all the work that faculty do. If teaching and service truly matter, that work should count in the tenure process.
- Reward quality, not just quantity. The academy needs to get beyond merely counting the number of articles in peer-reviewed journals.

Today, there many more outlets for publication, including online, and the quality of one's work should also be measured.

● Focus on outcomes more than face-time. It is important to tell Gen X faculty what is expected of them, and then let them figure out how. If they can produce at a high quality, and are accessible to students, it is unnecessary to count hours in the office.

CONCLUSION

While the policies codified by the AAUP early in the last century delineating a one-size-fits-all full-time tenure track, with a six years up-or-out probationary period, worked well for the GI, Silent, and Baby Boom Generations, they no longer do. The time is now to stop bemoaning what has been lost and what is past and get on with shaping the future with Gen X faculty and administrators leading the way. The Millennials (born 1981–99) are not far behind, and if we think the current academic employment policies and practices don't fit Gen Xers well, the problems will only grow more pronounced as the newcomers find their way into faculty positions.

NOTES

* The epigraphs for George Orwell, Florence E. Allen and Hervey Allen are taken from http://www.brainyquote.com

1. There are differences in the names given to each generation as is there variation in the specific start and end years that describe the various generations discussed in this chapter; I have chosen to use the names and dates listed here and used by Strauss and Howe (1997). Readers may also see the GI and Silent generations referred to as Matures—born prior to 1945 (Marston, 2007); as Veterans—born between 1922 and 1943 (Zemke, Raines and Filipczak, 2000); and as Traditionalists—born 1900–45 (Lancaster and Stillman, 2002).

2. Interpretive comments, mostly as regards academic freedom, amended the original 1940 Statement in 1970. In 1983, there were recommended procedures for increasing the number of minority persons and women on college and university faculty. In June 1999, the AAUP commented on post-tenure review. In November 1999, a statement "On Collegiality as a Criterion for Faculty Evaluation" was published. In May 2001, a "Statement of Principles on Family Responsibilities and Academic Work" provided "important relief for probationary faculty in their child-rearing years." In November 2003, the AAUP published its statement on "Contingent Appointments and the Academic Profession".

3. Quotes from Gen Xer/junior faculty utilized throughout this chapter, italicized and bulleted, are from unpublished interviews conducted as part of various research projects with which I have been associated over the past ten years—the Project on Faculty Appointments, the Study of New Scholars, and the Collaborative on Academic Careers in Higher Education (COACHE). See COACHE website at www.coache.org for more information.

REFERENCES

Bickel, Janet and Ann J. Brown (2005), "Generation X: implications for faculty recruitment and development in academic health centers," *Academic Medicine*, **80** (3), 205–10.

Bombardieri, Marcella (2005), "Reduced load lets faculty meld family, tenure track," *The Boston Globe*, 4 October, A1.

Brown, C. Stone (2005), "Avoiding stereotypes: four generations in the workplace," *DiversityInc.*, **4** (4), 28, 30–31.

Hewlett, Sylvia Ann and Carolyn Buck Luce (March 2005), "Off-ramps and on-ramps: keeping talented women on the road to success," *Harvard Business Review*, **83** (3), 43–54.

Howell, Lydia Pleotis, Gregg Servis, and Ann Bonham (2005), "Multigenerational challenges in academic medicine: UCDavis's responses," *Academic Medicine*, **80** (6), 527–32.

Knowledge@Wharton (2006), "Plateauing: redefining success at work," http://knowledge.wharton.upenn.edu/article.cfm?articleid=1564.

Lancaster, Lynne C. and David Stillman (2002), *When Generations Collide*, New York: HarperBusiness.

Lang, Molly Monahan and Barbara J. Risman (2007), "A stalled revolution or a still-unfolding one? The continuing convergence of men's and women's roles," http://www.contemporaryfamilies.org/subtemplate.php?t=briefingPapers&ext=stalledrevolution.

Marston, Cam (2007), *Motivating the "What's in it For Me?" Workforce*, Hoboken, NJ: John Wiley & Sons, Inc.

Quinn, Kate, Sheila Edwards Lange, and Steven G. Olswang (2004), "Family-friendly policies and the research university," *Academe: Bulletin of AAUP*, **90** (36), 32–4.

Radcliffe Public Policy Center (2000),"Study: for men, family comes first," *The Harvard University Gazette*, http://www.hno.harvard.edu/gazette/2000/05.04/radcliffe.html.

Strauss, William and Neil Howe (1997), *The Fourth Turning: An American Philosophy*, New York: Broadway Books.

Trower, Cathy A. (ed.) (2000), *Policies on Faculty Appointment: Standard Practice and Unusual Arrangements*, Bolton, MA: Anker Publishing Company, Inc.

Williams, Joan C. (2004), "Part-timers on the tenure-track," *The Chronicle of Higher Education*, http://chronicle.com/jobs/2004/10/2004101401c.htm.

Zemke, Ron, Claire Raines, and Bob Filipczak (2000), *Generations at Work: Managing the Clash of Veterans, Boomers, Xers, and Nexters in Your Workplace*, New York: AMACOM, American Management Association.

5. The impact of the Millennials on higher education

Donald W. Harward

INTRODUCTION

This session of the 2007 TIAA-CREF National Higher Education Leadership Conference focused on today's Millennial age students, and addressed such questions as what characteristics do these students share? How are our institutions preparing them for their future choices and challenges? What will be needed to recruit them and to educate them to be the next generation of faculty and institutional leaders?

The session participants included:

- Donald W. Harward (Moderator) is President Emeritus of Bates College, Senior Fellow of the Association of American Colleges and Universities and Director of the Bringing Theory to Practice Project supporting educational institutions as they address the integrated core outcomes of liberal education.
- Andrew K. Benton is President of Pepperdine University. His background is law and his multiple responsibilities at Pepperdine before becoming President in 2000 helped serve his objective of positioning Pepperdine as first in academic advancement and career preparation among American faith-based colleges and universities.
- Julie K. Little is Interim Director of EDUCAUSE, having recently served as Executive Director of Educational Technology at the Innovative Technology Center at the University of Tennessee. Her research interests focus on faculty development, facilitating communications and collaborations in distributed learning environments, and designing effective uses of instructional technologies.
- Debra W. Stewart is President of the Council of Graduate Schools, a position she has held since 2000. A national spokesperson for graduate education in America, Stewart served as Vice Chancellor and Dean of the Graduate School at North Carolina State University before joining the Council of Graduate Schools.

● Lou Anna K. Simon is President of Michigan State University, assuming that position in 2005. Prior to her appointment as President, she served as Provost and Vice President for Academic Affairs at Michigan State, as well as having earlier served in the University's Office of Institutional Research and the Office of Planning and Budgets.

Following the welcome of Ed Van Dolsen of TIAA-CREF to the afternoon session, Donald Harward began the session with remarks that helped to shape the context for the panelists' presentations and observations regarding the generation of the Millennials.

Beyond being wary of generalizations and stereotypes, an inclination to try to find the essential elements that characterize a generation should also be suspect. The metaphor of a strand of hemp rope offers the suggestion that instead of essential elements that run the whole course of the rope (that is, characterize the generation), there are multiple short strands, interlacing in complex ways that give the length of rope its strength and direction. The generation of Millennials, defined as the 75 million persons having been born in the United States between 1977 and 1998, do not share a common thread beyond the categorization of the boundaries of their birth years. But there are "short strands." And our objective in understanding how our educational institutions should be attending to Millennials resides in understanding the nature and complexity of those short strands.

This session brought to light key insights and perspectives regarding a few of those short strands, insights shared by four panelists with extensive experience and leadership in higher education. To begin, conference planners asked the panelists to consider the following characterization:

"Described as talented, sure of themselves, open-minded, collaborative, family-and-friends-oriented, technologically savvy, globally connected, and achievement-driven, the Millennials are, of course, wanted by everyone. Colleges and universities—branding and marketing—compete aggressively for them. Then, these Millennials and their 'helicopter' parents arrive, bringing with them multiple co-curricular desires and demands that have policy, facilities, and staffing requirements for institutions—all of which have financial implications. Upon graduation, some of the Millennials become part of our universities as graduate students, bringing again a new set of expectations."

We are also aware of other characterizations—less positive characterizations that emphasize the manifestation of disengagement exhibited by many Millennials attending colleges and universities today:

"The disengagement is cited in academic contexts, where many students are perceived as avoiding rigorous study, where faculty and students often mutually agree to a 'if you don't bother me, I won't bother you' compact, and where students and their families prefer to define education in terms of degree attainment—the cheaper and faster the better. Other patterns of disengagement are cited in student behavior and student culture. A variety of national surveys now suggest that over 40 percent of current Millennial age students self-report episodes of depression sufficient to interrupt their academic work; students report only occasional faculty awareness of the crises they, the students, see among their colleagues or the pain they themselves endure. Over 35 percent of current students report engaging in binging with alcohol or other drugs for the purpose of and with the intent of passing out—emotionally and physically disengaging. And for some observers, civic disengagement by students is so alarming as to question what and who will be preserving key democratic values in the future."

Positive or negative, characterizations do shape expectations, institutional responses, and student experiences. A third strand is found in a recent essay appearing in the *New York Times* September, 2007, Education Supplement. It is useful because it is a perspective from a Millennial himself, Nicholas Handler (2007), a Yale University sophomore. Among his observations, he wrote:

We are a generation that is riding on the tail-end of a century of war and revolution that toppled civilizations, overturned repressive social orders, and left us with more privilege and opportunity than any other society in history. Ours could be an era to accomplish anything. And yet do we take to the streets and the airwaves and say "here we are, and this is what we demand"? Do we plant our flag of youthful rebellion on the mall in Washington and say "we are not leaving until we see change!" Have our eyes been opened by our education and our conception of what is possible expanded by our privilege [so that] we demand a better world because of it? It would seem we do the opposite.

On campus, we sign petitions, join organizations, put our names on mailing lists, make small-money contributions, volunteer a spare hour to tutor, and sport an entire wardrobe's worth of Live Strong bracelets advertising our moderately priced opposition to everything from breast cancer to global warming. But what do we really stand for? (Handler, 2007, p. 36)

These several views set a context for our panelists who provided experienced and nuanced perspectives, each capturing some perspective on the Millennial Generation of students.

PERSPECTIVES ON THE MILLENNIAL GENERATION

Perspective I: The Strengths and Gifts of Many Millennials Now at Our Colleges and Universities

President Andrew Benton of Pepperdine picked up on how effective and engaging he finds this Millennial Generation, a perspective he has gained from over 20 years of leadership at Pepperdine, and from his, and his spouse's, parenting their own Millennial children. "At the end of my career, the heart of my work in education has been with the Millennial Generation, as they are the students and the people that I know best. I believe in this generation; I love this generation," he said.

Remarking that he found Millennials somewhat unaware of what may be expected of them someday, he did think them precocious, albeit often over-protected by their family—especially given the demographic reality that Millennials are often the only child, or one of only two children in the family. Millennials expect to be treated, and have been so, as an "only." They expect to be a name, not a number; they anticipate that they will confirm their own uniqueness. Those are consequences of their being at or near the center of attention for all their lives. They do not yet understand that the problems faced by the nation, are their problems.

Happily self-centered, Millennial students have "24-hour lives" and expect those in their orbits of contact, for example, faculty, to do the same—and to thereby be available to them. "They have an insatiable appetite for communicating and expect spontaneous dialogue, entertain-ment, or service," Benton reported. If generations need galvanizing events to characterize their initiatives and interests it must be 9/11 for Millennials and the location of selfless heroes among the respondents to that tragedy. Facing challenge or adversity, if a Millennial asks "Why me?," it is the ques-tion asked by one who sees the world (and has been encouraged to see the world) only from his or her own perspective. President Benton considered that our work as educators of the Millennials begins with the recognition of their chances for greatness, for rational choices, and for their enthusi-asm; then, he argued, "We must then help them to move beyond their current perspective."

Perspective II: The Millennial Generation's Facility, Preference, and Expectations in Using Digital Technology

Julie K. Little of EDUCAUSE began her remarks by asking the audience to read an "SMS" text message. Only a few could; even fewer could read a message in "Leet," a highly specialized form of electronic shorthand used in online games. The obvious point was that Millennials are not only likely to read "SMS" or "Leet," they use them frequently and effectively for communication in activities important to them. Over 80 percent of current Millennial teenagers are into online gaming, over 75 percent use instant messaging, and over 50 percent download music. They are extremely digital, and the next wave of our college students (those now four to six years of age) will be even more so.

Millennials are digital media users. They excel in using the media for self-expression as well as for social networking. They create blogs, Web pages, text and photo galleries; and they share those creations frequently and (perhaps some would caution) widely. Nearly 25 percent of current high school students use online tools to connect with other students around the United States and around the world. Daily contact between persons in different countries and certainly different time zones is ubiquitous—and 34 percent of those in frequent virtual contact report that they have *never* met in person.

As learners in a media-dominated context, Millennials are connected, experimental, self-confident, social, and above all, immediate. While preferring to work with others, their inclination is to use singular means of connecting—means they control. They are clearly visually stimulated and prefer documenting and linking theory and issues through experience. Interactive is the way Millennial students prefer to think, to work, and to socialize.

Little moved the focus of her presentation to the implications for education that follow from this characterization of Millennials. Her conclusions were that we as educators, and our educational institutions, have to make significant shifts that recognize what learning can mean for this generation. We must shift from linear presentation to hypermedia and from emphasizing instructing, to emphasizing discovery. Education must shift from teachers who present "one-size-fits-all" to customized learning, from being the "main source or answers" to being a guide.

Technical advances will and can be of assistance as these shifts in roles and responsibilities are achieved. But the shifts will not be the result of technology. The urgency for change is not that education must follow technical advances, gadgetry, or the popular choices of students. The argument for change begins with the recognition that teaching and learning must be contextualized and that Millennial learners can be stretched, challenged, and educated in ways that recognize and utilize their strengths.

Little concluded her remarks with several cautions: "Millennial students may be fluid with digital tools; but their understanding can be shallow. Understanding that includes seeing connections, and exploring applications, is the promise of education. And Millennial students, like students before them, need our help in understanding."

Perspective III: Millennials' Entrance into and their Effect upon Graduate Education as they Prepare to be the Future Faculties of our Colleges and Universities

Debra Stewart, President of the Council of Graduate Schools, was the only presenter at the conference who focused exclusively on graduate students. She began by observing that most people in America's graduate schools today will tell you that the students who have been entering in the last few years are different in a qualitative way. And the ways in which they are different are ways in which higher education is not particularly well positioned to respond effectively. They are multitasking and technologically savvy, which is good. They are also collaborative learners, which is also good. The problem is the faculty sometimes lag behind their students in technological prowess.

Today's graduate students are also more diverse in ways that go beyond conventional notions of diversity. They come to us with considerably more global experience and perspective than their predecessors did. And they are committed to maintaining balanced lives.

How are we doing in preparing for these different students? In Stewart's view, reform has taken place in graduate schools in this country, and is continuing to take place. "We in fact do know how to change; for change we must," she said.

In the last ten years we have seen a flurry of activity around the development at the faculty level of new interdisciplinary programs. We have introduced in graduate education life-skill courses (in Europe this is called the development of transferable skills). It means that PhD or Master's degree graduates need to be able to work meaningfully, to be able to manage projects, to communicate effectively, and to understand the ethical principles underlying their fields. Distance learning is now a straightforward element of many graduate education programs and a high percentage of the graduate students, particularly those in Master's programs, have experienced it.

By the mid-1990s, and certainly by the late 1990s, it was very clear that the American graduate faculty could no longer view what they were doing in doctoral education as only preparing students for the job they (the professors) had. There is now a new and very wide recognition that the graduate faculty of America must take seriously the obligation to prepare students for the job *they* (the students) will get, not the job the faculty currently have.

Millennials want to review and to evaluate the metrics for success of any graduate program that they consider. They want transparency and they want to understand completion rates. They want to understand job placement; and they want that information prior to making their decisions about graduate school. When they come to graduate school, they want to come into a community. And they want and expect to be globally connected so they can actually experience the world outside the United States, not just study it.

Will graduate schools meet the challenge presented by these different, these Millennial students? Stewart answered, "The answer of course has to be 'yes.' It has to be yes because graduate education is absolutely necessary to America's survival."

Perspective IV: What Educational Contexts Best Support, Encourage, and Maximize the Education, Development and Promise of the Millennial Generation?

President Lou Anna K. Simon of Michigan State University (MSU) began her remarks by reminding us that one of the best features of higher education is its pleasure in assailing the current and about-to-attend generation of attendees. The new generation will and must be different. The genius of the educational institution is that while taking pleasure in noticing and emphasizing the differences among generations, its responsibility and its success is in considering the uniqueness of the assets the new generation brings (or will bring) and how the institution can prepare itself and change itself to maximize those assets—not only for the students or their parents, but for the common or public good.

The discussion of Millennial students is really a prediction of the future, and a sense that we believe fundamentally that this permits us to meet our traditional responsibilities in new and different ways—ways that will have the profound possibility of benefiting our society. Millennials have enormous talent, but they lack a fundamental understanding of how to balance the tensions in their lives. We define them differently by place and space and globalization. But we in education must be able to take full advantage of the tensions in their lives in order that they may make more productive changes. That is essentially where the real role of the university comes into play. "We must think about not how they are different, but the dreams that they have not yet dreamt, and the doors that they don't even know exist. And with that in mind, we must ask what tools we have at institutions that will enable students to more effectively take advantage of their potential and to actualize their future dreams," Simon said.

How should parents of Millennials, the so-called "helicopter parents" be involved? President Simon's advice to parents:

Don't ask your student if he or she is homesick. Ask questions but not too many.
Expect change but not too much. Don't worry too much about emotional
phone calls or e-mails. Visit but not too often. Don't tell your students that
these are the best years of their life. They are not necessarily the best times of
their lives. In spite of their assertiveness, there is a lot of self-doubt among
Millennials.

Many Millennials don't know how to make mistakes, and are unprepared
to deal with the mistakes they will make. Technology provides anonymity
and safety from error, she argued. We must, and parents must, begin to let
them understand the role of making mistakes and being able then to take
full advantage of those mistakes. Parents should simply trust their students
and that trust will come out over a period of time.

Documenting the "space" needed for student development and learning,
President Simon shared several studies of MSU first-year students, considering specifically the 50 percent or more of those first-year students for 2000
and 2005 who reside in a living/learning community on campus. She made
a few observations based upon the survey results. The data confirm what
you have heard today: Millennials are team-oriented; they are overtly
confident (but may be harboring significant self-doubt); they are fascinated
by new technology; they are racially and ethnically diverse. They remark
that 9/11 did have an impact on them as does the continuing war in Iraq.

For all the similarities and common patterns, one difference is important.
This difference is even more telling when you notice that the demand and
the extent of contact with support services, including counseling, has
increased dramatically. Simon reported that:

We, like some other institutions, are asking how we can increase both the expectation and the reality of significant engagement with students (for example,
through involving students in research, through service-learning, and other
engaging pedagogies). Living and learning communities; greater mentoring;
study abroad collaborations; and many other initiatives are being considered. All
of these initiatives suggest that we have within our power (even in a place as large
as Michigan State) the capacity to break our environments down into meaningful learning contexts that take full advantage of the assets Millennials do and
will bring to us.

Finally, Dr. Simon commented on what we are all worried about and that
is how does all of the technology and its uses affect the human relationship
of understanding—of making connections to what is beyond ourselves? It
is through the translation of education into human relationships that educated citizens of our time will take on the roles of leadership and address
the most difficult problems of our society. So one of the things that is
troubling, as we think about this Millennial Generation, is how can that

condition of leadership (regarding constructing knowledge as a part of a human relationship) be nourished and not thwarted by technology? This takes us back to our fundamental challenge with the Millennial Generation: " How do we take full advantage of their assets, including their assets of facility with technology, and at the same time find a way to add the human dimension to produce the citizen leaders for the 21st century and beyond?"

Perspective V: Questions and Responses from the Audience

The panel's comments generated many thoughts, observations, and questions from the audience. An initial observation from an audience member focused on the fact that among all the shared perspectives regarding the Millennials, there did not appear to be bifurcated fault-lines distinguishing race and class. The remark called into question whether that was indeed true of Millennials (namely that the class/race fault lines were not as pronounced as in other generations), or that the analysis given regarding Millennials has to be deepened to reflect the reality of there being such bifurcation and we just have not discussed it. For example, what do we know about the impact of the paucity of computing equipment available for the children attending many inner-city elementary schools? Will those children reflect the qualities and assets of the Millennial Generation?

This was received as an important contribution to the discussion and was amplified by another member of the audience who presented the evidence that the demographics of Millennials now attending college reveals how those attending are becoming a more and more homogeneous class grouping. This suggests that such homogeneity is a real consequence of increasing costs and decreasing availability of support for students on the basis of "need" rather than "merit."

A new question was posed that suggests that a dimension of, or strand of, Millennials is their ambiguity regarding what constitutes honesty and individual responsibility—especially when considering the faculty lament that "many of today's students do not consider cheating or plagiarizing unethical." The response (measured by the fact that we must remember how general characterizations regarding a generation, is itself fraught with ambiguity) was that it is our task as educators to insist on authenticity and ethical behavior, and to design contexts where such authenticity is modeled. Any assessment strategy or grading used to measure student accomplishment must require such authenticity.

Another participant began by reminding the panel of the observation that Millennials "don't want to work 24/7; they want to have a life. They want and demand balance." This is interesting when posed in opposition to another observation made regarding Millennials—namely that they have an expectation of "24/7 service from anyone who is interacting with them to meet their needs." The consequence of their expectation places an extraordinary burden on today's faculty. They are not only trying to address the needs of students with different learning styles and students with increasing diversity of backgrounds; they are being expected to do so with immediacy—and some think with the additional expectation of being entertaining.

The complexity of responses made to this remark ranged from distress over the apparent "commodification" of education and the consideration of faculty as "service providers," to further discussion of the pedagogies of active learning that do challenge Millennial students and are seen as being at the core of the new role of educators.

Questioners asked whether or not there is a defining moment for the Millennial Generation. "Did 9/11, for example, galvanize reactions, ambitions, and values in a way that 'Sputnik' gelled a generation of activity and learning?" Panelists thought that this continues to be a provocative question for which there is no clear answer. The question asks what constitutes a "transformative moment" and whether such moments may not be sufficient, but are necessary, for the identity of a generation.

A last but lingering issue was posed by an audience member's question: "How do you go about characterizing what will drive change at our institutions, even when it is clear that we must change?" The questioner asked if the panelists thought that the several constituencies of educational institutions, including but not limited to faculty, can and often do, resist change. "They don't seek new ways to behave regardless of the incentives or the perceived need."

Responses from the panelists to this point varied. "We have to segment and to recall that the needs and the behaviors at one type of institution are very different from those at a different type of institution." Others suggested that the only method of getting an "engine" of change started is to "do so slowly and a little bit at a time. We, at colleges and universities, do 'get it'; and we are changing!"

REFERENCE

Handler, N. (2007), "The posteverything generation," *The New York Times College Issue*, 30 September, 36.

6. Attracting and retaining students: challenges and opportunities for today and tomorrow

Kenneth E. Redd

Thirty years ago Georgetown University in Washington, DC, received roughly 5000 applications for admission to its undergraduate programs, according to the *Washington Post* (Kinzie, 2008). This year, the number of applications for the fall 2008 entering class has leapt to more than 18 000. Georgetown is not alone—the *Washington Post* recently reported that colleges and universities all around the country, ranging from Harvard University to McDaniel College, are experiencing a surge in applications (ibid.). A 2007 report from the National Association of College Admissions Counseling (NACAC) found that approximately three-quarters of four-year colleges and universities reported increases in the number of undergraduate admissions applications they received from fall 2005 to 2006, and, remarkably, 18 percent of fall 2006 first-year undergraduates had applied to *seven or more* postsecondary institutions (Hawkins and Clinedinst, 2007). As a result, admissions personnel at four-year institutions will be busier than ever in 2008 and beyond.

The new generation of applicants is much different than any before it, and recruiting and retaining these students will be more difficult even for the most seasoned college admissions and financial aid administrators. In addition, a number of forces, particularly rising college prices and shifts in student financial aid, increasing racial diversity among the current and future traditional college-age population, and shifts in parental involvement in the college planning and financial aid process pose potentially daunting challenges in the future.

This chapter first takes a look at the characteristics and attitudes of current college students, and compares these with undergraduates from past generations. The chapter then describes the unique opportunities and challenges facing admissions officers as they try to recruit and admit more of traditional-age undergraduates. Admissions officers who prepare for the challenges represented by today's students will have a much better chance of gaining applicants and enrollees in the future, as the competition for these new students continues to increase in the years ahead.

THE MILLENNIAL GENERATION: RISING DIVERSITY, ASPIRATIONS, AND WEALTH

"Millennials" (defined as the 75 million persons born between 1977 and 1998) are poised to become the most educated generation in American history (Thielfordt and Scheef, 2004; Bagnaschi and Geraci, 2005). More of them are entering colleges and universities than at any time before. In 1980, just 49 percent of high school graduates enrolled in some form of postsecondary education within a year of receiving their diplomas, according to the National Center for Education Statistics (NCES, 1981). By 2005, the percentage of high school graduates immediately going onto college had jumped to 68 percent (NCES, 2006). And available evidence suggests that the percentages of high school seniors enrolling in college will continue to be large in the coming years. A 2005 opinion poll sponsored by Harris Interactive (Bagnaschi and Geraci, 2005) found that nearly two-thirds of college-bound high school graduates plan to earn a Master's degree or higher sometime in the future. And, with NCES predicting that the number of high school graduates will rise to a record 3.3 million in 2009 and remain at over 3 million in the five years thereafter (NCES, 2007c), the number of high school graduates entering college likely will continue rising for the foreseeable future.

But the rapidly rising number of postsecondary attendees is only part of the story concerning today's generation of traditional-age college students. These undergraduates have much different demographic characteristics than those of past generations. When compared with college first-years from 20 years ago, today's Millennial students:

- Are much more diverse. NCES's 1981 fall enrollment survey reveals that in 1980, 81 percent of first-time undergraduates at four-year colleges and universities were white, non-Hispanic. In 2005, the white share of first-year enrollment fell to 66 percent (Table 6.1). The greatest increase has been in the proportion of Latinos, which jumped from 5 percent to 10 percent. Women also made enrollment gains— rising from 51 percent of first-years to 55 percent.
- Come from higher-income families. The inflation-adjusted median family income of all undergraduates attending four-year colleges and universities rose from $60 828 in 1989–90 to $65 145 in 2003–04, and

Table 6.1 Demographic characteristics of first-time, full-time, degree-seeking first-years at four-year colleges and universities, 1980 and 2005

	1980	2005
Estimated enrollment	1 128 585	1 398 646
Gender distribution		
Male	49%	45%
Female	51%	55%
Racial/ethnic distribution		
White, non-Hispanic	81%	66%
African American	10%	11%
Hispanic	5%	10%
Asian/Pacific Islander	2%	6%
Native American/Alaska natives	1%	1%
Other and unknown	1%	6%

Source: NCES (1981 and 2006).

the percentage of students from families with income of $80 000 or higher jumped from 13 percent to 37 percent, according to the National Postsecondary Student Aid Study (NCES, 1990 and 2004; Bureau of Labor Statistics, 2008). These increases reflect national trends; the median income for all families with a head of household aged 45 to 54 (the typical age range of parents with college-age children) rose by about the same levels during this time span (US Census Bureau, 2008; Bureau of Labor Statistics, 2008). In addition, Harris Interactive (Crance, 2007) has found that the discretionary income of 18-to-30-year-old college students reached $48 billion ($3 593 per student) in 2007. The increasing economic clout of these students has undoubtedly altered life on many campuses.

- Are more academically prepared for higher education. NCES (2007a) reports that the average composite SAT score of college-bound high school seniors increased 6 percent over the past two decades. In addition, the College Board (2007a) reports that the share of high school seniors who took at least one Advance Placement exam jumped 64 percent between 2000 and 2006, and UCLA's *National Freshmen Norms* survey data (Higher Education Research Institute, 2007) reveal that the percentage of first-years who met or exceeded the recommended years of high school study has risen in nearly every subject area except history/American government since 1984 (the first year such data were collected). By these standards, today's high school students entering postsecondary education are more academically talented than any generation before them.

- Are more likely to integrate technology into their academic and personal lives. The great majority of current undergraduates have incorporated the Internet and other high-tech gadgets into their academic and personal lives. Harris Interactive (Crance, 2007) reports that cell phone ownership among college students has grown from a relative novelty to nearly universal, as has ownership of computers, MP3 players, and other electronic devices. Conversely, just 42 percent of undergraduates have a traditional land-line phone. Students use this new-found technical knowledge to improve their grades and to stay connected with family and friends through social networking sites such as MySpace and Facebook—both unheard of 20 years ago. And this trend will undoubtedly continue. An additional Harris Interactive survey reveals that nearly three-quarters of teenagers use instant messaging and 37 percent use text messaging to stay in touch with their friends (Harris Interactive, 2006).

Millennials also have radically different attitudes about and reasons for entering higher education than their parents. William Strauss and Neil Howe (2007), in a recent editorial in the *Chronicle of Higher Education*, write that the current generation views college as "a calculated market choice, with large rewards (obtaining the right credentials for a globalized economy)". Harris Interactive, in its 2005 survey of high school students (Bagnaschi and Geraci, 2005, p. 2), describes the different attitudes about college attendance between Millennials and their parents even more bluntly:

[The previous generation] went to college primarily out of inertia—their parents commanded them to, they hadn't considered other things to do post-high school, and college was viewed as a time of socialization and self-discovery to learn about career and life opportunities. [Today's generation] goes to college for plain and simple reasons: they want to learn and to enhance their job prospects. They do not go to college because of the expectations of others or because it is simply the next thing to do.

This changed attitude presents unique challenges and opportunities for admissions officers who seek to attract more of this new generation to their campuses.

APPLYING TO AND ATTENDING COLLEGE—THE "EXPLOSION OF CHOICE"

While students' reasons for choosing to go to college have changed, the criteria used to evaluate undergraduate admissions applications have remained remarkably stable. During the period from 1993 to 2006, the top criteria used by four-year colleges and universities to admit new undergraduates have been high school grades (particularly in college preparatory courses), admissions test scores, and class rank, according to NACAC's 2007 survey report (Hawkins and Clinedinst, 2007). In fact, while test scores have increased in importance over this time period, grades in college prep courses have consistently been rated as considerably more important by the most colleges. These NACAC results suggest that colleges will continue to compete fiercely for the "best and brightest" high school seniors. The pressure on admissions staff to quickly identify, recruit, and admit the most highly qualified applicants will thus remain enormously high in the future.

One recruitment challenge for college admissions staff is that today's top applicants have a much greater number of choices than ever when deciding which campus to attend. As Mark J. Penn and E. Kinney Zalesne point out in their 2007 book *Microtrends: The Small Forces Behind Tomorrow's Big Changes*, today's teens have grown up in a world in which they can choose products and services that fit their individual preferences. In nearly every industry, they can purchase items that are unique to their wants and needs; they can purchase these uniquely designed products whenever and wherever they want; and they can pay for them in a wide variety of ways (cash, credit, debit, Paypal, and so on).

This "explosion of choice" has certainly spread to higher education. With the advent of Web-based learning, students today can take courses at colleges and universities around the world, and they can choose the educational medium that best suits their needs—a "brick-and-mortar" campus, an online school, or a combination of the two. Today's current and prospective college students are just as brand-conscious as previous generations, but they are more likely to choose the college that best meets their unique, individual goals.

Current and prospective students are also much more focused on educational quality and outcomes than those of previous years. When asked by Harris Interactive (Bagnaschi and Geraci, 2005) to identify the factors that will be most important to them in choosing which college to attend in the future, the overwhelming majority of high school students in 2005 listed "program of study available" and "quality of teaching." Similarly, UCLA's most recent *Freshmen Norms* survey found that 63 percent of fall 2007 college first-years said "academic reputation" was a very important reason they selected the institution they chose to attend, while 52 percent listed "graduate with good jobs" (Higher Education Research Institute, 2008). Both percentages are at 35-year highs. University admissions officers and other personnel will thus be much more successful in recruiting and admitting students by emphasizing their diverse course offerings and the success of their recent alumni.

The message to admissions recruiters is clear—the students of tomorrow generally will choose to attend colleges that are the best fit for them academically and that will help them launch successful careers. As Harris Interactive's 2005 opinion poll points out: "Today's students are making decisions on a straightforward criteria [sic]: Does the college have the programs I want? Can I get a job when I graduate?" (Bagnaschi and Geraci, 2005, p. 3).

HIGH-TECH RECRUITMENT AND RETENTION EFFORTS

Admissions and recruitment strategies thus have had to change in order to meet these new students' expectations about college and the broad array of choices available. Students want more and more information about their prospective colleges, they want it instantly, and they want it from potential peers (current students) and professors rather than from administrators.

A number of institutions have begun to use new strategies to respond to the needs of potential applicants. As the *Boston Globe* points out, in their fall 2008 recruiting campaigns colleges have rapidly dumped their campus tours and glossy brochures and replaced them with Web-based efforts (Schworm, 2008). Colby College, for instance, now uses a student-run online magazine that features podcast interviews of students and professors. The Massachusetts Institute of Technology supports student blogs that allow prospective admissions candidates to get a first-hand look at life on campus. At a number of other institutions, prospective undergraduates can now instant message recruiters, take classes on iTunes, contact admissions officers on Facebook, and take campus tours on YouTube. NACAC's data show that 35 percent of institutions have chat rooms and 29 percent have blogs on their admission's websites (Hawkins and Clinedinst, 2007).

In all of these efforts, the emphasis has been on using technology to connect socially and academically with students, many of whom are now more interested in "meeting" and "chatting" online with their potential college classmates and professors before they decide which school to attend than they are in meeting them in person. While these new efforts respond to students' needs and desires, it suggests that institutions that are not as rich in resources will increasingly be pressured to adopt these new technologies to meet their enrollment targets.

Even with the increased efforts at student recruitment, retention of entering students may be an even bigger problem at many campuses. The 2006 *Beginning Postsecondary Students* longitudinal study found that one-fifth of all entering full-time first-years at four-year colleges and universities transfer to at least one new institution within their first two years of study (NCES, 2007c). Among students who transfer, the two most often cited reasons for leaving their original institutions were "personal reasons" (57 percent of transfers) and "dissatisfaction with program" (39 percent).

Admissions officers and other staff will thus continue to be challenged to help students stay connected to their campuses once they are enrolled. A number of colleges have adapted their high-tech recruitment strategies to help students deal with personal issues. The *Chronicle of Higher Education* reports that St. Olaf College in Minnesota recently installed a webcam in its student activities center so that homesick students could more easily stay in touch with their families and friends at home (Petrie, 2007). These and other high-tech efforts could make a difference in students' decisions to choose a college, and whether or not to stay after they enroll.

CHALLENGES AHEAD: COLLEGE COSTS AND FINANCIAL AID, PARENTAL INVOLVEMENT, AND RACIAL GAPS

Despite their higher incomes and greatly expanded institutional and other choices, high school seniors and young college students today feel more anxious and concerned about their futures than their parents were when they entered college, according to a 2007 survey from Key Educational Resource (*Chronicle of Higher Education*, 2007). Today's students have several good reasons to feel uneasy. They live in a post-9/11 world that has seen a rise in fears about terrorism; and media accounts of on-campus shootings and other violence have rapidly increased. It is no wonder that 65 percent of teenagers said they would choose a college based on its safety, according to Harris Interactive (Bagnaschi and Geraci, 2005).

But the issue that causes the greatest worry for prospective students and families is rising college costs. A 2006 *Wall Street Journal* poll (Cummings, 2006) found that the top concern among 13-to-21-year-olds was whether they could afford to attend higher education in the future. Students' concerns about college affordability are well founded. Average tuition and fee prices at four-year public colleges and universities rose 40 percent in inflation-adjusted value during the past decade, according to the College Board's *Trends in College Prices* report (2007b). Additionally, UCLA's most recent *Freshmen Norms* survey found that 39 percent of entering 2007 first-years listed their financial aid awards as an important factor in determining which school they attended, the highest share in 35 years (Higher Education Research Institute, 2008; Hoover, 2008a).

Many high school students are especially concerned about the amount they may have to borrow to attend college. The College Board's (2007c) *Trends in Student Aid* study shows that student loans account for the majority of financial aid that current students receive, and new baccalaureate recipients typically leave their institutions with $15 000 or more in education debt. With tuition prices continuing to rise and more aid coming from student loans, it is likely that financial aid and affordability will remain a challenge for both students and college personnel for many years to come.

A number of selective institutions (for example, Harvard University, University of North Carolina, University of Virginia) have responded to concerns about affordability by increasing their available funding for financial aid. But these institutions have large endowments and enroll a relatively small share of undergraduates nationally. Admissions officers and financial aid administrators at most other colleges and universities will be hard pressed to increase their aid budgets, and to provide more information about their tuition policies so that students' and parents' rapidly rising anxieties about college affordability are eased. Prospective applicants will want to learn about college financing options as well as admissions materials in a clear and concise manner, and they will want this information much earlier in the college application process. Admissions officers who are best able to coordinate their recruitment strategies with their financial aid information may be in the best position to gain prospective students in the future.

Rising college costs is just one of the top concerns admissions counselors will need to address if they are to meet their recruitment and retention goals. A second is the persistent gaps in college enrollment between white and racial/ethnic minority high school graduates. Despite some progress, African American and Latino high school students remain far less likely than their white peers to enroll in college, as Table 6.2 demonstrates. In 2005, 73 percent of white high school graduates entered postsecondary education after receiving their diplomas, compared with just 55 percent of African Americans and 54 percent of Latinos. More distressingly, the disparities between minority and white high school seniors entering higher education have actually grown larger between 2000 and 2005 than they were in the 1990s.

Table 6.2 College enrollment rates of recent high school graduates by race/ethnicity, 1980–2005

	African American (%)	Hispanic * (%)	White, non-Hispanic (%)
1980	42.7	52.3	49.8
1985	42.2	51.0	60.1
1990	46.8	42.7	63.0
1995	51.2	53.7	64.3
2000	54.9	52.9	65.7
2005	55.7	54.0	73.2

Note: * Due to small sample sizes, results for Hispanics should be interpreted cautiously.

Source: NCES (2007b).

Two main factors account for the lower incidence of minority high school students immediately attending college. First, minorities generally are less likely to meet the criteria many admissions offices use to recruit students. On average, according to the College Board (2007a), minorities score at lower levels on admissions tests and are less likely to attend high schools that offer Advanced Placement tests. Second, minorities also appear to have less access to information about college and financial aid options. A 2003 survey commissioned by the Sallie Mae Fund found that Latino parents and high school students are less likely to have ready access to the Internet, and thus do not learn about postsecondary enrollment and financing options at the same rates as whites (Sallie Mae Fund, 2003).

As colleges increasingly rely on the Internet, academic grades, and other criteria to recruit top students, minorities likely will remain behind whites in college access. These persistent gaps have had a negative effect on minority parents' views on the college admissions process. A 2005 Gallup poll revealed that nearly half of all African American parents believe their children do not have as good a chance at receiving a quality education as whites (Keifer, 2005). Admissions and financial aid staff will thus be even more pressured to develop ways to get information about funding and enrollment options for under-represented populations. One step institutions could take in this regard is to develop relationships with organizations that deliver information about financial aid and college opportunities to African Americans and Latinos. The Sallie Mae Fund's "First in My Family" campaign, which is aimed at closing the college access information gaps between minority and majority students, is one example of an effort that admissions personnel could use as a model for assisting students from under-represented populations (Sallie Mae Fund, 2003).

The third challenge for admissions staff is the lack of parents' involvement in their children's college planning and enrollment decisions. Despite the anecdotal evidence about the intrusiveness of "helicopter" parents on college campuses, it is clear that a number of current and prospective college students *want* their parents to be even more involved with college recruitment and enrollment activities (Rainey, 2006; Hoover, 2008b). In spite of this need, it is clear that in many instances, parental involvement comes too late to prepare prospective students adequately. In a 2007 study, the Institute for Higher Education Policy reported that fewer than 20 percent of parents of middle school children had begun to research college options, meet with teachers or counselors, or collect college admissions materials—all key parts of the college-planning process (Cunningham, Erisman, and Looney, 2007). And, in spite of the concerns about college prices, only one-third of parents had begun to save for their children's post-secondary expenses.

At the same time, the majority of teenagers and young college students view their parents as "their most trusted advisors," according to *The Chronicle of Higher Education* (Hoover, 2008b, p. A22), and want their mothers and fathers to be better equipped to help with college selection decisions. Admissions officers thus should begin to develop partnerships with middle and high schools so that parents feel more able to provide guidance to their children earlier in the college decision-making process. While families will increasingly turn to the Internet and other online resources to do college searches, they will still need the personal touches of admissions and financial aid officers. This result represents both a great challenge and opportunity for college admissions staff. Families clearly are looking for more guidance in preparing for college. Institutions that can provide materials to students earlier—starting in their middle school years—may be in the best position to gain advantages in the recruitment process.

THE FUTURE FOR COLLEGE ADMISSIONS

Today's current and prospective college students are more diverse, wealthy, academically and personally ambitious, and technologically advanced than any generation before them. The high educational aspirations of this new generation, combined with its entrepreneurial, independent spirit and technological savvy, promise to have long-lasting effects on college planning, recruitment, enrollment, and success. At the same time, worries about financial aid and student debt, combined with rising gaps between minority and white enrollments and lack of parental involvement in the college planning process during children's middle-school years, promise to test the abilities of many admissions and financial aid administrators. These staff members will need to make even greater efforts to recruit the high-ability high school seniors they have depended upon to keep their high rankings and reputations.

Two key demographic shifts will make it even harder to recruit new students in the future. First is the number of high school graduates, which will reach a peak in 2009 and then decline slightly in the following five to ten years (NCES, 2007a). A 2003 report from the Western Interstate Commission for Higher Education (WICHE, 2003) projects that the number of high school graduates will decline sharply in at least 20 states between 2009 and 2017. Second, and more importantly, a greater share of the high school seniors are predicted to be from racial/ethnic minority populations, particularly Latinos. WICHE data reveal that by 2014, white non-Hispanics will represent only one-half of all high school graduates, while Latinos will account for roughly 20 percent. In a number of Western and Southwestern states, Latinos and African Americans will constitute the majority of new high school diploma recipients, according to the WICHE study.

For college and university admissions and financial aid personnel, these demographic trends represent their greatest challenge for the coming years. How can they continue to recruit large numbers of high-ability students using the same measures of academic achievement as they have relied on in the past while the populations of such students may be declining? Will the financial aid and other resources needed to support the college-going rates of the emerging "majority-minority" populations be available? What new admissions criteria will be needed to help provide equal postsecondary education opportunities for the students of tomorrow? Colleges and universities that can quickly develop strategies to meet these challenges will prove to be the most successful in the coming years.

The future success of college admissions and financial aid efforts cannot be fully realized unless greater efforts are made to provide more information about postsecondary education opportunities to prospective students—particularly those from under-represented minority populations—during their middle and high school years. Admissions personnel can be at the forefront of these efforts by designing strategies that coordinate the delivery of information about college enrollment and financial aid opportunities in a concise and timely manner via the Internet and other means, and that help to bridge the widening racial gaps in postsecondary opportunity.

REFERENCES

Bagnaschi, K. and J. Geraci (eds) (2005), "How do high school students select a college?," *Trends & Tudes*, **4**(1), 1–4.

Bureau of Labor Statistics (2008), *Consumer Price Index—All Urban Consumers (CPI-U)*, dataset.

Chronicle of Higher Education (2007), "Prime numbers: yesterday's students vs. today's," 8 June, **53**(40), A7.

The College Board (2007a), *Advanced Placement Report to the Nation*, New York, NY: College Board.

The College Board (2007b), *Trends in College Prices*, Washington, DC: College Board.

The College Board (2007c), *Trends in Student Aid*, Washington, DC: College Board.

Crance, L. (2007), "On-campus: college students today," *Trends & Tudes*, **6**(6), 1–4.

Cummings, J. (ed.) (2006), "Majority of parents have set little or no money aside to cover children's college costs, according to new national survey," *Wall Street Journal Online Personal Finance Poll*, **2**(3).

Cunningham, A.F., W. Erisman, and S.M. Looney (2007), *From Aspirations to Action: The Role of Middle School Parents in Making the Dream of College a Reality*, Washington, DC: Institute for Higher Education Policy.

Harris Interactive (2006), "Teens set new rules of engagement in the age of social media," http://www.harrisinteractive.com/news/allnewsbydate.asp?NewsID=1114.

Hawkins, D.A. and M.E. Clinedinst (2007), *State of College Admission*, Alexandria, VA: National Association for College Admission Counseling.

Higher Education Research Institute (2007), *The American Freshman: Forty-year Trends—1966 to 2006*, HERI Research Brief, UCLA, Los Angeles, CA: HERI.

Higher Education Research Institute (2008), *The American Freshman: National Norms for Fall 2007*, HERI Research Brief, UCLA, Los Angeles, CA: HERI.

Hoover, E. (2008a), "Freshmen's concerns about quality, cost at 35-year high," *Chronicle of Higher Education*, http://chronicle.com/daily/2008/01/1361n.htm.

Hoover, E. (2008b), "Surveys of students' views complicate spin on 'helicopter parents,'" *Chronicle of Higher Education*, 1 February, A22.

Keifer, H.M. (2005), "Blacks: good education still out of reach for many," Gallup, http://www.gallup.com/poll/17734/Blacks-Good-Education-Still-Reach-Many.aspx?version.htm.

Kinzie, S. (2008), "Long lines at college gates" *Washington Post*, 26 January, B1 and B4.

National Center for Education Statistics (NCES) (1981), *Fall 1980 Integrated Postsecondary Education Data System (IPEDS) Enrollment Survey*, dataset.

NCES (1990), *1990 National Postsecondary Student Aid Study*, Undergraduate Data Analysis System dataset, Washington, DC: NCES.

NCES (2004), *National Postsecondary Student Aid Study*, Undergraduate Data Analysis System dataset, Washington, DC: NCES.

NCES (2006) *Fall 2005 Integrated Postsecondary Education Data System (IPEDS) Enrollment Survey*, dataset.

(NCES) (2007a), *Projections of Education Statistics to 2016*, Washington, DC: NCES.

NCES (2007b),   *Digest of Education Statistics: 2006*, Washington, DC: NCES.

NCES (2007c), *2003–04 Beginning Postsecondary Students Longitudinal Study (BPS:04/06)*, dataset.

Penn, M.J. and E.K. Zalesne (2007), *Microtrends: The Small Forces Behind Tomorrow's Big Changes*, New York, NY: Twelve.

Petrie, M. (2007), "Wave of the future?," *Chronicle of Higher Education*, http://chronicle.com/weekly/v54/i04/04a00703.htm.

Rainey, A. (2006), "Survey provides further evidence of high parental involvement with college students," *Chronicle of Higher Education*, 14 April, A39.

Sallie Mae Fund (2003), "Financial aid: the information divide survey key findings," news release, http://www.thesalliemaefund.org/smfnews/news/2003/news_nr184b.html.

Schworm, P. (2008), "Colleges turn to Web tools in hunt for '08 freshmen," *Boston Globe*, http://www.boston.com/news/local/articles/2008/01/07/college_turn_to_web_tools_in_hunt_for_08_freshmen.

Strauss, W. and N. Howe (2007), "Millennials as graduate students," *The Chronicle of Higher Education*, 30 March, B16.

Thielfordt, D. and D. Scheef (2004), "Generation X and the Millennials: what you need to know about mentoring the new generations," *Law Practice TODAY*, http://www.abanet.org/lpm/lpt/articles/mgt08044.html.

US Census Bureau (2008), *Historical Income Tables—Families*, dataset.

Western Interstate Commission for Higher Education (WICHE) (2003), *Knocking on the College Door: Projections of High School Graduates by State, Income, and Race/Ethnicity*, Boulder, CO: WICHE.

7. Recruiting and retaining the next generation of college faculty: negotiating the new playing field

Martin Finkelstein

THE PROBLEM IN CONTEXT

Recruiting—and retaining—the next generation of college faculty has risen to the top of our national agenda over the past decade no less than recruiting and retaining the next generation of nurses or the next generation of public school teachers. In the latter cases, of course, the shortages are acute right now—and have been longstanding; and the focus on recruitment is driven almost single-mindedly by the horrendous attrition rate among new nurses and teachers once on the job—a kind of revolving door (half have left the profession after three to five years). In the case of the college teaching professions, the rising concern is more "anticipatory" (although not far out in the future) and more focused, at least comparatively speaking, on recruitment—since retention in the academic professions has historically been very good (indeed, until not too long again, the ultra-high retention rate of tenured faculty was itself considered a major problem for American higher education).[1] And these concerns are being driven by stark demographics: the aging of the current corps of college and university teachers, the relentless expansion of student demand, and the leveling off (or even slight decline) in doctoral production in the United States, as well as the declining competitiveness of faculty compensation—all raising serious concerns about the quantity, but perhaps more importantly the quality, of future supply.

As concerns about faculty recruitment and retention in American higher education reach a level unprecedented since the 1960s, the logical place to begin in addressing those concerns (or, at least, scoping them out) would be with a few rudimentary questions: what have we learned from nearly a half-century of research about faculty recruitment and retention? And to what extent, and in what respects, do a variety of new developments—including the demographic revolution, the diversification of academic appointments and roles, and the changing academic labor market—challenge our conventional wisdom (understandings)? And to the extent that they do, what "new rules," if any, do we see emerging (or on the horizon)? And how will any such "new rules" likely play out over the coming decade? Generation?

THE LAST 50 YEARS

Studies of faculty recruitment and retention rose rapidly between the late 1950s and the early 1970s—roughly paralleling the great post-World War II expansion of higher education demand and the nearly 10–20-year lag in supply. Those studies sought to understand the choice of college teaching as a career (what attracted prospective faculty to college teaching careers and the timing of those decisions) and the factors that attracted faculty to one position rather than another and that then kept them at their employing institution or propelled them on to greener pastures—either inside or outside academe. Certain basic principles or understandings emerged from those studies (Finkelstein, 1984):

1. The people who became college teachers tended to be a readily identifiable "special breed." They had done well at school, had strong intellectual interests, deeply valued the opportunity to pursue those interests relatively unfettered (strong focus on autonomy), and tended to be relatively independent from parents' status concerns in making their career choice. If not quite a "calling," academic work was a not altogether objectionable (and even quite pleasant) means to fulfill certain very deep personal needs (Finkelstein, 1984).
2. Once in the saddle, academics tend to illustrate the principle of "inertia," that is, they stay put. While many test the job market, the proportion who actually change employment is small (no more than 10 percent a year at the height of the seller's market in the 1960s; see Brown, 1967; Carter, 1974). Mobility is the result of a complex combination of push (lack of opportunity to pursue one's interest, lack of collegial and administrative support, low salary) and pull (a significantly better opportunity, a significantly more prestigious institution). Salary tends to be of lesser importance. Most mobility is between academic institutions rather than between academe and other employment sectors (business/industry, government, and so on).
3. The academic career is an "exclusive" one, both in the sense of being the incumbent's sole occupational pursuit at a given moment and in the sense of remaining so over a substantial portion of the lifespan. Moreover, this "exclusive" career became highly structured and

routinized in the post-World War II period: intensive doctoral study, followed immediately by entry-level position, a six-year probationary period, a high-stakes "up or out" promotion decision, permanent tenure highlighted by only one further promotion opportunity during the ensuing career span. Faculty mobility tends to be shaped by career stage, rising predictably at entry-level appointment (some do not complete doctoral study or are unable or unwilling to take or find an entry-level position), the end of the probationary period just before the tenure decision and just before or just after ascending to the full professorship, the last promotion opportunity.

4. Institutional type and academic field shape the academic labor market. Caplow and McGee (1958) in their classic study showed that research universities constitute something of a closed and highly stratified subsociety in which prestige serves as the coin of the realm (that is, a substitute for money). The prestige of one's doctoral institution and/or one's doctoral mentor typically shape movement within the "old boy network"—a theme seconded by Wilson (1979).

Thirty years later, Burton Clark identified institutional type and academic field as the two central axes that defined the shape of academic work and careers. He conceptualized academic life as actually the aggregation of a multiplicity of "small worlds" defined by institution and discipline (Clark, 1987).

Since these "old rules" became established in the third quarter of the 20th century, and a seller's market yielded savagely to a buyer's market for faculty services, there have been periodic warnings issued about whether academe could continue to attract the "best and the brightest" (see most notably, Bowen and Schuster, 1986). The available data on the career choices of highly talented segments of the population including Phi Beta Kappa members, Harvard and other elite college seniors, Rhodes Scholars, and so on, did raise some initial alarm: their analyses demonstrate a precipitous decline in preferences for an academic career (vis-à-vis business, law, and medicine) during the 1970s and early 1980s—although, to be sure, the actual magnitude of such preferences has always been relatively small (declining from perhaps 5 percent to less than 1 percent of college seniors). The latest evidence (Schuster and Finkelstein, 2006) suggests a clear increase in such academic career interests during the 1990s, which while not matching the level of the 1960s, nonetheless has been sustained over more than a decade. Moreover, the latest available evidence from chairs of leading graduate departments suggests that they continue to see no decrement in talent among their graduate students and their new faculty hires (ibid.). The alarm bells seem to be muffled.

Such periodic warnings have taken on increased urgency in the past decade from two distinguishable vantage points. Professional organizations of academic scientists and engineers, led by the National Research Council (Freeman and Jin, 2003) have issued a series of reports identifying a crisis in the supply pipeline for scientists—noting that the majority of doctorates in mathematics, the natural sciences, and engineering are now being awarded to foreign-born scholars and non-citizens, the representation of native-born scholars has been declining. Scholars such as Eugene Rice, Ann Austin, and Cathy Trower (Austin and Rice, 1998; Rice, Sorcinelli, and Austin, 2000; Trower, 2000; Austin, 2002) have focused their attention on the conditions of doctoral study and the early faculty career years in terms less of the dearth of supply than in terms of inequities of treatment that may be accelerating early career attrition, especially among historically under-represented groups. Their findings generally paint a less sanguine picture: one of enormous performance pressures increasingly targeted on a new generation of academic women with largely unchanged "traditional" family and parental responsibilities, one of disjunction between the tenure and the "biological" clocks, one of limited opportunity for mobility and career success. Indeed, Mason and Goulden's (2002; 2004) large-scale long-itudinal analysis of new doctoral degree recipients showed quite conclu-sively that pre-tenure parenthood exacted a definable "price" in terms of subsequent career success for academic women, but not for academic men.

The message advanced in volumes such as Gappa, Austin, and Trice's recent *Rethinking Faculty Work* (2007) makes two interrelated arguments: (1) broad societal, technological, and demographic changes have reshaped the demographic composition of college faculties as well as the very nature of academic work and academic careers; and (2) those changes have largely obliterated the "old rules" and require that we develop a set of "new rules" to reshape our thinking and policies related to recruitment and retention of the future faculty.

Let's review each of these arguments in greater detail. So what are the major vectors of change? And to what extent and in what ways have they affected which of the "old rules"?

VECTORS OF CHANGE

Consider these contrasts in the profile of faculty *supply* in barely two generations:

Gender   Four out of five faculty in 1969 were men and new recruits barely differed from old hands. By the early 2000s, nearly two-fifths of all faculty were women, and among new recruits, the gender ratio is approaching 50–50. While earlier generations of academic women were predominantly single, the new generation is married, have children, and, more often than not, are part of a dual career couple.

Race/ethnicity In 1969, 90 percent of full-time faculty were white (and mostly male). By 2004, the overall figure had shrunk to 80 percent and lower among the newest recruits.

Nationality In 1969, barely 10 percent of the faculty were foreign-born, typically of European origin—refugees from Nazi Germany or the old Soviet Union. The vast majority of foreign-born faculty are now of East Asian (Chinese) or South Asian (Indian) origin with very different orientations to work than their native-born counterparts. Especially among new recruits in the natural sciences, mathematics, and engineering, perhaps as many as 25 to 50 percent are foreign-born Asians. And unlike native-born faculty, this group is disproportionately male. Moreover, while the behavior of these foreign nationals is shaped by labor market conditions in the United States, they are also being shaped by new economic developments in their native countries—a new "wild card" factor. As nations such as China, Korea, and to a lesser extent, India, have initiated major investments in their developing higher education systems to achieve "world-class" universities, conditions of academic life and prospects for academic careers are improving quickly and substantially—providing newly competitive opportunities for pursuing academic careers. The "playing field" upon which institutions are competing for faculty talent is thus expanding beyond other employment sectors in the United States to other national systems of higher education across the globe.

Weltanschauung (*world view*) In 1969, the American faculty was dominated by members of the World War II Generation and the newest recruits were members of the Baby Boom Generation. It is the Baby Boom Generation that are now at the end of their careers, being replaced at once by Generation Xers and members of the Millennial Generation (Howe and Strauss, 2000). This is a generation focused more self-consciously on family and work–life balance issues, a generation focused on teamwork and service in the name of the greater good. They pose a distinct challenge to the traditional norms of "blurring" lines between work and personal life, the valorization of professional autonomy over all else.

Consider at the same time these shifting axes of *demand*:

Academic field In 1969, more than two-thirds of faculty were in the traditional arts and sciences disciplines pursuing their graduate education and their early career in perfect lockstep pattern—a perfectly predictable (regularized) supply chain. By the early 2000s, the disciplinary balance had radically shifted towards the professions, especially the health professions. Among new faculty recruits, the *majority* were now in the professions— higher and lower—and drawn as frequently from professional practice as from an insular and clearly identifiable pre-service career track.

Institutional venue In 1969, about half the faculty were employed in research universities and the remainder distributed, for the most part, over other four-year institutions. Today, the proportion of faculty residing in research universities has shrunk to barely two-fifths; and most of the recruitment is being done by other than research universities for other than research roles.

Type of appointment In 1969, virtually all faculty positions were full-time, tenure-eligible career tracks. Every incumbent was expected to play roughly the same combined (integrated) role consisting of teaching, research, and service. Beginning with a vengeance in the 1970s, the ranks of part-time appointments swelled. And, beginning in the 1980s, full-time appointees were increasingly routed into fixed-contract appointments and off the tenure track. Indeed, for at least the last 15 years, the majority of all new full-time hires have been to fixed-contract, temporary appointments—the new "modal" faculty appointment in the United States. Moreover, the available evidence suggests that these appointments reflect not merely differences in the duration and permanence prospects of contracts, but a redefinition of the work role itself. Contract appointments typically entail more specialized roles—teaching only, research only, program director only—and often preclude formal involvement in academic governance— meaning a changed relationship to the employing institution.

DO VECTORS OF CHANGE NECESSITATE NEW RULES?

Assessing what these new developments and conditions mean for the future of the academic labor market depends, of course, on the context in which one interprets them: are they temporary dislocations or fallout from an extended academic depression (part of the academic business cycle)? Or, do they represent structural re-alignments, that is, the recasting of the academic marketplace in a globalized, knowledge-based economy? Up until quite recently, that matter of interpretation was hardly settled. Bowen and Schuster (1986) had predicted a widespread supply shortage of the "best and brightest" when the swelling Baby Boomlet hit college age in the first decade of the 21st century. Indeed, they seemed to suggest at that time the imminent restoration of the old academic equilibrium of the seller's market of the 1960s—with an impending rush to create new "tenure-track positions" and to do away with the lion's share of part-time appointments. Frances (1998) had predicted a surge in demand for faculty in response to continuing expansion of traditional student demand—albeit warning of the unpredictable effects of the new digital instructional technologies. And, most recently, Leslie (2007) predicted that widespread retirements of "Baby Boomer" faculty amid the relative underdevelopment of the "under 40" junior faculty ranks would drive a crisis in replenishing the faculty.

An increasing consensus, however, is emerging that while tenure and traditional academic appointments are not yet "dead" (Chait, 2002), we are witnessing a structural realignment that has little that is temporary about it. Finkelstein (2003) recently invoked Trow's (1973) concept of the structural transformation of national systems of higher education from elite to mass to universal access to remind us that broader transformations in the economy—industrialization, the emergence of the globalized, knowledge-based economy—have historically driven reconfigurations of higher education and the nature of academic work and careers. Developments such as feminization of the workforce, globalization of the labor market, the restructuring of work along the lines of greater "casualization" to insure competitiveness—reflect larger social forces that are transforming work in America—and the world. The restructuring of the college teaching force is, in this context, no different than the restructuring of professional work (including medicine and law) more broadly. Globalization, as Twigg (2002) has argued, has intensified competitive pressures and has forced entire industries to "restructure" themselves—now including higher education and its labor force.

If, then, these "new" developments are not going away and are (and will be) reshaping the faculty, what shape is it taking? On the face of it, these developments suggest nothing less than a wholesale reconfiguration of both demand and supply in ways that we do not yet fully comprehend. Higher education is increasingly hiring practicing professionals who have not experienced extensive pre-service socialization to the academic role during traditional doctoral education. Indeed, many of these professionals may best be described as "accidental" academics. It is increasingly hiring married women with families who are insisting on a reasonable work–family-life balance—as indeed are the shrinking core of Millennial males. It is increasingly hiring foreign-born and racial/ethnic minorities. It is increasingly hiring retirees from business and industry and from academic positions at other institutions. It is increasingly redefining traditional research university roles. We are seeing clear lines of stratification among the faculty ranks among a core permanent "traditional" academic staff and a larger contingent staff serving more specialized functions. It is increasingly bringing into the academy a new sociological generation in terms of orientation to self, society, and work.

THE NEW FACULTY TOPOGRAPHY

So, how do these developments affect the "old rules"? Most fundamentally, these developments undermine the basic underlying assumption of the "old rules," that is, that there is, in some meaningful sense, a corporate faculty that has a fundamental unity of mission, background, motivation, and talent level. In that sense, the "old-line" faculty no longer exists. We have rather a highly differentiated academic *workforce* (including an exploding number of non-faculty professionals—the fastest-growing segment of the academic workforce; see Frances, 1998). How can we describe the basic lines of differentiation of this new faculty workforce, those Rhoades (1998) called "managed professionals"? Before we can assess how the "old rules" are changing, we need to describe clearly the topography of the new faculty workforce. Once the cells are named, we are then in a position to assess how the various faculty sub-groups are likely to behave. That topographical mapping exercise is best applied to recent recruits to the college teaching force—insofar as these represent the future of the profession—and allow us to extrapolate with greater confidence. Graphically, the topography of new recruits since at least the early 1990s is displayed in Figure 7.1.

Writ large, the new academic generation is about evenly divided between full-timers and part-timers. But neither of these groups is of a piece. Among the full-timers, the basic divide is between those on and off the tenure track—roughly half and half. But there are clear cleavages that criss-cross this basic one: the divide between men and women; the divide between those in the professions and those in the traditional arts and sciences; the divide between the younger entrants fresh out of graduate school (in their thirties) and the older entrants (frequently practicing professionals in their forties or fifties or "early" retirees from business/industry or the military); the divide between those in research universities and those outside. Indeed, among the professionals and older new recruits are a majority of "accidental" academics in the professions.

The part-timers are nearly as diverse internally as they are in comparison to the full-timers. While the part-time professoriate has always included practicing professionals (architects, engineers, attorneys), many doctorally

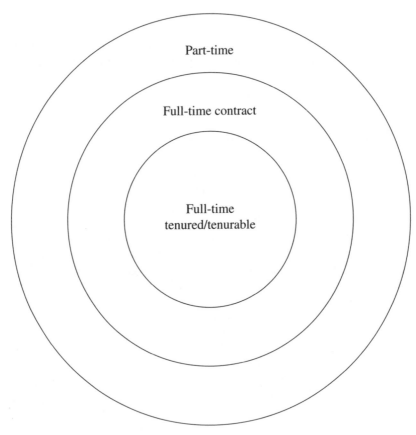

Figure 7.1   Topography of new faculty hires

trained, who teach a course in their area of specialized expertise (Tuckman, 1978), Schuster and Finkelstein (2006) identified at least two growing segments of the part-time professoriate. These include:

- *Career enders.* Individuals who have retired from institutions of higher education or from business and industry and are either pursuing a second career or transitioning to retirement (this group has swelled to nearly one-sixth of part-timers).
- *Freelancers.* Individuals, including homemakers and disproportionately women, who weave one or more part-time teaching gigs into a multi-component career. These individuals include the "freeway flyers," that is, those who have pieced together courses at multiple

institutions, those who have developed "home businesses," and those just hanging in there, sometimes quite unhappily, while prospecting for a full-time position. They now constitute as much as one-third of the part-timer professorate in several fields.

What then can we say about faculty recruitment and retention as it applies differentially to these many and varied faculty sub-groups? Will all sub-groups be affected equally by new developments? Will some be relatively insulated? Will the interests of others be advanced rather than aggravated?

NEW TOPOGRAPHY: PROSPECTS FOR TRADITIONAL TENURABLE FACULTY

To begin with, what can we say about the recruitment and retention of that one-quarter of the newly entering college teaching force that can be classified as traditional tenure-eligible or tenured, full-time faculty—understanding that somewhere between 40 and 50 percent of them are now likely to be young married women? First, it seems to me that the most basic of the "old rules"—that academic careerists are a "special breed" whose unique confluence of values and interests, including intellectual interest and achievement, the quest for autonomy even at the risk of foregoing pecuniary benefit—still holds. All the available evidence suggests that those unique individuals are still being attracted to academic careers in about the same small, but unchanging, measure. Moreover, these individuals are, judging from the available recent evidence, working harder than ever (58 hours weekly in 2004 vs. 53 hours in 1988) and are subject at once to increased expectations for scholarship and publication (Schuster and Finkelstein, 2006; Leslie, 2007), on the one hand, and heightened expectations for teaching performance, on the other. What may, however, be changing is the value orientation that mediates how these tenure-trackers fulfill these deep personal needs—and at what price. Academic women and Millennials, generally, are more oriented to family and achieving a reasonable work–life balance than has historically been the case for Baby Boomers (see Howe and Strauss, 2000). Anecdotal evidence suggests that they are less willing to sacrifice everything on the altar of work. Behavioral evidence is less clear. There are some data that suggest that women and minority faculty are leaving academic jobs at a higher rate than white men— although the actual magnitude of that rate is not clear (Trower and Chait, 2002 cited by Gappa et al., 2007; Leslie, 2007). To the extent that this does not reflect the sort of hemorrhaging we see in nursing or K–12 teaching, however, uneven retention represents more an *equity* issue than purely a *supply* issue. Modestly higher pre-tenure attrition rates for women are likely to be more than compensated for by recruiting new members (and are not entirely unexpected as we know from the "career stage" rule about the period immediately preceding the tenure decision). Moreover, the restructured academic workforce provides a new diversity of opportunities including less stressful, more specialized fixed contract positions as well as a variety of part-time positions for those seeking alternatives to the tenure-track straitjacket.

This is *not* meant to minimize the serious equity issues that are raised by the unique situation of newly entering women faculty. They do indeed have a tougher road to hoe with fewer immediate rewards (although compensation rates are improving slightly); and academic institutions do need to consider how they will address such issues from an equity perspective. At the same time, it is important to keep in mind that tenure-track vacancies account for a shrinking proportion of academic job openings— not quite half of the full-time vacancies over the past 15 years. Indeed, Leslie (2007) recently demonstrated using National Center for Education Statistics sources just how little the number of new tenure-track positions had grown—for men as well as women—over the past generation for those under 40. It is critically important to emphasize that the share of these regular full-time positions has not only declined proportionately, but that actual numbers of "traditional" positions show almost no growth. Current supply in the aggregate is more than likely to fulfill quite adequately that reduced demand—assuming that the old-line faculty do not, as a group, retire all at once (certainly an unlikely scenario!).

More troubling from a purely supply perspective—and receiving much less attention—are the changing prospects of foreign-born faculty, especially Asian men in the natural sciences and engineering. While graduate programs in these disciplines have for at least the past quarter-century been stocked by foreign-born scholars, there is new evidence suggesting that young scholars who once completed their doctorates in the United States and routinely stayed there to pursue academic and research careers are now less likely to come (a function at least in part of post-9/11 immigration restrictions) and increasingly returning home to pursue academic careers in the rapidly developing higher education systems of their home countries (Hong, 2008). Per capita research and development expenditures are increasing much more rapidly in China and other parts of Asia than in the United States (Cummings, 2008). Indeed, while the United States still maintained a global lead in production of scholarly papers and research, the center of gravity is discernibly shifting as by far the greatest growth in scholarly production moves to Asia (ibid.). While the magnitude of this reversal of the "brain drain" is not yet clear, the emerging signs are unmistakable, especially among Chinese academics. Moreover, there is no evidence whatever that the proportion of native-born American students in these fields is on anything but the continued wane (Leslie, 2007).

Future prospects for foreign-born faculty underline the larger issue of discipline-specific variation in the actual numbers and proportionate representation of tenure-track and tenured faculty positions. Leslie (ibid.) recently examined disciplinary differences in the proportion of tenure-track vs. fixed-term positions between 1988 and 2004. He reported a clear bifurcation between those fields that showed continued growth in tenure-track positions and those that were growing primarily through the proliferation of fixed-contract positions. Generally, the natural sciences were the only group of disciplines showing considerable growth in tenure-track appointments—although they also grew in the number of contingent appointments. The health sciences, the humanities, and education, on the other hand, grew almost entirely in terms of contingent positions while the number of tenured positions actually declined. Faculty in the "high-tenure-gain" fields have higher pay, lower undergraduate teaching loads, and produce more publications than faculty in "low-tenure-gain" fields. They are also more likely to receive research funding and spend more time on research. Moreover, the fields that have gained in the proportion of tenured/tenurable positions have tended to reduce reliance on part-time faculty while those who have lost tenured faculty have come to rely increasingly on part-time faculty.

These analyses suggest four things:

1. The traditional tenured/tenurable faculty is shrinking and is likely to continue to do so. The demand for tenured/tenurable faculty is actually declining; and available supplies, despite some minor downturn in PhD production, seem likely more than adequate to meet demand. Moreover, currently practicing professionals and retirees seeking second careers constitute new and promising sources of supply.
2. Developments are increasingly uneven across fields. Certain fields in the natural sciences and engineering are certain to require an increased need for recruitment for tenure-track positions; most other fields are decreasing their recruitment of tenurable/tenured traditional faculty. The academic landscape is increasingly differentiated by academic field or groups of academic fields—stratification lines that began to be drawn in the 1980s have now taken a second-order leap forward. Very different recruitment and retention policies will be required in these situations.
3. Foreign-born scholars have over the past 20 years played an important role in American graduate education in the natural sciences and

engineering and have allowed the national scientific research enterprise
to be adequately staffed. There are emerging signs that over the next
generation there will be increasing competition for that supply from
rapidly developing higher education systems, especially in Asia (that is,
China's world-class universities initiative). In the context of current
federal immigration policies, the recruitment of foreign-born scholars
becomes particularly problematic.

4. If the supply issues are of modest scope overall, they are nonetheless
    quite acute in specific fields and in the case of foreign-born scholars.
    While not strictly speaking a matter of supply, the changing demo-
    graphic composition of new recruits to the profession raises new equity
    issues that will need to be addressed.

NEW TOPOGRAPHY: PROSPECTS FOR THE NEW CONTINGENT MAJORITY

What can we say about the one-quarter of new academic positions that are
fixed-term contract positions? In the first place, it is helpful to recap the
major sub-categories that exist within this broad area: full-time faculty in
the professions, especially the health professions, who are "accidental" academics; women faculty who deliberately seek more circumscribed positions
that do not involve open-ended research commitments (in some cases,
moving from a tenure-track to a fixed-contract position or even to a part-
time position, typically for family reasons); and aspiring, full-time tenure-
track faculty, males as well as females, who have been unable to land
tenure-track positions, especially in certain "oversupplied" fields like the
humanities and education.

Recruitment and retention issues, I would argue, vary considerably
depending on which of these three sub-groups one is talking about. The
"aspiring tenure-trackers" are the most single-mindedly motivated of the
three sub-groups: while some may abandon the hope of a traditional academic career at some point (and economic concerns are likely to accelerate that "tipping point"), they typically represent that "special breed" of
individual for whom academic work represents a rare occupational
opportunity to fulfill deep personal needs. While some women may fall
into this category of aspirants, there are many more who can be classified
as "life balancers" for whom such term-limited and work-circumscribed
positions are indeed a positive inducement to a species of academic life
that minimizes its greatest disadvantages/costs. For those new faculty
recruits who have retired from a first career and who are seeking renewal
or reinvention in a second career (often coming with attractive pension in

hand), contingent academic life may offer just the right blend of meaning and (marginally acceptable) compensation. The critical supply implications here tend to be field-specific. That is, there are a handful of fields where a significant segment of the entry-level academic track is functionally specialized, fixed-contract positions. They include English, foreign languages, mathematics, basic business courses, introductory general education requirements (drawing on social science and humanities faculty), and certain professional fields, including the health sciences. While American higher education may not, in the short or intermediate term, be in danger of "running out" of such individuals, there are troubling long-term implications for the survival and prosperity of these fields for whom academic careers have historically provided a modal venue.

The sub-group of professional field faculty—the "accidental" academics —are probably the most challenging of the three sub-groups in terms of recruitment and, especially retention. Many of these individuals will have been practicing their profession before assuming a faculty position, are doing so while concurrently holding a faculty position, or will return to professional practice after a stint in a faculty position. Issues of competitive compensation will be greatest here.

Then of course, there are the part-time faculty. They rarely constitute much of a recruitment problem—although this obviously varies by field and by geographic location (relatively easy in the major urban areas, much more difficult in rural areas). Retention can be a problem, but the available data suggests that nearly one-tenth of part-timers are actually tenured and as much as half may be classified as long-term part-timers, that is, individuals who teach one or two courses a year over a significant stretch of time. It is important to be clear that the labor market for contingent faculty is likely quite different than that for tenure-track faculty.[2] It may be local or regional, but is rarely national or international; or, as Twombly (2005) has described it in relation to the hiring of full-time tenure-track faculty at major community colleges, "recruit nationally, but hire locally or regionally" (p. 438). This means that institutions may not be self-consciously seeking the absolute "best and brightest" in filling different sorts of faculty positions, so much as seeking to match the requirements of a particular position (which may, for example, focus on clinical teaching) to the talents of a particular individual. Many, depending on location, will test the local and regional market—even while placing advertisements in the national media. It is a critical piece of reality—testing that only a bare majority of vacancies may be filled these days by national search *and* national hiring processes focused on a prospective recruit's scholarly accomplishments and potential.

SOME FINAL THOUGHTS

In any discussion of faculty recruitment and retention, it is important to remember that we are discussing recruitment to "the best job there is" and one for whom demand in its pure form has been drastically—and, probably, permanently—reduced. However precipitous the decline in the academic estate over the past generation, 80 percent of faculty are still "satisfied" with their jobs and would choose an academic career all over again (Schuster and Finkelstein, 2006; Leslie, 2007). While we may lament the passing of the good old days, it is important to assess contemporary academic careers in the context of the broader restructuring of work in the global economy. The American economy is losing many good jobs, and, while gaining others, there is very little security in those new positions. The prospect of job security symbolized by tenure is an increasingly rare and precious commodity in the new global economy.

Having said that, we should also be clear that there are major issues in recruiting segments of the college teaching and research force looming on the horizon. Thus far we have alluded to the following:

1. Equity for women and racial/ethnic minorities—whether they be in tenure-track or contingent positions. There are equity issues in both contexts. In the tenure-track situation, will there be opportunities for women, minorities, and other Millennials who may be unwilling to sacrifice everything for their careers? In contingent appointments, will incumbents be exploited by institutions?
2. The situation of faculty in a handful of "competitive" fields in the natural sciences, engineering, and some professions where both recruitment and retention are likely to pose real challenges to colleges and universities. The potential impending siphoning off of foreign-born faculty in the natural sciences and engineering by rapidly developing systems at home represent a particular specialized threat here.
3. Beyond these issues, there are major faculty on-the-job socialization issues to which colleges and universities will need to attend. Historically, most institutions depended on American graduate education for the pre-service socialization of new recruits. It was assumed that graduate professors in the traditional arts and sciences had socialized their students to research and teaching norms in the field through teaching and research apprenticeships and through the opportunities for participant observation offered by full-time doctoral study. Such pre-service socialization is much less the norm with the new varieties of non-tenure-track faculty outside the traditional arts and sciences. A great deal more attention will need to be given to in-service

socialization of faculty on the job. That will mean that functions such as "faculty development" will assume an increasingly important role on our increasingly balkanized campuses.

IN SUM: OLD RULES, NEW RULES?

What then can we say about the relevance of the old rules? What new rules may be required? And how must they be applied? The major concluding observation that needs to be made is, of course, that the academic profession as we have known it since World War II—a relatively homogeneous workforce united by a common background, a common mission, a common career trajectory, albeit with significant variation among institutional types and academic fields—has transformed itself, perhaps under our collective radar, into a highly differentiated workforce segmented by diverse backgrounds, career trajectories, motivation, talents, and work roles. The heretofore (historic) core of that workforce, the tenured and tenure-track faculty, is shrinking overall and subject to increased workload pressures. That shrinkage varies widely by academic field, creating very different market situations for the traditional faculty labor. While these new conditions pose challenges to the large entering cohort of women faculty and Millennials, and may indeed be exacerbating attrition among these groups, entirely new sources of supply—practicing professionals and retired individuals seeking second careers—are emerging that nicely match emerging curricular needs/student preferences in ways that promise to offset any modest attrition increases among traditional new recruits.

This differentiation of the profession, we have argued, represents an irreversible structural shift in response to larger economic forces transforming the world of work. Some of the basic "old rules" will either disappear or will become much more restrictive in their application. Clearly, the notion of academics as a "special breed" will become increasingly limited in its application to a shrinking core. And certainly, academic careers are becoming less exclusive and less subject to the rules of inertia. If, in some respects, the shaping influence of institutional type becomes attenuated as a "research and publication" culture extends beyond research universities to many four-year institutions, that influence of academic field becomes stronger as disciplinary markets balkanize ever further along the lines of "market" value.

As the academic workforce balkanizes, we will need to think about faculty recruitment and retention in much more field-specific and nuanced ways. A crisis in one area may not be a crisis in all—but depending on its specific location, a crisis nonetheless. Over the coming decade, colleges and universities will be weighing to what extent they can recruit and manage a highly differentiated workforce that supports institutional mission without weakening the traditional core of their academic staff—the tenured/tenurable faculty.

If campuses face one imperative in the short and medium term, it is to come to grips publicly and deliberatively (self-consciously) with the new academic order. Institutions need to think long and hard—and collectively—about what kinds of faculty roles support which aspects of their mission. To what extent can the requirements and contours of traditional tenurable positions be modified to accommodate the new Millennial Generation of academic women? To what extent ought accommodation be achieved not by modifying traditional faculty roles, but by constructing and strengthening new types of more specialized roles? What is the right proportion of faculty appointments to optimize institutional mission and individual career development and satisfaction? To the extent that the academic workforce is diversifying its background and pre-service socialization, what new structures will institutions need to design in order to socialize an increasingly heterogeneous group of professionals to some set of traditional academic norms? Or, to what extent should the traditional norms that bound the tenured faculty simply be allowed to disintegrate? Which norms or elements are mission-critical—in the short and or long term? Which are simply gratuitous vestiges of an old order?

There are no easy answers or ready prescriptions. Our highly decentralized academic system in the United States demands that we take broad and individualized responsibility for shaping an academic labor force that well serves our institutions and the national research and development enterprise.

NOTES

1. There are, to be sure, issues related to who is retained and who is lost, reflecting disproportionate attrition among women and minorities, but that issue will be addressed later.
2. And even among tenure-track faculty outside the university sector.

REFERENCES

Austin, Ann E. (2002), "Preparing the next generation of college faculty; graduate education as socialization to the academic career," *Journal of Higher Education*, **73**(1), 94–122.

Austin, Ann E. and R. Eugene Rice (1998), "Making tenure viable: listening to early career faculty," *American Behavioral Scientist*, **41**(5), 736–54.

Bowen, Howard and Jack Schuster (1986), *American Professors: A National Resource Imperiled*, New York: Oxford University Press.

Brown, David (1967), *The Mobile Professors*, Washington, DC: American Council on Education.

Caplow, Theodore and Reece McGee (1958), *The Academic Marketplace*, Garden City, NY: Doubleday.

Carter, Alan (1974), *PhDs and the Academic Marketplace*, New York: McGraw-Hill.

Chait, Richard (2002), *Questions of Tenure*, Cambridge, MA: Harvard University Press.

Clark, Burton (1987), *The Academic Life: Small Worlds, Different Worlds*, Princeton: Princeton University Press.

Cummings, William K. (2008), "The context for the changing academic profession: a survey of international indicators," keynote address at the International Conference on the Changing Academic Profession, Hiroshima, Japan, 28–30 January.

Finkelstein, Martin (1984), *The American Academic Profession*, Columbus, OH: Ohio State University Press.

Finkelstein, Martin (2003), "The morphing of the American academic profession," *Liberal Education*, **89**(4).

Frances, Carol (1998), "Higher education: enrollment trends and staffing needs," *TIAA-CREF Research Dialogues*, No. 55 (March).

Freeman, Richard B. and Emily Jin (2003), "Where do new US trained science-engineering PhDs come from?," paper presented at the American Academy of Arts and Sciences, Washington, DC.

Gappa, Judith, Ann Austin, and Andrea Trice (2007), *Rethinking Faculty Work*, San Francisco: Jossey-Bass.

Hong, Shen (2008), "Development of the academic profession in China: results of a national survey," paper presented at an International Conference on the Changing Academic Profession (co-sponsored by Hiyajima and Hiroshima Universities), Hiroshima, Japan, 28–30 January.

Howe, Neil, William Strauss, with R.B. Matson (Illustrator) (2000), *Millennials Rising: The Next Great Generation*, New York: Vintage Press.

Leslie, David (2007), "The reshaping of America's academic workforce," *TIAA-CREF Research Dialogues* No. 87 (March).

Mason, Mary Ann and Marc Goulden (2002), "Do babies matter? The effect of family formation on the lifelong careers of academic men and women," *Academe*, **88**(6), 21–7.

Mason, Mary Ann and Marc Goulden (2004), "Do babies matter (Part II): closing the baby gap," *Academe*, **90**(6), 11–15.

Rhoades, Gary (1998), *Managed Professionals: Unionized Faculty and Restructuring Academic Labor*, Albany, NY: State University of New York Press.

Rice, R. Eugene, Mary D. Sorcinelli and Ann Austin (2000), "Heeding new voices: academic careers for a new generation," *New Pathways Working Paper No. 7*, Washington, DC: American Association for Higher Education.

Schuster, Jack and Martin Finkelstein (2006), *The American Faculty: The Restructuring of Academic Work and Careers*, Baltimore, MD: Johns Hopkins University Press.

Trow, Martin (1973), "The transition from elite to mass to universal higher education," in *Policies for Higher Education, from the General Report on the Conference on Future Structures of Postsecondary Education*, Paris: OECD.

Trower, Cathy (2000), *Policies on Faculty Appointments: Standard Practices and Unusual Arrangements*, Bolton, MA: Anker Publishing.

Trower, C.A. and R.P. Chait (2002), "Faculty diversity: Too little for too long?" *Harvard Magazine*, **104** (March/April), 33–7.

Tuckman, Howard (1978), "Who is part-time in academe?," *AAUP Bulletin*, **64**(4), 305–15.

Twigg, Carol (2002), "The impact of the changing economy on four-year institutions of higher education: the importance of the Internet," in P. Graham and N. Stacey (eds), *The Knowledge Economy and Postsecondary Education: Report of a Workshop*, Washington, DC: National Academy Press.

Twombly, Susan (2005), "Values, policies and practices affecting the hiring process for full-time arts and science faculty in community colleges," *Journal of Higher Education*, **76**(4) (July/August), 423–47.

Wilson, Logan (1979), *American Academics: Then and Now*, New York: Oxford University Press.

8. Baby Boomers

Carol A. Cartwright

Members of the Baby Boomer Generation touch higher education at many points. They serve as faculty, staff, and administrators of colleges and universities. They are alumni, corporate partners, legislators, and donors. They are parents of traditional-aged students and many are students themselves. As the Baby Boomers begin to retire, discussion is needed about the possible effects of their decisions on various aspects of higher education. Boomers are expected to influence our thinking, and our actions, in areas such as providing opportunities for mature learners, determining appropriate approaches to philanthropy, and providing for retiree health care.

The Baby Boomer panel was moderated by President Emeritus Carol Cartwright from Kent State University who framed the discussion by briefly describing some key differences between the pre-Boomer Generation and the Boomers. Referencing the work of David Stillman of BridgeWorks, she noted that Boomers are "raging against aging" and will have different attitudes and behaviors toward staying engaged and transferring wealth.

While Boomers are committed to causes and are generally described as optimistic and idealistic, they are generally not as loyal and committed to institutions (as opposed to causes) as prior generations and will likely need to be involved and cultivated in different ways for their philanthropic support. Their energy and interest in staying active could translate into a desire to continue working and less predictability about retirement patterns. It could also create a large group of educated and enthusiastic volunteers for higher education and other organizations. However, Boomers' interest in continuing involvement, whether in professional positions or pursuing volunteer activities and engaging in hobbies, will often be constrained by their dual roles as parents and caregivers of their own aging parents.

Carol Cartwright also reminded the group that lenses in addition to generational ones emerged in the presentations and discussions from the prior day. For example, earlier in the conference Joan Girgus suggested that stages of life are as relevant as generational differences in considering implications for higher education. She described, for example, the prominence of developmental characteristics of the adolescent life stage regardless of generation. While the specifics may vary from decade to decade, similar adolescent developmental characteristics and challenges remain basically the same from generation to generation. In effect, the teenage characteristics prevail over the generational attributes. Some life stages may not be as volatile as adolescence and may not override generational differences to the same extent. The significance of intra-group as well as inter-group differences was also mentioned.

Panelists in this conference session included Dr. Nancy Uscher, Provost of the California Institute of the Arts (CalArts), who is also an accomplished violinist and faculty member of the School of Music. Dr. Uscher assumed her responsibilities as Provost in 2004, following faculty and academic administrative positions at the University of New Mexico. Her academic degrees, all in music, are from the Eastman School of Music, SUNY at Stony Brook, and New York University, where she earned her PhD. Father Lawrence Biondi, SJ, President of Saint Louis University since 1987, also served as a panelist. Prior to his service at Saint Louis University, he was Dean of the College of Arts and Sciences at Loyola University in Chicago. An ordained priest, he has earned six academic degrees, including a Master's degree in linguistics and a doctorate in sociolinguistics from Georgetown University. University of Utah President, Michael Young completed the panel. Prior to his appointment at the University of Utah in 2004, he was Dean of the George Washington University Law School and before that, a professor of law at Columbia University for 20 years. President Young earned degrees from Brigham Young University and Harvard Law School and is widely recognized as a scholar of the Japanese legal system, dispute resolution, labor relations, and international trade law. Two of the three panelists are members of the Boomer Generation.

PANELISTS' PRESENTATIONS

Provost Nancy Uscher initiated the discussion with a brief description of CalArts, which was founded by Walt Disney in 1960. Disney wanted to create a community of artists in Los Angeles that would become a laboratory for the arts. A relevant aspect of the institution for this discussion is that CalArts does not have a tenure system, but uses multi-year renewable contracts. Nancy Uscher focused the majority of her remarks on the leadership role of the six deans at CalArts who all continue to be actively engaged in their artistic work as well as their administrative responsibilities. Wondering if these Boomer deans would slow down as they aged, and acknowledging some early skepticism about the deans' abilities to lead "double lives," she reflected that their passion for their work and their commitment to the unique role and mission of CalArts appear to have kept every dean involved and they are "not planning on retiring any time soon." She noted that the deans, who are all from the Baby Boomer Generation, "exude vitality and are exceptional role models for students and faculty members."

Based on her review of scholarly work regarding the generations, Dr. Uscher noted that Boomers are characterized as wanting peers who share their passions and interests and as desiring a group affiliation in which members want to make a difference in their own lives and in the larger community. This understanding from the research, combined with the unique mission of CalArts, led her to the conclusion that the deans have committed to form a special kind of leadership community—one that requires an understanding of the intensity of the solitary activities associated with the artistic process as well as the peer engagement needed to be strong academic administrators and leaders of their schools. A strong theme emerged in Provost Uscher's remarks about very high degrees of connectivity between and among the deans and the faculty, staff, and students of the six schools of CalArts. She described several exemplary projects to demonstrate enterprising and synergistic collaborations in dance, music, theater, art, film, and video.

Over the nearly 40 years of its existence, CalArts has encouraged its leaders to think conceptually that their administrative positions are part of their practice of art. An ethnological study of the early years described the conceptualization of the school as individual works of art and the embodiment of the unique visions of the deans. Regardless of the level of leadership, hiring at CalArts is driven primarily by excellence in artistic expression.

Recognizing that the melding of administrative and artistic practice that characterizes the culture of CalArts is somewhat unique in higher education, Nancy Uscher offered insights that may be relevant to other institutions and other disciplines in terms of the relationships between Boomer faculty and younger colleagues and students. The decanal leadership team was described as engaging in a creative process that crosses generational boundaries and regards students as young colleagues. Students actively collaborate with faculty members, arts-focused relationships are developed with alumni across generations, and the boundaries of the arts disciplines become blurred as deans and faculty join to meet the needs of Millennial artists who champion interdisciplinary work. To illustrate this, Uscher provided an example:

> One particularly interesting example of creative activity that crosses generational boundaries took place in New York just last week when David

Rosenboom, Dean of the CalArts School of Music presented at the meeting focusing on arts and technology with Grisha Coleman, a recent alumna who regularly works with a team of collaborative artists and is a current research fellow at the Studio for Creative Inquiry at Carnegie Mellon University. Together, David and Grisha explored the role of artist as cultural producer in society and reminisced about the unique intergenerational student-faculty artistic interaction that defined Grisha's years as a graduate student.

While other institutions may not have such distinctive missions, these experiences will no doubt transfer to many faculty–student interactions in which Boomers are working with Millennials. Furthermore, there may be implications for ways to encourage interdisciplinary work, which will be increasingly more important as we acknowledge the multifaceted nature of today's problems.

Provost Uscher noted the difficulties of succession planning in light of the deans' active work as artists and their attitudes toward retirement. However, she also stated that the institution ultimately benefits if these active leaders and artists choose to stay involved. She believes that they are not only putting off retirement, but that they are actually building new momentum in their careers even though this appears to be contrary to trends for members of the Boomer Generation working in more traditional disciplines and at more traditional institutions. In her words, "These colleagues are fully immersed in the global world of the arts. Their energy level is high and there is virtually no burnout. One might say that there is a constant replenishment of what John Sexton, President of New York University . . . called 'Attitudinal Endowment'."

She concluded by cautioning against over-generalization about any group and reminded the audience—as did many other speakers—that any generation represents a broad range of behaviors and a rich complexity of desires and future aspirations.

Father Biondi of Saint Louis University echoed the theme of vitality from Nancy Uscher's remarks as he noted that Baby Boomers are far from the stereotypical picture of retirees with their feet up or heading to the beach or the golf course. In his view, Boomers are retiring because their professional success has provided them with financial resources and the freedom to pursue personal fulfillment. Father Biondi has found that the powerful idea of worthwhile personal engagement has profound implications for higher education. He stated:

We know that the Baby Boomers are the wealthiest generation in the United States' history. We also know that they do not approach wealth or retirement with the same attitudes as their parents. They do not look at philanthropy in the same way either. Their giving only begins with their checkbook. In fact, often the skills and the knowledge that they contribute are much more valuable than the dollars they donate. The gift of their time and expertise is more valuable to the Boomers themselves in terms of personal satisfaction and legacy, and, therefore, certainly more valuable to our institution.

Building on the idea of personal involvement, and on the contributions of wealth, wisdom, and work, Father Biondi argued that we should embrace the Boomers and show them that they are valued and that we should make good use of the time they wish to give us. The gift of time can be substantial because, according to the University of Maryland Survey Research Center, retirements free up 25 hours per week for men and 18 hours for women. As described by Marc Freedman in his book, *Prime Time, How Baby Boomers Will Revolutionize Retirement and Transform America* (2000), Boomers have two things that only maturity can provide— experience and perspective on the meaning of life. Freedman notes that as Boomers age, they increasingly understand their own mortality and feel a need to ensure that their legacy is carried out after they are gone.

Father Biondi suggested that there is no better way for Boomers to do this than to pass on what they have learned in their lives. He pointed out that Baby Boomers are not only the healthiest and most vigorous, but also the best educated, of any group of older adults in America's history. He provided several examples of ways that Saint Louis University found to partner with Boomer alumni by providing them with opportunities to use their skills to benefit, not just the university, but the greater St. Louis area. He finds that there is synergy as these contributions benefit the university, the metropolitan St. Louis area, and the Boomers themselves.

Alumnus Terry Donohue exemplifies such collaborations. He was a successful executive with Enterprise Rent-a-Car and was recruited by a fellow alumnus to create a non-profit organization to promote retail business in a low-income neighborhood in St. Louis. With the purpose of sparking economic revitalization, the organization is both a business and social incubator. The Cook School of Business at SLU helps to manage the programs, and retired business executives donate their talent to mentor budding entrepreneurs. Mr. Donohue also gives back by serving as an executive-in-residence and a mentor for the MBA program capstone course. This generous contribution of time and expertise improves the educational experiences and the professional prospects of the MBA graduates.

Recognizing that colleges and universities are sometimes criticized for being out of touch with the real world, President Biondi described the current workloads of faculty and administrators as leaving little time to work in the real world. However, he argued that, with the involvement of Boomer volunteers who may still be in the professional world or are retired from it, the real world could easily be brought into the classroom. Both students and faculty benefit from this type of first-person contact.

Based on the success of programs such as the non-profit organization described above, President Biondi recommended that the first step to financial commitments is to get Boomer alumni involved and help them feel invested in what is happening at their alma mater. He stated, "First, ask them to give their expertise rather than their money. It shows these Boomers that you value what they have accomplished in their lives and that you believe that your university can benefit from them. Their gift of treasure will truly follow."

Father Biondi expanded on the value of ensuring that engagement precedes requests for donations by characterizing the traditional generation (pre-Boomer) as passive donors and Boomers as the opposite. He cited the rise of family foundations and donor-advised funds as evidence of active donors, who also become satisfied donors. He described the significant financial contributions of one alumnus who supports need-based scholarships at SLU. This alumnus does far more, however, than donate his personal wealth. He is also an enthusiastic member of the board of trustees and has provided his company's expertise to assist the university with its employee assistance program.

In concluding, President Biondi reaffirmed his earlier remarks about the importance of genuine involvement to ensure strong connections to the institution. He put his ideas in the framework of the mission of Saint Louis University: "As leaders of higher education, we do have the opportunity to give them the guidance, the purpose, the gentle push in the right direction by presenting them with the opportunities to be women and men as servant leaders and to become instruments of positive change in their communities."

The final panelist, and the only representative from public higher education, was Michael Young, President of the University of Utah. He announced that he intended to be a bit of a contrarian and began with statements of two caveats. First, he suggested that we are in uncharted waters regarding how well we understand the shifts and changes that are going to occur as Baby Boomers age and engage our universities. In addition, he asserted that what is really transformative is the fundamental aging of the American population, not generational differences. By 2020, 33 percent of the population will be over the age of 50, and, by 2050, the number of people over 65 will outnumber those aged 14 and under.

Regarding the transfer of wealth that was discussed many times throughout the conference, he noted that it will be a disparate transfer: "That is to say, there will be those who have a great deal of wealth to transfer and those who will not be able to retire because they don't have the resources." In his view, both ends of the spectrum are relevant for higher education.

In terms of those who have wealth, Michael Young agreed with Father Biondi that we have a different kind of entrepreneurial philanthropist who engages with institutions in different ways from prior generations. There are also significant differences among the engaged Boomer donors as some are well aligned with institutional missions and needs as they make their contributions and others are not. This latter group presents greater challenges in working through the tension that is inherent in a situation in which the donor has ideas that are not helpful to mission and institutional purpose.

For those at the end of the spectrum who do not have adequate resources to retire, there are interesting educational opportunities. For example, they may want or need to change jobs and this will require different responses from universities. Educational opportunities abound for those who have wealth as well. This could mean an expansion of courses, more specialized courses, arts experiences, and in President Young's words: "more humanities because they may actually be interested in Shakespeare." A recent AARP (formerly, American Association of Retired Persons) study suggested that 73 percent of those over age 50 anticipate having an additional new interest or hobby during retirement—that's 60–70 million people who might be looking to our institutions for some new learning experiences. President Young described these as opportunities for retraining as well as entertaining. Furthermore, he reminded us that these learners will not be passive, suggesting that they will want to be active participants who shape their own educational experiences. Suggesting that this change will not always be easy, he stated: "It will also present some challenges as many of these students will think they know better than our professors, and indeed in many cases, they may actually know more than our professors."

The challenges presented by multiple generations in the same classroom will also create new teaching and learning situations. However, Michael Young indicated that since about 40 percent of students now enrolled in American higher education are non-traditional-age students, this is not an entirely new problem. What will be new is the significant increase of such situations in the future. He regarded this as a wonderful opportunity to put the experiences of mature students together with the optimism and idealism of younger students and try to meld the two to create exciting learning experiences. It goes without saying that younger generations (digital natives) are securing information in very different ways than Boomers (digital immigrants) and this context also influences the learning process, as well as ways of social interaction.

President Young introduced the concept of diversity as another point of contrast between younger generations and Boomers. Today's traditional-age students have grown up in an environment in which 35–40 percent of the people they interact with are members of minority groups, and they are very comfortable accepting diversity of many types. He characterized the differences as between what has had to be learned by Boomers because they typically grew up in less diverse environments, and what has been acquired naturally by younger generations. Noting that these differences will also manifest themselves in classroom experiences, as well as ways in which alumni engage with academic programs, he believes that we must deal with these additional challenges and opportunities.

Finally, referencing earlier information that the Baby Boomers are more skeptical of government and less sure of the value of historic institutions, President Young suggested that this will translate into declining support for public institutions, including higher education. He contrasted the public opinion of 10–15 years ago when people would likely state that they believed that the primary benefit of higher education was a social—or public—good, with current trends that place more value on the individual benefit.

In conclusion, he related these thoughts to higher education's historic role of providing access to higher education for all groups. Access to opportunities for education created very porous social structures and enabled the United States to achieve 24 percent of the world's GDP for almost 100 years. He stated: "Much of that is due to higher education. But that's because, in part, there has been a kind of public compassion and support and commitment." In his view, that is at risk when there is increasing influence of generations who are not loyal to the historic values of public education. Still, he argued, the Boomer Generation has an enormous range of experiences and we should not lose that history.

AUDIENCE INTERACTION

As she opened the session for audience questions, Carol Cartwright asked the panelists to reflect on the topic of leadership, which surfaced in a variety of ways in each panelist's formal remarks. She asked for their perspectives on approaches or models of leadership that would likely be most effective in bridging differences among generations and also between those Boomers who have the means to retire and give back and those who do not.

Michael Young initiated the conversation by noting the need for inclusiveness in leadership and the complications that are added when people come to the table with different life experiences, different perceptions, and different views of what institutions ought to be accomplishing. The difficulty of creating shared visions and, at the same time, preserving core values, struck him as a significant leadership challenge.

Nancy Uscher took a different tack and recommended that we should encourage students and young colleagues to examine their own leadership talents. Since students and younger generations may be unaware of their potential for leadership, she suggested that Boomers in leadership positions should take responsibility for creating opportunities to develop leadership potential—and not just for higher education.

Father Biondi took yet another approach to the question and drew our attention to the leaderless situations in corporate America in which individuals lack ethical and value-centered principles. Saint Louis University is committed to developing students who graduate with discipline knowledge and an academic degree, but also with a developed conscience that encourages them to think carefully about what they will do with their knowledge. Furthermore, he noted the value of teaching ethics as part of the curriculum. He sees this as part of the opportunity for higher education to inform and transform students into leaders.

This discussion of leadership transitioned to a discussion of governing boards through a question raised about Boomers as board members. The questioner wondered if Boomer trustees are more interested in strategic work and if the comments from panelists about Boomers as donors (who want to be engaged as well as provide financial resources) related to how they behave as members of governing boards. Father Biondi began by referencing the differences between public and private universities in terms of the selection of board members. At Saint Louis University, presidents of other Jesuit institutions serve on the board and this can create a different dynamic with between 6 and 11 of the 55 members from other—and sometimes competing—universities. In the end, though, he is convinced that board members must buy into the vision in order to be successful. For this reason, SLU has a two-day orientation to explain the vision, mission, and tradition of the university. Potential board members are cultivated in much the same way as donors to assure their understanding of their role and the type of participation that is expected.

As president of a public university, Michael Young described a very different model. Board members are appointed by the Governor and confirmed by the Senate and they are a very small group compared with the size of the board at most private institutions. He noted the importance of a good relationship with the Governor and the significant value of transparency to guard against political fallout. He also mentioned the important role of advisory boards that function more like boards of private universities in terms of engagement and giving.

Yet another model was presented by Nancy Uscher who described the CalArts board as representing the entertainment industry, which fits with the unique mission of the institution, but presents interesting intergenerational challenges. At least three generations are currently members of the board. Boomers may serve on several boards and understand expectations while Gen Xers have different attitudes about their board responsibilities. The challenge of finding a common sense of responsibility is exacerbated by time constraints when people are working in a global entertainment industry.

Turning to a new line of questioning, the lack of attention in the session to Boomers as faculty members was introduced and issues were posed about the relative merits of delaying retirement or encouraging it and about retiree health benefits. A 2005 American Association of University Professors (AAUP) survey (supported by the TIAA-CREF Institute) suggested that administrators were more concerned about attracting the next generation of faculty than about Boomer faculty postponing retirement. The speaker noted that postponing retirement may benefit universities because of difficulties of attracting new faculty in some fields. He also noted that pensions are safe whereas retiree health benefits can be changed at any time. Faculties are concerned about unfunded liabilities of retiree health insurance.

Provost Uscher described a bridge plan that provides an incentive to retire by assuring health insurance until age 65 when Medicare kicks in. While she described the deans and faculty of CalArts as not yet interested in retiring, she noted that their artistic work prevails and they may want to retire from the institution so they can pursue their art in other ways. The bridge incentive provides for these situations and enables CalArts to help faculty create the best possible futures for them.

Presidents Biondi and Young offered similar information about early buy-outs as well as views that productive and enthusiastic faculty should be encouraged to stay. All panelists urged flexibility and referenced the individual nature of each case and the obvious challenge of finding ways to continue funding for productive faculty and ways to urge those who are less productive to move on. Michael Young told the story of Nobel Prize Winner, Mario Capecchi, from the University of Utah who said it took 22 years to do the work that won the prize and, at age 70, he was starting a new project that would likely take 20 years to come to fruition.

Panelists indicated that they felt personally unprepared to address technical issues related to retiree health insurance and referred to their reliance on their human resources professionals to help them understand this topic.

Following this general line of discussion, another member of the audience noted that a majority of American workers retire gradually. He characterized the older labor force as including some members (like the alumni described by the panelists) who have something to contribute and want to stay engaged and others who cannot stop working, but also having a large majority in the middle. He described this group as having talent, time, and a willingness to contribute but as not having an inclination to do so or an organization to which they are connected. How will we take advantage of the wave of Boomers who might be encouraged to get involved and give back but do not know how or where to start?

Father Biondi suggested that the seeds of service are planted early, perhaps in the undergraduate curriculum with service learning projects. In this regard, it is interesting that a characteristic of Millennials is a commitment to service and a willingness to volunteer. Provost Uscher recommended that we find ways to urge retirees from universities to teach in the public schools—in effect, create a Teach for America program for Boomers.

President Young reinforced the need for service learning to build habits of volunteering and reaffirmed a point that he made earlier—that we need to disaggregate the generation and focus more on individual circumstances and needs. There are different circumstances, expectations, and needs of sub-groups of the generation. He also took the conversation in a new direction by suggesting that higher education needs to structure itself to retrain those who would like to continue to contribute. In terms of public policy, change is also needed when, for example, an engineer with 30 years of experience has to spend a year and a half to get a credential to teach high school mathematics.

Two questioners returned to the discussion of leadership development. One reminded us that the Boomers cross a broad range of ages and the last of the group will not retire until 2030, and the other focused on the larger issue of identifying and developing leadership talent at all ages. People are often rejuvenated by trying something new in their mid-fifties or sixties and universities tend not to be very creative in moving people into new opportunities within the same institution. This participant continued and expressed an interest in discussing higher education's opportunities to enable individuals to take a new lease on life and contribute to their institutions while they still have 10 to 15 years of working lives. This point was made in the context of the arts communities in Nancy Uscher's presentation when she described the vitality of the Boomer artists she works with.

Succession planning for leadership was also addressed. The panelists agreed with the importance of the topic and each described leadership development programs at their institutions, most of them focused on younger generations and rising stars. Father Biondi described a program in which the 28 Jesuit colleges and universities collaborate on an eight-week summer leadership program for faculty who are interested in administration.

Boomers who are not on the front end of the retirement curve and still have 10 to 15 years of university service left were also thought to be appropriate subjects of leadership education. In the context of this discussion, an interesting idea emerged about whether people "stumble" into leadership positions or are intentionally groomed for them. One panelist suggested that senior leaders are at fault if they allow this phenomenon of stumbling into administration to apply to women and minorities. He said that we need to expand our minds about viewpoints toward leadership, who has those characteristics and how to put them in positions where they can test themselves to see if they want such positions and are good at them. The bottom line was that all panelists agreed that presidents and provosts must take responsibility for succession planning—a responsibility that has not typically been embraced in higher education as it has been in corporate life.

At this point, a questioner changed the direction of the conversation by asking about disengaged faculty, especially related to how to get them invested in the careers of younger faculty and transmit their expertise and experience before they retire. This led to a lively debate about whether differentiated staffing patterns were realistic in the research-oriented academic cultures of most institutions. Obviously, with differential assignments, rather than expectations of balanced workloads in teaching, research, and service, faculty could be deployed in optimal ways relative to their particular strengths. However, most in the audience believed that faculty would be unlikely to approve such arrangements.

Predictably, the discussion segued to a discussion of tenure and the proliferation of alternative models of faculty contracts. Provost Uscher pointed out that CalArts did not have a tenure system and acknowledged it was easier to start an institution without tenure than to dismantle it. An audience participant (from the AAUP) suggested that the major change with respect to tenure over the past 20 to 30 years is the percentage of faculty on the tenure track. About 60 percent of faculty was on the tenure track 30 years ago and about 30 percent are now. Clearly, the system is eroding and it may be that the market will seek a correction in terms of recruitment of new faculty. Another participant wondered if discussions about tenure are really more about managerial challenges of dealing with unproductive faculty who are tenured. This quickly led to several comments about the rarity of such cases and the extraordinary commitments made by those who choose to become faculty members when much more money can be made in the private sector. The fundamental issue is how to light up faculty and ask them to work long hours when there are "virtually no carrots and no sticks."

Several comments followed about the fundamental nature of the management challenge and the value of open debate about how to manage and deploy faculty most effectively. The role of tenure in supporting academic freedom and the democratic essential of a free exchange of ideas and new insights to contribute to society were often mentioned as well. As the academic leader of an institution without tenure, Provost Uscher pointed out that value systems that ensure academic freedom can be developed and quickly become part of the culture.

In closing, Carol Cartwright thanked everyone for the robust discussion and indicated that the conversation was more comprehensive than other sessions because significantly more time was available. The discussion benefitted from the important contributions of the panelists as well as the lively participation by the audience. Significant themes introduced in the panelists' presentations were built on in interesting ways through the audience participation. Points of difference were also introduced and woven into the conversation in important ways.

SUMMARY AND CONCLUSIONS

The three panelists represented remarkably different institutions of higher education in terms of mission, history, and governance structures. All of them, however, exhibited strong consensus about the pivotal role of institutional mission. Regardless of the specific topic, Provost Uscher and Presidents Biondi and Young were quick to note that decisions must be driven in light of mission and overall purpose. Whether considering issues of faculty appointment, alumni relations, curriculum, or governance, policies and decisions must be aligned with mission. This strong thread of staying true to mission was woven throughout the presentations and discussions.

Commitments to understanding their own personal leadership approaches and the effects of their styles of management on their institutions also emerged as a significant similarity among the panelists. While each supported different types of leadership development for younger faculty and administrators, all were firm in their convictions about the necessity of programs such as leadership academies, summer leadership experiences, and other intentional leadership mentoring programs. In addition, all panelists as well as several audience members pointed to the value of capturing the talents of Boomer faculty and administrators who are on the late side of the retirement curve. Since the age span of the Baby Boomer Generation is so wide, many in the group will not retire until 2030, and their talents should not be overlooked or wasted. However, we cannot leave their opportunities for new contributions to chance and must also invest deliberately in helping these faculty and administrators learn about the potential of new responsibilities.

A strong consensus was evident throughout the discussion about the active nature of Boomers. While most of the commentary involved Boomers outside of the institutions and focused on ways to encourage them to become engaged as volunteers and donors, some discussion occurred about ways to rejuvenate members of the faculty and staff who may be from the Baby Boomer Generation. However, the Boomer characteristic of active rather than passive participation did not carry over from the alumni group to the faculty group. This basic description of active and engaged Boomers, which is reflected over and over in the research literature, should be helpful in rethinking faculty and staff roles just as it is in rethinking ways to engage alumni and other supporters from outside the institutions.

Differences in approaches to learning, harkening back to the idea of Boomers as desiring active engagement, surfaced in several parts of the discussion, and frequent comparisons were made between older Boomers, younger Boomers, and younger generations in terms of learning styles. Interesting challenges presented by several generations of learners, with diverse learning preferences and experiences and comfort levels with technology, working in the same classroom were noted Not enough attention was given in this session to the differences between approaches to teaching and learning exhibited by faculty and students, especially when wide variations in learning preferences exist. This topic was addressed more fully in other conference sessions.

Discussions of the active versus passive nature of Boomers as donors and volunteers also included many references to the beliefs of Boomers in causes as opposed to institutions. They are much more likely to want to be directly involved in planning for their volunteer activities and directing their philanthropy than their predecessors. In addition, they want their engagement to be personally worthwhile and want to feel that a legacy is being created. These feelings have significant implications for their service on governing boards and on how they are cultivated for both their gifts of time and treasure. The commitment to causes rather than institutions also has implications for their support for public institutions, including higher education and K–12 public schools.

Retirement planning was addressed in several different ways and represents an area of considerable complexity. On the one hand, universities are looking for ways to encourage senior faculty to stay because of the difficulties of recruiting new faculty in some areas. On the other hand, they are looking for incentives to encourage faculty to retire so they can staff new areas of expertise and increase diversity. Plans to assist in bridging toward retirement as well as the potential for differentiated staffing models were discussed. Underlying the discussion was the role of academic cultures that are slow to accept change.

Everyone acknowledged that the situation of retiree health insurance is very worrisome and that few have identified good long-term solutions.

None of the panelists felt capable of addressing the technical issues of post-retirement benefits, but all acknowledged that this is an area that requires serious study. The behavior of public school teachers might be indicative of the decisions to be made by those in higher education. If this is true, then those employed in higher education are likely to time retirement decisions in large measure in light of access to low-cost health insurance.

The age span of members of the Baby Boomer Generation is about 20 years and likely means that different characteristics will emerge for those on the leading edge of the generation who are beginning to retire and those at the tail end who will retire closer to 2030. Boomers are clearly not a homogeneous group, regardless of their age and position as early or late in the generational age span. All panelists and most audience commentators reinforced the importance of recognizing differences within the group as well as between the Baby Boomers and other generations. For example, while attention needs to be given to new approaches to recruiting alumni volunteers and cultivating donors, equal attention is required for those who do not have wealth and do not feel able to retire. Both groups may turn to colleges and universities for education, but for some it will be retraining and for others it will be for life enrichment.

REFERENCE

Freedman, Marc (2000), *Prime Time, How Baby Boomers Will Revolutionize Retirement and Transform America*, New York: PublicAffairs.

9. The "boom" heard round the campus: how the retirement of the Baby Boomers will affect colleges and universities

Karen Steinberg, Phyllis Snyder, and Rebecca Klein-Collins

Asked to consider "Baby Boom retirees," Americans are most likely to think about the hot topics of the political arena: Social Security and Medicare. In truth, however, the impact of the enormous wave of Baby Boomers reaching retirement age will be even more far reaching, affecting housing, health care, and even transportation. And the size of this group of retirees, along with their long track record of influencing our culture by behaving in unprecedented ways, is likely to challenge the world of colleges and universities as well.

Higher education, according to projections, will be affected in terms of both supply and demand. Many faculty and administrators will leave academia at the same time that there is predicted to be a great surge in demand for higher education from this influential generation.

And that is not the only surprise. While earlier generations of retirees might have turned to college and universities primarily to pursue hobbies, read the Great Books or otherwise make good use of their leisure time, Baby Boomers are expected to demand that plus much more. They will also turn to higher education to gain the skills they need to help them prepare for new ways of working. The challenge facing colleges and universities is big, but it is not insurmountable. Many of the strategies colleges and universities use for their adult students more generally can be adapted to serve the specific needs of the Boomers in their quest for "encore careers."

BABY BOOMERS: THE PHENOMENON AND THE IMPACT

To understand fully the phenomenon that we are facing with an aging Baby Boomer population, we need to consider the size of this generation, relative to the generations that came before it. Prior to the late 1940s, the United States had experienced a long period of declining birth rates, first due to the influences of the Industrial Revolution, followed shortly thereafter by further declines due to the Great Depression and World War II.

Once the war was over, soldiers came home and the country also experienced a booming economy. The result was what the Population Research Bureau has called an 18-year "fertility splurge." Women married younger and had their first babies much younger than at any other time in modern history. In addition, they had more babies on average: a high of 3.7 children by the late 1950s, compared with only 2.1 children during the 1930s (Light, 1988 as cited in Greenblat, 2007, p. 873–4).

The result was a sharp increase in the population, with the generation born between 1946 and 1964 significantly larger than the generations that came before. Today, we see that sharp increase as we look at Census data of the number of older residents, past and projected. In 1970, for example, there were 20.1 million people over age 65 in the United States. In 2010, when the first Baby Boomers reach retirement age, there are projected to be 40 million in that age group. Twenty years after that, in 2030, the number is projected to be more than 70 million (Figure 9.1).

Noteworthy is the fact that the baby boom eventually came to an end, with fertility rates again declining. Subsequent generations—known by the nicknames Generation X and Generation Y—are not nearly as large as the Baby Boomers. Therefore, in the coming years, in addition to having an ever larger number of older people, we will be seeing older people making up a proportionately larger segment of our overall population. Census data and projections show that in 2000, people age 65 and over made up only 12.4 percent of the overall US population, but that will rise to nearly 20 percent after 2030.

The Mark of a Generation

It is not as if this is the first time that our society has taken notice of the Baby Boom Generation. We have long been influenced by this group because of its size and the different ways in which it has shaped our culture. Baby Boomers were the first group of children raised in homes with television, they taught the rest of us how to question authority during the Vietnam War years, and their interests helped shape cultural phenomena

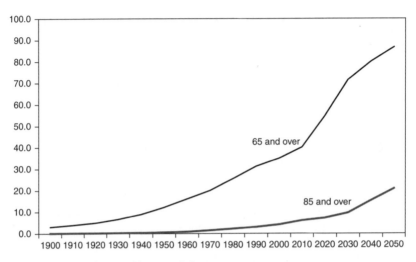

Note: Numbers refer to resident population.

Source: US Census Bureau, Decennial Census and Projections.

Figure 9.1   *Number of people aged 65 and over and 85 and over, selected*
years 1900–2000 and projected, 2010–50 (in millions)

ranging from rock and roll to film, and from the sexual revolution to the
fitness craze.

The influence of the Baby Boomers also touched higher education in
important ways. From the 1960s through the 1980s, colleges and universities
instituted a number of changes that resulted in part from the influence of
this generation. Students took greater control of their learning experiences,
and departments embraced different views influenced by the Civil Rights
and Women's Rights movements, expanding their curricula to incorporate
African-American, Native American and women's studies. But the biggest
change during this time was the size of the college-going population. A
greater proportion of the Baby Boom Generation pursued postsecondary
learning opportunities than was the case with previous generations. Greater
access to and interest in education combined with the sheer size of the group
to create an enormous demand for higher education (Kasper, 2002–03).

One result of this enrollment boom was the growth of community colleges nationwide. During the period when Baby Boomers reached adulthood, enrollment in community colleges grew exponentially: from about
1 million students in 1965 to 2.2 million by 1970, and then almost doubling
to 4.3 million by 1980 (ibid.). Data from the American Association of
Community Colleges show that the number of community colleges in the

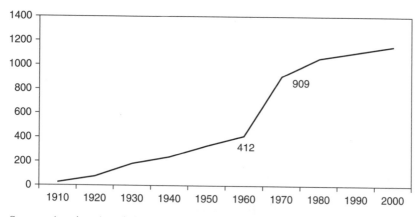

Source: American Association of Community Colleges (2008).

Figure 9.2   Number of community colleges, 1910–2000

United States more than doubled between 1960 and 1970, from 412 colleges in 1960 to 909 in 1970, precisely the time when the first of the Boomers were reaching college age (Figure 9.2).

THE COMING TALENT CRUNCH

The Baby Boomers are positioned to have just as large an impact on higher education today as they did 30 years ago. One significant way that they will have an impact will be in the large numbers of retiring faculty and administrators within higher education. Not too long ago, there was a concern within higher education about the glut of older faculty due to the fact that the mandatory retirement age had been abolished in 1994. The law permitting faculty to teach beyond the traditional retirement age was for many a wonderful development that allowed older professors to continue their contributions to higher education. But, on the other hand, it made it difficult for colleges and universities to make room for younger talent (Pant, 2007).

Today the challenge looks different. The American Association of University Professors (AAUP) reported last year that colleges and universities are less concerned about getting their faculty to retire than they are about recruiting new talent and retaining their current faculty. Only 19 percent of responding institutions said that strategies to encourage faculty retirement were important, while in contrast, 96 percent viewed recruitment of new faculty as important, and 89 percent viewed faculty retention as important (Conley, 2007).

Just as challenging will be the task of finding people to serve as senior administrators in higher education. The Bureau of Labor Statistics is projecting approximately 6000 new job openings in postsecondary education administration between 2004 and 2014, and individual institutions are anticipating turnover rates of 50 percent or higher in the next five to ten years. The proposed solutions for filling these roles resemble some of the strategies being used in the private sector for positions facing shortages—a hope for delayed retirement to age 67 or higher, and recruiting higher education retirees to serve as part-time administrators or consultants (Leubsdorf, 2006).

Retirees Enrolling As Students

The second key way that the Baby Boom Generation is expected to have an impact on higher education institutions is through enrollments. As more Boomers reach or approach retirement age, more are finding their way to colleges and universities—either as returning or first-time students. *U.S. News* recently reported that the number of college students over age 40 has grown by 20 percent in the last decade. This number is expected to rise even more dramatically with the aging of the Boomers (Clark, 2007).

Hundreds of colleges and universities have anticipated this increase in older learners by developing special centers, or Lifelong Learning Institutes, that cater to the learning needs of older students. However, it would probably be a mistake to assume that this generation is going to follow the pattern of their parents, who, when pursuing learning in retirement, have typically enrolled in classes like art, history, literature, and philosophy (Brandon, 2006).

Instead, Boomers have been warning us that they have no intention of being typical retirees. Jokes about 60 being the new 40 aside, people of this generation generally do not see themselves entering an "end stage" of their lives. They know that they have a longer life expectancy than any generation that has come before, and they believe they have many productive years ahead. Going to college for many of this group, then, is seen not as entertainment, but rather as the ticket to what they want to do or need to do in their "third stage" in life. As the Boomer Generation enters this "third stage" what sorts of demands will they make on colleges and universities, and how might higher education respond?

THE INTENTIONS OF THIS GENERATION

In recent years, there have been a number of studies, which are discussed here, that have asked the Baby Boom Generation exactly how they view

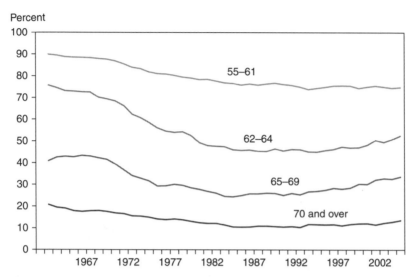

Note: Data for 1994 and later years are not strictly comparable with data for 1993 and earlier years due to a redesign of the survey and methodology of the CPS (Current Population Survey). Beginning in 2000, data incorporate population controls from Census 2000.

Source: Bureau of Labor Statistics (2008).

Figure 9.3 Labor force participation rates of men aged 55 and over, by age group, annual averages 1963–2005

their own retirement and what it is they plan to do when they do reach the traditional retirement age. Many of these studies have reached some degree of consensus on two main points. First, most agree that compared with earlier generations, more Baby Boomers will likely work past the traditional retirement age of 65. Second, while many of the working retirees will likely continue doing what they have always done in terms of paid work, a significant number is expecting to do something completely different.

Working Beyond 65

Not everyone gets to retirement age and hangs up their work shoes for good. From the 1960s through the end of the 1980s, the United States saw a fairly consistent decline in labor force participation of men over age 50, while labor force participation of women over 50 experienced little change (Figures 9.3 and 9.4). However, beginning in the 1990s, we see that picture changing rather dramatically, with men in their sixties and women over age 55 experiencing an increase in labor force participation. Men aged 62–64,

Percent

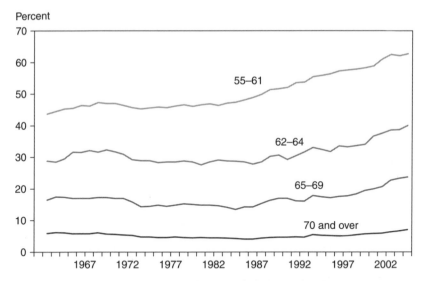

Note: Data for 1994 and later years are not strictly comparable with data for 1993 and earlier years due to a redesign of the survey and methodology of the CPS (Current Population Survey). Beginning in 2000, data incorporate population controls from Census 2000.

Source: Bureau of Labor Statistics (2008).

Figure 9.4   Labor force participation rates of women aged 55 and over, by age group, annual averages 1963–2005

for example, had a labor force participation rate of more than 75 percent in 1963. This dropped to a low of 45 percent by 1995, but steadily rose to just over 52 percent in 2005.

Similarly, women aged 62–64 had a labor participation rate in the high 20 percent to low 30 percent rate between the mid-1960s and mid-1990s. Since then, however, the participation rate has also been rising, reaching 40 percent in 2005. Women aged 55–61 and 65–69 have also experienced rising labor force participation rates since the mid-1990s.

The Merrill Lynch (2006) *New Retirement Study* reported that adults in the United States are expecting to retire later than the traditional 65-year milestone age. Today, the average age at which people expect to stop working completely is 70 or beyond, and almost half (45 percent) say they do not plan to ever stop working. The "average" person expects to officially retire at age 61 but then work in some capacity for an average of nine years in retirement.

A number of different studies have expanded on how this new view of retirement could play out with the Baby Boom Generation:

- An AARP (Zapolsky, 2004) survey found that almost 80 percent of Baby Boomers planned to work at least part-time in retirement.
- The *New Face of Work Survey* conducted by Princeton Survey Research Associates International found that 65 percent of people aged 50 to 59 (what they called the "leading edge Boomers") say that work will continue to be a part of their life throughout what used to be the retirement years (MetLife Foundation and Civic Ventures, 2005).
- The *2006 Merrill Lynch New Retirement Study* found that, on the one hand, one-third of Boomers aged 51–59 and three-quarters of adults aged 60–70 consider themselves retired, even though more than one-third of current retirees aged 51–70 are working for pay.

The MetLife Mature Market Institute has outlined a number of reasons for this expectation of work in retirement, including:

- increased longevity;
- changing economic factors such as increased health care costs;
- a growing skills shortage in many industries;
- different beliefs about work among the aging Baby Boomer Generation;
- [lack of] financial resources available for retirement (David DeLong & Associates and Zogby International, 2006).

Findings from a Pulte Homes (builder of the Del Webb communities) Baby Boomer survey from 2005 support these reasons, with 37 percent of respondents aged 50–59 saying that they planned to keep working because they needed the money, 26 percent saying simply that they enjoy their work, and 15 percent expressing concern about losing health care benefits if they retire (Figure 9.5).

Going in New Directions: Why Many Boomers Will Need Education and Training for Retirement

The reasons Boomers give for plans to continue working past the traditional retirement age are not a surprise to those who have been following the trend of delayed retirement for almost two decades now. But what may be a surprise is the type of work that Baby Boomers say they want to do in their Sixties and Seventies and the role that education may play in helping them to get there. Many Baby Boomers will continue doing what they have always done in terms of paid work—perhaps they will negotiate shorter hours or a more flexible schedule. However, a significant number are telling researchers that they want to do something different in retirement, what

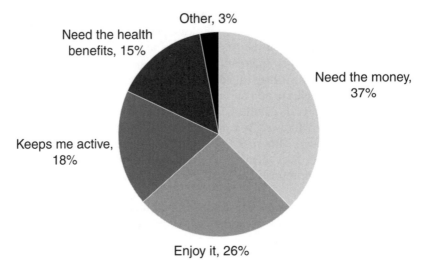

Other, 3%

Need the health
benefits, 15%

Need the money,
37%

Keeps me active,
18%

Enjoy it, 26%

Source: Pulte Homes (2005).

Figure 9.5   Reasons for working in retirement for those aged 50–59

many have come to call "encore careers." (For more on encore careers, see
Freedman, 2007.) The *Merrill Lynch Retirement Study* (2006) found that as
many as 65 percent of Boomers expect to change their line of work after
they retire from their current career.

For these Boomers, education and training will play a key role in helping
with such transitions. For a retiree interested in a new career, coursework
that provides some additional skills for that next job may be really valuable—or it may be a requirement. Half of all adults aged 50 to 70, according to another survey by the MetLife Foundation and Civic Ventures
(2005), want to do work that contributes to the greater good, particularly
education and social services. A recent Experience Wave survey found that
more than three-quarters of the respondents agreed that people over 50
could stay engaged if they had access to training (Wofford, 2008). Retirees
wanting to serve as teachers, for example, may need several semesters of
college in order to gain teacher certification, or to complete the coursework
that is part of alternative teacher certification programs. In addition, many
career options will require a high level of computer skills and this is another
area in which Boomers may seek additional training.

Our organization, the Council for Adult and Experiential Learning
(CAEL) recently conducted a survey of the older employees of a large
insurance company. The responses from these individuals typified the
trends outlined above, with over half of the respondents (58 percent)

expecting to work part-time during retirement, and 61 percent viewing retirement as an opportunity to volunteer or work with community, civic, or special interest groups. Sixty-two percent of the respondents said that training to update skills would be helpful as they begin to contemplate and determine the next stage of their career.

IMPLICATIONS FOR COLLEGES AND UNIVERSITIES

While many Baby Boomers appear to be interested in pursuing postsecondary learning during what is considered the typical retirement years, there are a number of barriers that will make education and training a difficult undertaking for some. If colleges and universities find ways to remove those barriers, they could realize a significant new source of enrollments (and revenue) over the next 20 to 30 years (Yankelovich, 2005).

CAEL views lifelong learning as central to the vitality of both individuals and organizations and has set as part of its mission removing policy and organizational barriers to learning opportunities for adults. Like many other organizations, we are listening to the expectations of this generation and are interested in their particular needs in relation to lifelong learning. One set of barriers facing older learners is, in fact, the same set of barriers that all adult learners face. The standard classification of barriers includes personal, attitudinal, and structural barriers (Cross, 1981). *Personal or situational barriers* include barriers such as the lack of time (due to work schedules, family obligations, dependant care, health issues, and so on), and lack of money. *Attitudinal or dispositional barriers* have to do with how people view their ability to succeed at education and training, with many people burdened by fear of failure, particularly if they had not been successful in school earlier in their lives. *Structural or institutional barriers* are the barriers that the schools themselves may create, for example, by offering classes only during the daytime or only in 16-week semesters.

For many years, leading institutions have worked hard to remove barriers to adults, in many cases implementing some or all of what CAEL has come to call the Principles of Effectiveness for Serving Adult Learners (CAEL, 2000). We call the colleges and universities that implement these principles Adult Learner Focused Institutions (ALFIs). Initially developed in 1999 from benchmarking research with the American Productivity and Quality Center (APQC), the principles address learning barriers through a variety of policies and practices. The ALFI principles are described below and adapted to include examples of policies and practices that colleges and universities could embrace in order to prepare for and welcome the coming return of the Baby Boom Generation.

Outreach

In the standard ALFI model, special outreach designed to engage adult learners helps to overcome barriers in time, place, and tradition to create better access to educational opportunities. Potential students need to be aware of programs that meet their needs and need to know how to access these programs. Strategies to reach out in a concerted way to older populations could include specialized marketing materials (for example, with photos of older learners) and ad campaigns and colleges may need to rethink where they can reach this audience. Civic Ventures has noted that this kind of marketing and outreach needs to show how a college's services will meet the range of needs of Boomers—at all skill and income levels— and should avoid "any taint of euphemism or condescension" (Bank, 2007). Older learners are not just interested in personal enrichment but also in retraining, refreshing workplace skills, and preparing for new careers. The outreach strategies need to acknowledge those very real goals and how the institution is prepared to help the older learner reach them.

Life and Career Planning

Providing and equipping career and educational advisors to help with decision-making is an important strategy for helping adults, many of whom do not know what kind of program to pursue, how to get started, and how to make it all happen given individual life circumstances. Advising that keeps the special concerns of older learners in mind is similarly important. Their learning goals need to be achievable and get them where they want to be in within their timeframe. Having someone help them identify the range of options available to them, and provide them with information on labor market demands for their skills even as an older worker, is critical to ensuring a successful learning experience. This may mean finding ways to ensure that college advisors are well trained in a range of career opportunities, particularly those that could be appealing and appropriate for an older worker.

Like most other adult learners, and like all learners who work, Baby Boomers will likely need to have access to these educational and career advising services during non-work hours or have options such as phone appointments to accommodate their busy schedules.

While the Baby Boomer population is typically seen as a generation that is more highly educated than previous generations, this is a very large and diverse population with a wide range of educational attainment. Many older adults have only a high school diploma or less and have spent their lives working in low-skill jobs. As the American Council on Education has noted, when these individuals plan for their future, any lifelong learning goals need to take their previous education—and previous educational experiences—into account (Lakin et al., 2008). It will be even more critical for institutions to offer educational and career planning services to help these individuals determine how education and training can help them access jobs that can give them greater financial security even as they get older. College-based career and educational advisors will need to widen their network of business contacts to include those who are interested in employing and using the skills of the more mature worker as well as those who are interested in their younger classmates.

Financing

Baby Boomers are known for being one of the most affluent generations of our time, but it would be a mistake to draw the conclusion that older learners do not need financial help in returning to learning. In fact, while fewer older people may be living in poverty than did 30 years ago, it is also true that there is greater income inequality within this generation than ever before (Lakin et al., 2008).

Some mature workers may be able to rely on help from employers through tuition assistance benefits to pursue college degrees, but these benefits will not be available to all individuals seeking lifelong learning. Even those who have tuition assistance benefits may not be able to use them to pursue a completely different line of work. Baby Boomers will therefore face many of the same financial barriers to learning as do other adult learners. In addition, once they have retired, their fixed incomes will probably make it less likely that they can afford the cost of tuition or that they will seek loans to pay for their education.

Colleges and universities serving adult learners of all ages may already provide them with assistance with financial aid or payment plans and with information about what options are available for part-time students. Such strategies will be equally beneficial to older adults as well. In addition, some institutions already offer tuition waivers for senior citizens. A 2006 study found that individual institutions in 21 states offered such waivers, and tuition waivers for seniors were also available statewide in 18 states under state statutes and ten states through formal policies (Boatman and L'Orange, 2006). However, as a recent ACE report notes, many restrictions may apply, including space availability, instructor permission, or audit-only registration (Lakin et al., 2008). One could expect further restrictions should the number of older learners increase significantly and add to capacity issues at already stretched institutions. It will be important for states and colleges within states to re-examine their aid policies for older adults to respond to demand from Boomers and workforce and skills shortages within their borders that this generation could help to relieve with the right education and training programs.

Other financial assistance options may be on the horizon as policy-makers and stakeholders begin to realize the value of the older workforce to local economies. For example, CAEL is currently piloting Lifelong Learning Accounts (LiLAs) targeted to older and minority health care workers in the San Francisco Bay Area. A LiLA account is an employer-matched, portable, worker-owned account used to finance career-related education and training. It is similar in concept to a 401(k)[1]; employee contributions to LiLA education and training accounts are matched by their employers. In the Bay Area LiLA pilot, CAEL, in partnership with the Jewish Vocational Service, is exploring how LiLAs can be helpful in supporting Boomers wanting to explore new avenues for work—a strategy that could be important for retaining workers in the health care field, which has a long history of both workforce and skills shortages.

Assessment of Learning Outcomes

One way that adult-focused institutions earn their reputations for serving adult learners well is by providing alternatives to a focus simply on how many credits someone has, or how many hours they have sat in a class-room, in order to gain credentials, certificates, or degrees. A focus on what an individual has actually learned with the goal of recognizing and credentialing learning outcomes such as measurable skills, competencies, and knowledge is important to those returning to the academy with a rich set of experiences that often includes real knowledge and skills from other places. Important for Baby Boomers will be finding educational providers that help them document and credential that knowledge quickly and appropriately without requiring them to start over again.

Adults, for example, often have little patience with entry-level courses (often required to advance to courses that apply more directly to real life and the workplace) or courses that cover material that the student may have dealt with every day in their careers. As Baby Boomers near retirement, they will return to college with an abundance of life and work experiences. One institutional strategy to try to capture the college-level knowledge that the Boomers already have gained from their experience is prior learning assessment, or PLA, a term for a variety of approaches that evaluate an individual's learning from work and life experience for college credit. PLA comes in many forms—including written exams and portfolio evaluations—and many colleges and universities nationwide already offer some kind of PLA to their students. Expanding these services and making them more widely available and known will be important for helping Baby Boomers reach their learning and career goals more quickly.

A second assessment-related hurdle for some Baby Boomers may be an over-reliance by some institutions on the results of placement exams and traditional methods of remediation. A report by the Portland Community College Taskforce on Aging (2007) found that some older learners were being placed in lower-level courses that they felt they were "well beyond." These learners suggested that short-term refresher workshops in subjects like math might be a better use of time for such individuals, rather than requiring them to sit through entire courses again.

Teaching–Learning Process

The way in which instruction is delivered is an important factor that can contribute to an adult learner's success, with some of the best strategies being those that treat the learner's own life and work experiences as valuable contributions to the learning process. With older adult learners, making connections to life experiences may become even more important, both to facilitate learning and to minimize feelings of alienation that some older learners have experienced in classrooms of younger students and faculty (Portland Community College Taskforce on Aging, 2007).

For Boomers using education to prepare for and pursue new careers, it may also be more effective for the material to be presented using the language of and drawing upon the issues that arise in a new workplace. They will also want the courses to be delivered in smaller and more accelerated modules than the traditional 16-week semester—a kind of "no-nonsense approach" favored by many community colleges that specialize in helping adult students get in, get the learning they need, and get out again (Portland Community College Taskforce on Aging, 2007; Sander, 2008).

Student Support Systems

In our 34 years of working with adult learners, CAEL has found that they have many life challenges and responsibilities to manage while trying to pursue education. In addition to working, they often have young dependants, they may need to care for ailing parents, manage a household, deal with family crises or illnesses, and so on. Those various layers of life issues rarely disappear just because someone reaches age 55—and in some cases, life can become even more challenging. Systems for supporting the older learner and helping them succeed despite all of these challenges are very important and can include things like advising, mentoring, financial advising and assistance, and new student expectations and orientation. Clear curricular maps and career pathways, as well as prior learning assessment can also help them see a way to navigate toward their goals.

The older learner may also need the human connection outside of the classroom to help them feel like they belong at the institution and that they have people to whom they can turn for help and guidance. The feelings of alienation can be quite acute for many adults, particularly when significant age differences exist.

Technology

In the general ALFI framework, technology is an important factor in providing adult learners with what they need to succeed in college and in the workplace. The institution uses information technology to provide relevant and timely information and to enhance the learning experience. Exemplary practices include using technology to bridge geographical barriers to learning, provide flexible and timely administrative services, and to expand the choices for learning modes. But the importance of technology presents two problems for Baby Boomers. First, many retirees enroll in higher education in part to have direct social interaction with people (Lehman, 2006; Lakin et al., 2008) and in many cases these technologies will seem counterintuitive to that need. For some Boomers, distance and hybrid classes may suit their needs well; for others, these technology-assisted options will not hold any appeal.

The second concern is that none of these exemplary technology practices do any good if the older student is not comfortable with technology in the first place. This concern is one that colleges and universities will need to address for many older learners. Baby Boomers have become far more comfortable with technology than the generation before, but facility with computers is hardly a universal skill among older people. For example, the Pew Internet and American Life Project found that Internet usage declines steadily with age, with more than 80 percent of people in their thirties spending time online compared with 73 to 76 percent of people in their forties, 68 percent of people in their fifties, and 55 to 57 percent of people in their sixties (Fox and Madden, 2005). For those returning to school in order to pursue a second or third career, having or developing a high comfort level with technology will be critical. Colleges and universities will need to find ways to reach out to those students, determine their needs, and help them develop the technology skills they will need to succeed both in class and in their hoped-for career (Sander, 2008).

Strategic Partnerships for Career Transitions

Adult-learner-focused institutions succeed by forming strategic alliances with local organizations and employers to ensure that workers learn about educational opportunities, and that students learn about work opportunities and what is needed to succeed in today's workplace. Colleges and universities use these relationships to ensure that their curricula and practices remain relevant and current. As colleges and universities consider the return of Baby Boomers, and the reasons for their return to learning, these partnerships become even more important.

Colleges will want to ally with several different kinds of employers: employers needing to fill high-skill, high-demand jobs such as those in health care; employers needing to find workers interested in part-time or cyclical jobs; and social service organizations or schools that offer both paid and unpaid work opportunities for the many Boomers interested in "making a difference" in their retirement years.

There may also be opportunities to form partnerships with employers who want to help their workers make successful transitions to their "encore careers." One program model for this kind of approach is IBM's "Transition to Teaching" program, which is focused on training mid-career employees to become teachers—mostly in math and science subjects—after their tenure at IBM. The company's goal is both to help the existing workers make successful transitions to their next career, while also helping to strengthen science and math instruction in the nation's schools. IBM's Chief Learning Officer, Ted Hoff, explains that this addresses "both the issue of how we build a better workforce while also helping our own people who might be looking for a change, but not necessarily looking to retire" (Klein-Collins, 2007).

Civic Ventures, which has been working to help older Americans put their experience to good use in retirement, recently announced the MetLife Foundation/Civic Ventures Community College Encore Career Grants, which have been awarded to ten community colleges that will work to develop initiatives designed to match Boomers' experience, skills, and interests to "encore careers" in critical service fields (Civic Ventures, 2007). Some of these encore college programs have established strategic partnerships to meet demand for such programs. Civic Ventures has provided examples of its grantees' programs, which help to illustrate the kinds of partnerships that will help meet the needs of older learners:

- A program at Collin Community College near Plano, Texas is working with local employers to help telecommunications engineers and other downsized technology professionals become math teachers through a fast-track program.

- Owensboro Community and Technical College in Kentucky is working with a local hospital to recruit retiring nurses and train them for encore careers as nursing instructors.
- Baltimore City Community College is providing a full-service out-placement program for African-American women over 50 interested in pursuing encore careers in public school education, health care, and social services (Bank, 2007).

Partnerships with philanthropic organizations may help to provide resources needed to establish special programs and outreach for Boomers. The Civic Ventures grants, for example, have been funded by the MetLife Foundation, and CAEL's Bay Area LiLA program targeting mature workers has been funded by Atlantic Philanthropies. These investments help to demonstrate the importance that the broader community is beginning to place on the need for career education programs for mature workers and learners.

SUMMARY

The post-war Baby Boom created a generation that has broken new ground at every stage of its life. Now poised to become the largest older population in our nation's history, Boomers are preparing to obliterate our preconceptions about retirement and life after age 65. Harris Wofford (2008), former US Senator and current spokesperson for Experience Wave, has noted that the public focus on the burden created by such a large older population has completely overshadowed the fact that this group of people has the potential to make significant contributions to our communities, if we only learn how to tap their time and talent in a new way. But in order to see the Boomers fully as contributors, we will need to help many of them find their way back to school and be successful there.

Colleges and universities can help this population by recognizing their learning needs, addressing their barriers, and honoring the experience that they bring to the learning environment. Institutions could consider a number of different kinds of strategies including:

- adopting marketing strategies that reflect older learners' concerns, respect their ambitions, and recognize their learning goals, especially those related to the pursuit of encore careers;
- assisting Boomers in identifying jobs and related educational paths for what it is they want to achieve in an encore career;

- providing training and support services at times and in places that are accessible to all adults who may be working full-time;
- assisting with new strategies for financing learning such as Lifelong Learning Accounts;
- providing avenues for older learners to accelerate the learning process, or at least minimize the need for them to sit through what they already learned elsewhere;
- honoring the life and work experiences of older learners, both in the classroom and in campus life generally;
- helping to close the generational digital divide, so that Baby Boomers are more comfortable with the technology that they will need to use both for education and in an encore career;
- working closely with employers, community-based organizations, economic development agencies, and governments to design and offer new workforce learning programs that meet the labor force needs of local economies and the "encore ambitions" of the Boomer Generation.

With these strategies, colleges and universities will pave the way for Baby Boomers to return to learning in large numbers, once again shaping our learning communities in positive and memorable ways.

NOTE

1. Type of employer-sponsored defined contribution retirement plan under Section 401(k) of the Internal Revenue Code.

REFERENCES

AARP (2000), AARP Survey on Lifelong Learning, www.aarp.org/research/reference/publicopinions/aresearch-import-490.html.

American Association of Community Colleges (2008), "Community college growth by decade," http://www.aacc.nche.edu/Content/NavigationMenu/AboutCommunityColleges/HistoricalInformation/CCGrowth/CCGrowth.htm

Bank, David (2007) "Training for 'encore careers'." Civic Ventures, http://www.civicventures.org/communitycolleges/Encore_Colleges.pdf.

Boatman, A. and H. L'Orange (2006), *State Tuition, Fees, and Financial Assistance Policies for Public Colleges and Universities, 2005–06*, Boulder, CO: State Higher Education Executive Officers, www.sheeo.org/Finance/tuitionfee06.pdf.

Brandon, Emily (2006), "The class goes gray. Retirees head back to college, and what's not to like? They often don't need to study for exams—or even pay tuition," *U.S. News*, http://www.usnews.com/usnews/biztech/articles/061029/ 6prime.htm.

Bureau of Labor Statistics (2008), "Older Americans update 2006: key indicators of well-being," www.agingstats.gov/agingstatsdotnet/Main_Site/Data/2006_Documents/ CBeconomics.xls.

CAEL (2000), *Serving Adult Learners in Higher Education: Principles of Effectiveness: An Executive Summary*, www.cael.org/alfi/PDF%20files/Summary %20of%20Alfi%20Principles%20of%20Effectiveness.pdf.

Civic Ventures (2007), "First major community college effort launches to help Baby Boomers prepare for second, 'encore' careers. Civic Ventures, MetLife Foundation invest in 10 leading institutions training Boomers for jobs benefiting the greater good," press release, 13 August, http://www.civicventures.org/news/releases/index.cfm?date=2007_08_13.

Clark, Kim (2007), "Heading back to college. Universities are doing more than ever to attract older students," *U.S. News*, http://www.usnews.com/articles/business/retirement/2007/10/26/heading-back-to-college.html.

Conley, Valerie Martin (2007), *Survey of Changes in Faculty Retirement Policies 2007*, American Association of University Professors. Funded by the TIAA-CREF Institute, and the Cornell Higher Education Research Institute.

Cross, K. Patricia (1981), *Adults as Learners: Increasing Participation and Facilitating Learning*, San Francisco: Jossey Bass.

David DeLong & Associates and Zogby International (2006), *Living Longer, Working Longer: The Changing Landscape of the Aging Workforce*, a MetLife study, http://www.metlife.com/WPSAssets/13497229201173736554V1FLivingLonger.pdf.

Fox, Susannah and Mary Madden (2005), "The Pew Internet and American Life Project," http://www.pewinternet.org/pdfs/PIP_Generations_Memo.pdf.

Freedman, Marc (2007), *Encore: Finding Work That Matters in the Second Half of Life*, Cambridge, MA: PublicAffairs.

Greenblat, Alan (2007), "Aging Baby Boomers. Will the 'youth generation' redefine old age?" *CQ Researcher*, **17**(37), 865–88.

Kasper, Henry T. (2002–03), "The changing role of community college", *Occupational Outlook Quarterly*, winter 2002–03, http://www.bls.gov/opub/ooq/2002/winter/art02.pdf.

Klein-Collins, Becky (2007), "A conversation with IBM's Ted Hoff," *CAEL Forum and News,* Winter.

Lakin, Mary Beth, Laura Mullane, and Susan Porter Robinson (2008), *Framing New Terrain: Older Adults and Higher Education*, American Council on Education.

Lehman, Jim (2006), "Three retirement challenges the experts never told you about," *CAEL Forum and News*, Spring.

Leubsdorf, Ben (2006), "Boomers' retirement may create talent squeeze," *The Chronicle of Higher Education*, **53**(2), A51, http://chronicle.com/weekly/v53/i02/02a05101.htm.

Light, Paul C. (1998), *Baby Boomers*, New York: W.W. Norton.

Merrill Lynch (2006), *2006 Merrill Lynch New Retirement Study*, http://www.ml.com/media/66482.pdf.

MetLife Foundation and Civic Ventures (2005), *New Face of Work Survey*, www.civicventures.org/publications/surveys/new-face-of-work.cfm.

Pant, Paula (2007), "As Baby Boomers ready for retirement, colleges look for replacement faculty," *Colorado Daily* (U. Colorado), 16 March, http://media.www.thebridgenewspaper.com/media/storage/paper1120/news/2007/03/16/News/As.Baby.Boomers.Ready.For.Retirement.Colleges.Look.For.Replacement.Faculty-2777670.shtml.

Portland Community College Task Force on Aging (2007), "Boomers go to college. A report on the survey of students 40 and older conducted by the Portland Community College Taskforce on Aging draft report for comment and review," http://www.pcc.edu/about/commitments/aging/documents/boomer-report-033007.pdf.

Pulte Homes (2005), *Pulte Homes Baby Boomer Study 2005*, May.

Sander, Libby (2008), "Blue-collar Boomers take work ethic to college," *The Chronicle of Higher Education*, **54**(19), A1, http://chronicle.com/free/v54/i19/19a00101.htm.

Wofford, Harris (2008), "Why colleges should welcome the return of the Boomers," *The Chronicle of Higher Education*, 8 February, **54**(22), A1.

Yankelovich, Daniel (2005), "Ferment and change: higher education in 2015," *The Chronicle of Higher Education*, 25 November, **52**(14), 86–89.

Zapolsky, Sarah (2004), "Baby Boomers envision retirement II: survey of Baby Boomers' expectations for retirement," *Research Report*, RoperASW, AARP, http://www.aarp.org/research/work/retirement/aresearch-import-865.html.

10.   As Baby Boomers retire

Valerie Martin Conley

Will you still need me?
Will you still feed me?
When I'm sixty-four? (Beatles, "When I'm Sixty-Four," written by Paul McCartney, released 1967)

INTRODUCTION

What about 65? 70? 80? When a new faculty member joins an institution there is a sense of excitement and anticipation. Everything is new. There are typically several programs designed to welcome and orient the faculty member to their new community—at the institution, college, and department. Sometimes there are even receptions hosted by organizations within the surrounding community. After all, a lot of effort, including a substantial monetary investment has been made to recruit the faculty member (and sometimes his or her spouse or partner as well) to the institution. When all of the negotiations are finally said and done, everyone is committed to the individual's success. But, the lyrics from the popular Beatles song capture the sentiment many older faculty members, including those from the Baby Boom Generation, may be feeling as they age. To what extent do institutions continue to demonstrate commitment to individual faculty members' success throughout their career?

In a policy environment where legislators are looking for ways to keep experienced workers working, higher education policy-makers may be headed in the opposite direction. For example, the National Governor's Association is studying ways to engage Baby Boomers and "build an experience dividend" (Greenya, 2008). Former senator, Harris Wofford, D-Pa, is working with states to find ways to tap older workers' skills. In a feature story in *USA Today* about the "Experience Wave" Boomer initiatives, Wofford was quoted as saying: "We're retiring the concept of retirement" (El Nasser, 2008). However, among higher education institutions, retirement incentives—or buy-outs as they are often referred to—have become commonplace since mandatory retirement was eliminated for tenured faculty members. More than a third of institutions in a recent survey of higher education administrators reported that one or more institution-wide financial incentive programs for retirement had been offered since 2000 (Conley, 2007a).

Administrators, particularly human resource professionals, recognize recruitment, selection (that is, hiring), orientation, and retention as important aspects of the staffing process. When asked to rate key areas related to staffing, the majority of institutions rated recruitment (96 percent) and retention (89 percent) "very important." Much less attention is placed on leaving or separating from the institution, however. Only 19 percent of institutions in the same survey rated retiring older faculty members "very important" (Conley, 2007a). We can only speculate why this may be the case. It may be because large numbers of older faculty have not yet begun to retire and so it is not yet a priority for institutional administrators. Or it may be that institutions see retiring older faculty as inevitable, and are more concerned about recruiting and retaining faculty than managing or supporting retiring older faculty (Conley, 2008). Regardless of why, the fact is, as Baby Boomers retire, more attention will be placed on staffing practices and processes related to retiring or separating from an academic career, and in particular managing Baby Boomer retirement. As the television commercial for Liberty Mutual reminds us, when people do the right thing they call it being responsible. The people responsible for helping faculty transition into retirement and for protecting the interests of individuals and institutions have an important role to play in the future of higher education.

KEY QUESTIONS AND ISSUES

There are too few resources available to help individuals in these positions make good decisions. In an effort to fill this gap, I explore key questions and issues in this chapter that administrators need to consider as they carry out the important responsibility of managing Boomers' retirement. A series of questions may guide the decision-making process:

1. What is the age distribution of employees by planning unit? How many individuals are projected to retire each year? What is the optimal time to offer retirement incentive packages? How generous should retirement incentives be? What is the supply and demand of employees by primary occupation and desired demographic composition?
2. What are the institution's policies and procedures related to retirement? How have the policies and procedures changed over time? What are the

Table 10.1   Summary of retirement management issues

Demographic Context	Policy Issues	Plan Characteristics and Services	Legal Issues
Age by discipline	National issues Social Security Health Care	Flexibility Equity	Age Discrimination in Employment Act Older Workers
Supply and demand by age	State issues Economic Outlook Pension design –Defined benefit/ defined contribution Health insurance Institutional trends Strategic planning/ management –Replacement –Reallocation –Renewal	Cost-effectiveness Financial planning Non-financial planning Retirement readiness	Benefit Protection Act of 1990 Pension Protection Act of 2006 Employee Retirement Income Security Act Termination for cause Reporting regulations

push/pull factors associated with the policies and procedures from the perspective of the individual and from the institution? In other words, what aspects of the institution's retirement process are particularly attractive to individuals? What aspects most benefit the institution? Are there disincentives (for example, related to the availability of retiree health care)? What are the characteristics of pension plans available in the state? How do the plans compare across comparable institutions, whether public or private?

3. What is the economic and political landscape in the state? How do state and national laws impact the institution? What are the applicable reporting regulations?

In general, these issues fall into three categories: the demographic context and associated policy issues, individual and organizational concerns, and the legal landscape. The scope of the chapter precludes definitive treatment of these issues, but I close with a series of recommendations intended to provide a direction for future conversations and research. Table 10.1 summarizes the major themes.

DEMOGRAPHICS, SOCIAL SECURITY, AND POLITICS

Now that the first of the Baby Boom Generation, a retired school teacher, has filed for Social Security benefits, managing Baby Boomers' retirement will begin to increase in importance as an integral aspect of human resource planning for several years to come—becoming more of a priority for organizations from all sectors of the economy.

Being hailed a "silver tsunami," the US Census Bureau defines the Baby Boom Generation as people born between 1946 and 1964 (US Census Bureau, 2006b). The estimated number of Baby Boomers as of 1 July, 2005 was 78.2 million. The Census Bureau has been tracking the impact this group of individuals is having on the aging of the US population and has compiled a fact sheet about Baby Boomers available from the online Question and Answer Center. The "Population profile of the United States: 2000," records that the median age of the US population reached a new high in 2000 (US Census Bureau, 2008), and continues to increase. "On July 1, 2005, the median age of the population was 36.2 years—older than the highest median age ever recorded in a census (35.3 in Census 2000)" (US Census Bureau, updated January 2007). The number of older Americans will begin to increase at an even faster pace as the Baby Boom Generation reaches age 65 between 2010 and 2030. Over the next 25 years, the US population aged 65 and over is expected to double in size. By 2030, almost one out of five Americans will be 65 years or older. What is the fastest-growing segment of the US population? The answer is the age group 85 and older (US Census Bureau, 2006a).

In the *Older Americans Update 2006: Key Indicators of Well-being*, the Federal Interagency Forum on Aging-related Statistics (2006) provides compelling evidence that the elderly will live longer, healthier lives. It is almost certain that these demographic shifts will challenge assumptions we hold as a society regarding aging and the elderly.

Those within academe may experience an acute awareness these issues bring because of the way higher education experienced growth during the 1960s and 1970s and because of the way higher education—in particular public higher education—is staffed and funded, creating unique challenges for those responsible for managing Baby Boomers' retirement. The average age of faculty has increased along with the US population—from 47 in fall 1987 to 50 in fall 2003 (the most recent year data are available) (National Study of Postsecondary Faculty). The average age of full-time tenured faculty members has also been increasing and was 54 in 2004. As of 2004, more than one-third (35 percent) of faculty members were 55 years old or older (Conley, 2007b). Figure 10.1 shows the average age of faculty

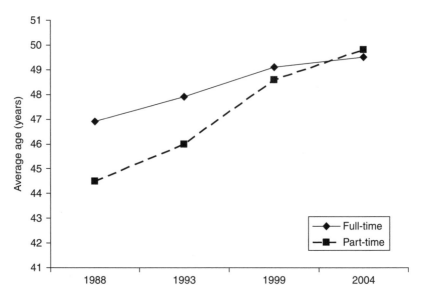

Sources: US Department of Education, National Center for Education Statistics, National Study of Postsecondary Faculty (NSOPF).

Figure 10.1   *Average age of instructional faculty and staff in four-year institutions, by employment status: 1988, 1993, 1999, and 2004*

members in four-year institutions is increasing for both full- and part-time faculty (tenured and untenured), respectively. The average age of part-time faculty has increased from 44 to 50 years old during the time period.

Furthermore, there has been a dramatic increase in the percentage of part-time faculty relative to full-time faculty in colleges and universities over the past three decades (US Department of Education, 2006). Given the size of the part-time faculty population overall, administrators may want to focus some attention on the retirement policies and processes related to retirement for this group of employees in particular. There are inherent challenges in doing so, however. There are many reasons why faculty work part-time and many reasons why institutions employ faculty part-time. Many part-time faculty members do not have access to employer-sponsored retirement benefit programs. Part-time faculty members are less likely to be eligible for benefits than full-time faculty—and even when they are eligible, fewer elect to participate. About half of institutions (57 percent) indicated that part-time faculty members were eligible to participate in institutionally sponsored retirement savings plans and only about half (53 percent) of those were doing so (Conley, 2007a). Although not all part-time faculty members need or want access to these programs, administrators responsible for managing retirement benefits and programs may want to consider increasing the availability of retirement plans for part-time faculty and look for ways to increase understanding of the factors contributing to the reasons part-time faculty are not participating when they are eligible.

Age is the main determinant of when an individual will retire, so institutions should have good data on the age profile of their faculty, by a variety of characteristics including academic discipline (Leslie, Janson, and Conley, 2006). When the size of a discipline is small and the age of faculty in the program is similar, several faculty members may elect to retire at the same time. This may lead to immense challenges or strategic opportunities, depending upon the program and institution. Understanding the demographic characteristics of faculty within the context of the institution is vital, not only in managing retirement, but also in contributing to comprehensive planning efforts and the strategic direction of the institution. The authors observed, "Institutions may want to encourage retirements or encourage retention, depending on their strategic position" (p. 82). Managing Boomers' retirement is an important human resources strategic imperative, requiring a sophisticated level of understanding of the demographic context and associated policy issues. The next sub-section focuses on two policy issues of growing concern: Social Security reform and health care.

Social Security and Health Care

As the age of the population increases, issues of interest to older Americans are beginning to receive the spotlight on the political stage. Social Security reform and health care, for example, are two issues of growing concern. "Social Security faces a shortfall over the indefinite future of $13.6 trillion in present-value terms, an amount equal to 3.5 percent of future taxable payrolls" (US Department of the Treasury, 2007a). In an effort to stimulate and guide conversation—and action—related to the need for Social Security reform, the US Department of the Treasury has released three *Issue Briefs* covering the following topics:

1. The Nature of the Problem;
2. A Framework for Analysis;
3. Benchmarks for Assessing Fairness and Benefit Adequacy.

There is little, if any, disagreement that Social Security reform is needed, but consensus that there is a problem is not enough. The first brief demonstrates there is a significant cost for delay and that not taking action is unfair because it exempts additional generations from sharing in the financial consequences of reform (US Department of the Treasury, 2007a). A simple, but powerful message is contained in the brief: increased economic growth can make reform easier, but by itself cannot solve the problem. The second brief offers a framework for designing and evaluating reform plans, which hinges on the ability to safeguard Social Security surpluses. The framework includes four key components: fairness across generations, fairness within generations, size of the safety net, and pre-funding future benefits (US Department of the Treasury, 2007b). The third brief provides concrete examples of how the framework could be applied to determine fairness and benefit adequacy (US Department of the Treasury, 2007c).

Although faculty members are typically not dependent solely upon Social Security during retirement, administrators responsible for managing Boomers' retirement should still monitor Social Security reform debates because of the potential impact they may have on retirement policies and practices in higher education. Current proposals for reform include "limiting benefits for wealthy retirees, indexing benefits to prices rather than wages, increasing the retirement age, discouraging early collection of retirement benefits, and changing the way benefits are calculated" (The White House, 2005). While these changes would not likely affect anyone born prior to 1950, the reforms may have as large an impact on higher education as eliminating mandatory retirement ages for tenured faculty did in the mid-1990s. In particular, increasing the eligibility age for Social Security and discouraging early collection of benefits may cause individuals to alter their retirement decisions, causing colleges and universities to have to further adapt to multiple retirement patterns.

An added complexity inherent in inevitable Social Security reform is what might happen to the availability of Medicare and the rising cost of health care. One only needs to listen to the campaign speeches of presidential candidates to realize that the rising cost of health care is on people's minds. The percentage of large private-sector employers offering health benefits to retirees declined between 1988 and 2004 (Henry J. Kaiser Family Foundation and Hewitt Associates, 2004). Similarly, many colleges and universities have begun re-examining benefits offered to active and retired faculty. Many institutions are shifting more of the responsibility for the cost of coverage to the individual and are offering fewer benefits. The majority of institutions reported that faculty retirees continue to be eligible for group health insurance upon retirement. However, the share of the cost borne by the individual and the institution varies. Fifty-one percent of institutions paid part of the cost for the faculty retiree and their spouse. Thirty-three percent of institutions required the individual to pay 100 percent of the cost and 17 percent of institutions paid the entire cost of medical insurance for the retiree. Almost all institutions (96 percent) reported that individuals were responsible for 100 percent of long-term care. Less than one-half of institutions (45 percent) reported that their health insurance benefits had stayed the same for both active and retired faculty members since 2000. "Twenty-six percent of institutions reported reducing benefits for both groups equally, while 8 percent indicated that benefits for retired faculty had been reduced more than those for active faculty" (Conley, 2007a, pp. 26–7).

Berberet et al. (2005) found senior faculty members are concerned about the cost of health care and the availability of university-provided health insurance in retirement. Administrators responsible for managing Boomers' retirement may want to consider the extent to which availability and cost of health care may impact individuals' decisions about retirement. It is necessary to strike a balance between individual and organizational concerns. In the next section, I highlight some of the individual and organizational concerns regarding faculty retirement.

INDIVIDUAL AND ORGANIZATIONAL CONCERNS

Although not definitive, there is evidence to suggest the number and percentage of faculty retiring has been increasing. Between fall 1997 and fall 1998, 29 percent of full-time faculty who left their institutions retired (Berger, Kirshstein, and Rowe, 2001). Between fall 2002 and fall 2003, 36 percent of those who left retired—a seven percentage point increase. While some of these departures were prompted by actions taken by institutions, such as early retirement incentive offers, the number of retirements and the proportion of departures from institutions due to retirements appear to be increasing steadily too. Higher education may be faced with a barrage of retirements as Baby Boomers approach retirement age. Or they may be faced with the challenge of responding to an ever-faster-paced changing environment characterized by changing student characteristics, increased competition for scarce resources, and more and more calls for accountability in an environment absent mandatory retirement. Undoubtedly, different institutions will face varying challenges and will be more or less prepared to respond to those challenges. There is little systematically collected information to help those responsible make good decisions. Sufficient data are not available from any source, for example, to estimate supply and demand of faculty. The diversity of institutions, disciplines, and employment relationships that would need to be taken into consideration makes the task daunting. Without the benefit of a national context, institutions are left with a multitude of unknown variables.

Institutions must track faculty demand on their own, but they can get a fairly good picture of supply from a combination of federal data sources: Integrated Postsecondary Education Data System (IPEDS) Completions (degrees conferred by level), IPEDS Human Resources (new hires), and the National Science Foundation (NSF) Survey of Earned Doctorates (SED). Information on exits from an institution—either for retirement or any other reason is not collected through the IPEDS surveys, however. The processes for accessing these resources have improved, but nonetheless require an in-depth understanding of the data to use it for decision-making. Many institutions use these resources to aid in the development of availability pool information already. Administrators responsible for managing Boomers' retirement may want to integrate retirement projection planning into these processes with a goal of developing an overall human resource planning model for the institution.

Prior to the passage of the Age Discrimination in Employment Act (ADEA), institutions could set mandatory retirement ages for tenured faculty members, with most institutions setting the age at 70. The ADEA put the timing of retirement in the hands of the individual. Many were concerned that allowing individual faculty members, particularly those with tenure, to decide when they would retire would restrict the institution's ability to hire new faculty members and put additional financial burdens on institutions because they would have to maintain the higher salaries of these personnel and continue retirement contributions for longer periods. These concerns gave rise to early retirement incentive programs, which take a variety of forms. There are three basic goals of early retirement incentive programs:

1. getting the right number of older workers to accept the incentive;
2. getting the right older workers to accept the incentive;
3. obtaining older workers' commitment to accept the incentive at the right cost to the organization (Feldman, 2003).

Applied to retirement in general, the goals might be:

1. projecting the number of workers who will retire at a given time;
2. helping individuals plan for and transition to retirement;
3. optimizing the timing/level of benefit of retirement incentives and maintaining competitive retirement benefits (including health care).

In accomplishing these goals, policies and programs should take into consideration both individual and organizational concerns, while at the same time maximizing desirable characteristics including flexibility, equity, and cost-effectiveness.

Flexibility and Equity

Although the largest percentage of full-time faculty and instructional staff said they expect to retire "on-time"—that is—between the ages of 65 and 67 (37 percent), about one-quarter of faculty reported expected ages of retirement that may be considered "early" (55–64) or "late" (68–74), respectively (Figure 10.2). This distribution depicts the diverse expectations about retirement that are emerging in higher education since mandatory retirement ages were eliminated for tenured faculty members through amendments to the ADEA (Conley, 2007b).

The distribution also underscores that understanding the age distribution of faculty is no longer enough. Institutions should collect information from faculty about their desire for various retirement options such as early or phased retirement. Administrators need a variety of tools in order to manage Boomers' retirement successfully. To date, institutions have typically used early retirement incentives in the form of lump sum cash payments or phased retirement options to entice older faculty to retire. Large-scale analysis regarding the effectiveness of these programs in higher education is scarce. Individual institutional analyses suggest these programs are at least somewhat successful in attaining the stated goals and intended outcomes.

Standardized policies, rather than ad-hoc arrangements provide equity. Leslie and Conley (2006) edited an issue of *New Directions for Higher Education* focusing specifically on phased retirement as an option that provides flexibility. Janson (2006) noted that phased retirement policies have been in place in some institutions for 30 years or more. She describes one institution's decision to move away from a largely discretionary and informal process to a formal phased retirement policy to stop "wheeling and dealing" and to ensure equity and fairness. Leslie et al. (2006), offer specific policy recommendations supporting increasingly varied choices that individual faculty members are making about when and how to retire. Some of the recommendations apply to retirement in general: "Faculty approaching retirement may need comprehensive financial planning support, and some may need more personal counseling" (p. 83). They recommend that, "Long-term planning should allow an increasing interest in flexible employment options" (p. 84), and they also point out that, "Individual circumstances may require special consideration . . . Institutions should be prepared to be flexible in exceptional cases" (p. 83). Knowing how and when to be flexible requires an understanding of the history of the institution and its culture, but it also requires an understanding of legal constraints. The next section focuses on faculty retirement and the law.

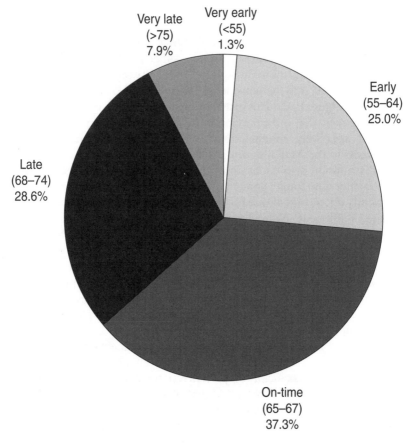

Note: From "Retirement and benefits: expectations and realities," by V.M. Conley (2007),
The NEA 2007 Almanac of Higher Education, p. 91. Copyright 2007 by the National
Education Association. Reprinted with permission.

Sources: US Department of Education, National Center for Education Statistics, National
Study of Postsecondary Faculty (NSOPF).

*Figure 10.2   Percentage distribution of expected timing of retirement of
             full-time instructional faculty and staff: 2003–04*

FACULTY RETIREMENT AND THE LAW

Consideration of retirement in higher education benefits from a review
of the legal issues associated with it. These legal issues generally include
an understanding of the historical view taken by the courts, primary
legislation, and interpretation of the legislation by the courts in subse-

quent rulings within both a local and a broader context. The seminal legislation affecting retirement in the United States is the Age Discrimination in Employment Act (ADEA) of 1967 and its amendments. Several researchers studied the events leading to the passage of the 1974, 1978, and 1986 Amendments to ADEA (Ford, 1978–79; Pratt, 1989; Hammond and Morgan, 1991; DiGiovanni, 1993). In summary, prior to the passage of ADEA, institutions were free to set policies that required faculty members to retire when they reached a certain age. Most institutions that had mandatory retirement policies set the age at 70. The original provisions of the ADEA prohibited discrimination on the basis of age with respect to individuals between the ages of 40 and 65, but held exemptions for public employers and tenured faculty. Yet, the courts did not interpret this to have any bearing on mandatory retirement policies. The 1974 Amendments to the ADEA extended the earlier provisions to public employers. The 1978 Amendments raised the upper age limit to 70. The 1986 Amendments eliminated the upper age limit altogether (DiGiovanni, 1993). The ADEA Amendments have specific relevance to higher education because they ultimately eliminated mandatory retirement ages for tenured faculty.

Prior to the passage of ADEA Amendments, eliminating mandatory retirement ages for all but a select group of professions, federal courts heard several cases that challenged the constitutionality of mandatory retirement policies under the due process and equal protection clauses of the Fourteenth Amendment. Perhaps the seminal case, *Massachusetts Board of Retirement* v. *Murgia* (1976), was decided by the US Supreme Court when it "refused to declare a public employer's policy of mandatory retirement unconstitutional" (Ford, 1978–79, p. 162). While not a case involving higher education, it is important because it sets the tone of approval by the courts of mandatory retirement ages in general.

In this case, Robert Murgia challenged the constitutionality of a Massachusetts statute that required state police officers to retire at age 50. Murgia passed the required annual physical examination without difficulty. The case was strengthened by the low mandatory retirement age being enforced (*Massachusetts Board of Retirement* v. *Murgia*, 1976).

To decide the case, the Supreme Court applied two tests that had been used repeatedly in Fourteenth Amendment cases. The two tests were (1) the strict scrutiny test and (2) the rational basis test. The strict scrutiny test determines whether the statute or policy invades a "fundamental right" or discriminates against a "suspect class." The rational basis test determines whether the classification is rationally related to a legitimate state purpose. The court ruled that age was not a "suspect classification." It further ruled in favor of a "rational basis" since a legitimate state objective was found in protecting the public (Ford, 1978–79). This case was seen as a refusal by the federal courts to entertain challenges to the constitutionality of public employers' mandatory retirement policies. Further disagreements about the intention of Congress to outlaw mandatory retirement for employees within the protected age group would lead Congress to amend the ADEA.

The principal case involving higher education decided before the ADEA legislation was amended was *Weiss* v. *Walsh* (1971). In this case, a prominent philosophy professor at Catholic University sued after he was offered a prestigious humanities chair by Fordham University, only to have the offer withdrawn solely because of his age. He was 69. There was no question that the plaintiff possessed the qualifications for the job. In addition, Fordham University admitted that the only reason that the offer was withdrawn was because of the plaintiff's age—at the request of the New York Board of Regents. The Board of Regents had statutory authority in this case because the position was a state-supported chair.

The court rejected the Fourteenth Amendment claim saying that age generally bears some relation to mental and physical capacity and as a classification cuts across racial, religious, and economic lines (*Weiss* v. *Walsh*, 1971). The language of the court's ruling is interesting given the failed attempts by some legislators to include age in Title VII of the Civil Rights Act of 1964. This ruling provided a clear indication of the position of the courts with respect to age and employment. Even when there is no evidence to suggest that age impairs the individual's ability to do the job, the courts recognized the employer's right to have mandatory retirement policies. The Second Circuit upheld this ruling (461 F. 2d 846, 1972), the Supreme Court denied certiorari (409 US 1129, 1973), and refused to reconsider the denial (410 US 970, 1973).

Furthermore, state courts found in favor of disparate mandatory retirement ages between types of institutions. For example, faculty in community colleges in California were required to retire at age 65, whereas faculty in the state universities and four-year colleges were not required to retire until age 67 (*American Federation of Teachers College Guild* v. *Board of Trustees*, 1976). The court ruled "the distinction made by the state had a rational basis in the essential difference between the two types of academic institutions" (Ford, 1978–79, p. 166).

The only example of a case in which a constitutional challenge to mandatory retirement policies in higher education institutions was successful was in *Nelson* v. *Miwa* (1976), a case decided by the Hawaii courts. The ruling, however, was very specific to the facts of the case. The board of the University of Hawaii had established a policy that set the mandatory retirement age at 65, but that permitted renewals on a year-to-year basis until age

70. The renewals were based on a two-part test. The first test determined whether the current faculty member was more qualified than any applicant for the job. The second test was supposed to determine whether the individual provided "essential" services to the university. The court found no rational basis for the second test for persons who had passed the first test. This case did not refute the constitutionality of mandatory retirement policies at educational institutions; rather it found that the policy, through the use of the second test, violated the plaintiff's right to equal protection because there was no rational basis for it.

If the courts generally favored mandatory retirement ages, why was the exemption for tenured faculty members allowed to expire? In "Uncapping mandatory retirement: the lobbyists' influence," Pratt (1989) provides an account of the events that led up to both the 1978 and 1986 ADEA Amendments that pertain specifically to higher education. Pratt (ibid.) describes higher education as "almost totally uninvolved in the anti-age discrimination movement" before 1977 and the academic sector as "surprised by the 1977–78 legislation" (p. 15). He describes the higher education lobby as "unable to exert political influence a decade later, when legislation on total uncapping of the MRA was introduced" (p. 15). As a final point, he describes the leadership of the primary higher education lobbying organizations as in "disarray" (p. 20).

The higher education lobby finally became sufficiently motivated to mount a campaign to exempt tenured faculty members from the provisions of the proposed legislation. The campaign advanced several reasons why the exemption was necessary: (1) the number of job openings for young faculty would be reduced because older faculty would remain in the workforce, (2) affirmative action efforts on the part of women and faculty of color would be thwarted, and (3) institutions would experience additional financial pressures because they would have to sustain higher-paid faculty salaries and continue retirement contributions for longer periods (Pratt, 1989).

Congressional representatives made it clear that they had heard these arguments before from members of the business community and had not been persuaded. However, the higher education lobby was able to advance two convincing arguments that demonstrated academe was different from other large employers. The first argument was based on the demographics of the faculty population. Projections indicated that there would be an oversupply of tenured older professors because of the number of faculty members hired during the expansion of the 1950s and the 1960s.

The second argument dealt with the complexities that tenure brought into the discussion. Lobbyists argued that if mandatory retirements were abolished or the upper age limit was raised, tenure would be threatened.

The difficulty of determining when a faculty member's performance had declined enough to justify terminating employment "for cause" might force universities to conduct frequent evaluations of all faculty members. These anticipated reviews were described by the higher education lobby as potentially "costly, demoralizing, and inconclusive" (ibid., p. 21). Faculty retirement was recognized as different from retirement in other professions primarily because of the process of job evaluation.

In addition, researchers found many retired faculty from all types of institutions favored mandatory retirement because it provided clarity and equitable treatment since there was "an official, universally applicable cutoff time" for ending the employment relationship (Dorfman et al., 1984, p. 98). Retired faculty also favored retiring gradually to retiring all at once (ibid.).

In light of these arguments, the American Council on Education (ACE) lobbied for a 15-year extension, "which would be designed to ease out of the tenured ranks the large 'bulge' of faculty members who initially had been recruited into academe in the 1960s and who were scheduled to retire in large numbers only in the late 1990s and beyond" (Pratt, 1989, p. 28). The ADEA is a hybrid statute, which draws its anti-discrimination language from Title VII of the Civil Rights Act of 1964, and its enforcement procedures from the Fair Labor Standards Act (Ford, 1978–79). The other, much stronger, voice in this debate was the American Association of Retired Persons (now known as AARP) and the National Retired Teachers Association united lobby who were successful in characterizing uncapping "as the greatest civil rights legislation for the elderly in the past 20 years" (Pratt, 1989, p. 28). The final result was a short reprieve (seven years) to allow institutions some time to plan for the implications associated with eliminating the mandatory retirement age.

A series of debates regarding the implications for tenure ensued, most notably between Oscar M. Ruebhausen, Chairperson of the Commission on College Retirement from 1984–87 and Matthew W. Finkin, Professor of Law, University of Illinois. Ruebhausen (1988) wrote about the contractual nature of tenure and challenged higher education to reform the tenure system or replace it with fixed-term contracts. Finkin (1988), on the other hand, felt that replacing traditional tenure arrangements with fixed-term contracts would threaten academic freedom.

The Committee on Mandatory Retirement in Higher Education concluded that "eliminating mandatory retirement would not pose a threat to tenure" (Hammond and Morgan, 1991, p. 105). They reasoned that tenure does not, nor should it, protect faculty against dismissal for inadequate performance. They also did not find any evidence that the number of inadequate faculty would increase if faculty were allowed to work past age 70 (Hammond and Morgan, 1991). Finally, the committee acknowledged that "colleges and universities hoping to hire scholars in new fields or to change the balance of faculty research and teaching interests will need to encourage turnover using mechanisms other than performance evaluation and dismissal" (ibid., p. 106).

Regardless of the debate, there was little activity with respect to case law after uncapping mandatory retirement in higher education occurred. Most of the cases that have been heard have been brought as termination for cause cases, not ADEA cases (Hendrickson, 1999). An example that does involve ADEA litigation is *Fisher* v. *Asheville-Buncombe Technical Community College* (1993). This case can be used to outline the criteria applied by the courts in disparate treatment theory. First, the plaintiff established a prima facie case of age discrimination. Then, the burden of proof shifted to the institution. In this case, the institution provided valid reasons for the dismissal based on poor job performance. Finally, the plaintiff had an opportunity to show that the reason was a pretext for discrimination based on age.

Even though it is still seen as a rare event in higher education, there have been numerous cases where the courts have ruled on the termination of tenured faculty for cause. The relationship between these cases and ADEA is unclear because they have not been brought as ADEA cases. At the time of this writing, there were several relevant cases pending. Administrators responsible for managing Boomers' retirement should be aware of the decisions.

In part, institutions have adapted to uncapping mandatory retirement age policies by offering early retirement programs. To date, they still use termination for cause only as a last resort (Hendrickson, 1999). It will be interesting to see if the new era of accountability that is sweeping over higher education will impact the number of tenured faculty members who are dismissed for cause and subsequently the number of court cases being heard to arbitrate the decisions. While not everyone agrees with Ruebhausen's (1988) views on tenure, it is hard not to see some merit in his assessment that the challenge to higher education is to operate tenure and retirement systems that "encourage both continuity and change" (p. 573). Monitoring the legal issues may provide a lens through which to view their success.

Other legislation affecting retirement includes the Omnibus Budget Reconciliation Act of 1986, the Older Workers Benefit Protection Act of 1990, the Employee Retirement Income Security Act, and the Pension Protection Act of 2006. These acts strengthened workers' rights with respect to employee benefits plans. The earlier legislation made it clear that "pension benefit accruals and/or contributions cannot be reduced or discontinued because of the attainment of any age" and that "the ADEA is intended to bar age discrimination in employee benefit plans with certain narrow exceptions"

(Martin, 1993, p. 49). According to a White House Fact Sheet, the Pension Protection Act of 2006 requires that companies measure obligations of pension plans more accurately and stipulates that they must pay additional premiums if plans are underfunded (The White House, 2006).

Pension plans and laws are extremely complex. Administrators responsible for managing Boomers' retirement need to understand the applicable statutes at the national and state level. In addition to federal legislation, state law must also be examined. In Ohio, for example, there have been legislated criteria for buy-outs. To assist staff, leaders, and members to understand the variations in public education pension plans across the United States the National Education Association regularly compiles *Characteristics of Large Public Education Pension Plans*. In 2006, for the first time, the study included retirement benefits for higher education faculty and higher education support professionals (National Education Association, 2006). The resource contains data on 99 different retirement systems. Legal issues associated with each system or plan must be interpreted within the context of the type of institution and the state. Perhaps this is one reason why there are so few comparative sources of information available to help administrators make good decisions about managing the retirement process in higher education.

RECOMMENDATIONS

Managing Baby Boomers' retirement is recognized as a significant leadership challenge for higher education. I conclude with some recommendations for practice:

1. Monitor relevant policy debates, particularly related to Social Security reform and health care.
2. Get in the conversation—locally, at the state level, and nationally.
3. Collect and analyze data including detailed information on age by selected characteristics important to the context of the institution. Consider calculating a Retiree Benefit Risk index for groups of employees and collecting data geared toward understanding employees' concerns related to retirement, such as the availability of health care.
4. Implement policies and practices that will ensure faculty members work longer because they want to, not because they have to in order to maintain access to affordable health care for themselves, their spouse, or partner. Savvy institutions recognize that retirement benefits—including affordable, quality health insurance—are a mechanism for attracting and retaining high-quality faculty and a tool for

controlling the flow of older faculty out of the workforce. Key questions to consider include: how do we pay for it? What is the appropriate distribution between the individual and the institution? What difference does timing for retirement decisions make?

5. Consider benefits for all employees—are part-time faculty members eligible? If they are eligible, are they participating? Why or why not?
6. Understand retirement as a process. One size does not fit all when it comes to retirement. There are many ways to retire: early, phased, on-time, or postponed.
7. Invest in education and services to increase individual knowledge and understanding regarding retirement planning, both financial and non-financial.
8. Engage in human resources planning.
9. Model retirement projections including optimal timing for offering retirement incentives and the most cost-effective level of benefit.
10. Integrate human resource planning into other planning processes at the institution (that is, tie enrollment, budget, and human resources planning models together in a comprehensive planning process).

The process of retiring from an academic career today is both different from and the same as it was 30 or 40 years ago. Much has changed. Shifting responsibility for retirement from the institution to the individual poses a significant administrative and leadership challenge for institutions. Individuals must be knowledgeable about their options and the outcomes of the decisions they make. At the same time, much has stayed the same. Dorfman et al. (1984) studied retired professors from liberal arts colleges, a comprehensive university, and a major research university. Their results showed that a majority of faculty from all types of institutions had planned for retirement and were positive about retirement. These retired professors gave some suggestions for improving institutional retirement policy. Their recommendations included: (1) help in planning, (2) more information about retirement, (3) support for continued work, and (4) gradual retirement. Twenty-five years later, this is still good advice.

REFERENCES

American Federation of Teachers College Guild v. *Board of Trustees*, 63 Cal. App. 3d 800, (1976).

Berberet, J., C.J. Bland, B.E. Brown, and K.R. Risbey (2005), "Late career faculty perceptions: implications for retirement planning and policymaking" [electronic version], *Research Dialogue*, No. 84, 1–12, http://www.tiaa-crefinstitute.org/research/dialogue/docs/84.pdf.

Berger, A., R. Kirshstein, and E. Rowe (2001), "Institutional policies and practices: results from the 1999 National Study of Postsecondary Faculty, Institution Survey," Washington, DC: National Center for Education Statistics, http://nces.ed.gov/pubsearch/pubsinfo.asp?pubid=2001201.

Conley, V.M. (2007a), "Of incentive plans, health benefits, library privileges, and retirement," *Academe*, **93**(3), 20–27.

Conley, V.M. (2007b), "Retirement and benefits: expectations and realities," *The NEA 2007 Almanac of Higher Education*, Washington, DC: National Education Association.

Conley, V. M. (2008), "Regenerating the faculty workforce: A significant leadership challenge and a public policy concern," *Advancing Higher Education*, February, New York: TIAA-CREF Institute.

DiGiovanni, Jr., Esq., N. (1993), "Legal aspects of the aging work force," in N. Julius and H. Krauss (eds), *The Aging Work Force: A Guide for Higher Education Administrators*, Washington, DC: College and University Personnel Association pp. 189–116.

Dorfman, L.T., K.A. Conner, W. Ward, and J.B. Tompkins (1984), "Reactions of professors to retirement: a comparison of retired faculty from three types of institutions", *Research in Higher Education*, **20**(1), 89–102.

El Nasser, H. (2008), "States want to tap boomers' skills," *USA Today*, 22 February, 1A.

Federal Interagency Forum on Aging-related Statistics (2006), *Older Americans Update 2006: Key Indicators of Well-being*, Federal Interagency Forum on Aging-related Statistics, Washington, DC: US Government Printing Office.

Feldman, D.D. (2003),"Endgame: the design and implementation of early retirement incentive programs," in G.A. Adams and T.A. Beehr (eds), *Retirement: Reasons, Processes, and Results*, New York: Springer, pp. 83–114.

Finkin, M.W. (1988), "Tenure after an uncapped ADEA: a different view," *The Journal of College and University Law*, **15**(1), 43–60.

Fisher v. *Asheville-Buncombe Technical Community College*, 857 F. Supp. 465 (W.D.N.C. 1993).

Ford, L.C. (1978–79), "The implications of the age discrimination in employment act amendments of 1978 for colleges and universities," *The Journal of College and University Law*, **5**(3), 161–209.

Greenya, J. (with I. Golin) (2008), "Building an experience dividend: state governments lead the call to engage boomers" (Civic Ventures Policy Series), http://www.civicventures.org/publications/policy_papers/pdfs/BldingExpDiv.pdf.

Hammond, P.B. and H.P. Morgan (eds) (1991), *Ending Mandatory Retirement for Tenured Faculty: The Consequences for Higher Education*, Washington, DC: National Academy Press.

Hendrickson, R.M. (1999), *The Colleges, Their Constituencies and the Courts* (2nd edition), Dayton, Ohio: Education Law Association.

Henry J. Kaiser Family Foundation and Hewitt Associates (2004), "Current trends and future outlook for retiree health benefits: findings from the Kaiser/Hewitt 2004 survey on retiree health benefits," http://www.kff.org/medicare/7194/ upload/ Current-Trends-and-Future-Outlook-for-Retiree-Health-Benefits-Findings-from-the-Kaiser-Hewitt-2004-Survey-on-Retiree-Health-Benefits.pdf.

Janson, N. (2006), "Phased retirement policies," in D.W. Leslie and V.M. Conley (eds), *New Ways to Phase into Retirement: Options for Faculty and Institutions, New Directions for Higher Education*, No. 132 (Winter 2005), 31–46.

Leslie, D.W. and V.M. Conley (2006), *New Ways to Phase into Retirement: Options for Faculty and Institutions, New Directions for Higher Education*, No. 132 (Winter 2005), San Francisco: Jossey-Bass.

Leslie, D.W., N. Janson and V.M. Conley (2006), "Policy-related issues and recommendations," in D.W. Leslie and V.M. Conley (eds), *New Ways to Phase into Retirement: Options for Faculty and Institutions, New Directions for Higher Education*, No. 132 (Winter 2005), 73–85.

Martin, D.W. (1993), "Faculty early retirement incentive programs in selected Virginia universities," unpublished doctoral dissertation, Virginia Polytechnic Institute and State University, Blacksburg.

Massachusetts Board of Retirement v. Murgia, 427 US 307 (1976).

National Education Association (2006), *Characteristics of Large Public Education Pension Plans*, NEA Stock No. 3451-1-00, Washington, DC: NEA.

National Study of Postsecondary Faculty, *Faculty Survey* [data file], Washington, DC: National Center for Education Statistics.

National Study of Postsecondary Faculty, *Institution Survey* [data file], Washington, DC: National Center for Education Statistics.

Nelson v. Miwa, 56 Hawaii 601, 546 P. 2d 1005, 81 ALR 3d 799 (1976).

Pratt, H.J. (1989), "Uncapping mandatory retirement: the lobbyists' influence," in K.C. Holden and W.L. Hansen (eds), *The End of Mandatory Retirement: Effects on Higher Education, New Directions for Higher Education* No. 65, San Francisco: Jossey-Bass, (pp. 15–31).

Ruebhausen, O.M. (1988), "The age discrimination in employment act amendments of 1986: implications for tenure and retirement," *The Journal of College and University Law*, **14**(4), 561–74.

US Census Bureau (2006a), "Dramatic changes in U.S. aging highlighted in new Census, NIH report: impact of baby boomers anticipated," http://www.census.gov/Press-Release/www/releases/archives/aging_population/006544.html.

US Census Bureau (2006b), "Facts for features: oldest baby boomers turn 60!," http://www.census.gov/Press-Release/www/releases/archives/facts_for_features_special_editions/006105.html.

US Census Bureau (updated January 2007), "Population profile of the United States: dynamic version. Age and sex distribution in 2005," http://www.census.gov/population/pop-profile/dynamic/AgeSex.pdf.

US Census Bureau (2008), "Population profile of the United States: 2000," http://www.census.gov/population/www/pop-profile/profile2000.html#cont.

US Department of Education (2006), "Digest of education statistics 2005," Washington, DC: National Center for Education Statistics, http://nces.ed.gov/programs/digest/2005menu_tables.asp.

US Department of the Treasury (2007a), "Social Security reform: the nature of the problem," *Issue Brief No. 1*, http://www.treas.gov/offices/economic-policy/briefs/SSIssueBrief1.pdf.

US Department of the Treasury (2007b), "Social Security reform: a framework for analysis," *Issue Brief No. 2*, http://www.treas.gov/offices/economic-policy/briefs/SSIssueBrief2.pdf.

US Department of Treasury (2007c), "Social Security reform: benchmarks for assessing fairness and benefit adequacy," *Issue Brief No. 3*, http://www.treas.gov/offices/economic-policy/briefs/SSIssueBrief_3.pdf.

Weiss v. *Walsh*, 324 F. Supp. 75 (S.D.N.Y. 1971), aff'd, 461 F. 2d 846 (1972).

The White House (2005), "Strengthening Social Security for the 21st century," [electronic version], http://www.whitehouse.gov/infocus/social-security/200501/strengthening-socialsecurity.html.

The White House (2006), "The Pension Protection Act of 2006: ensuring greater retirement security for American workers" [electronic version], http://www.whitehouse.gov/news/releases/2006/08/20060817.html.

11. Generational impacts—the views of symposium participants

Mark Heckler, Virginia Michelich, and Teresa A. Sullivan

The TIAA-CREF Institute 2007 National Higher Education Leadership Conference included a breakout session where the participants were provided with the opportunity to discuss what the speakers had said about the impact of the different generations on higher education. The breakout sessions were facilitated by Mark Heckler of the University of Colorado at Denver and Health Sciences Center; Virginia Michelich of Georgia Perimeter College; and Teresa Sullivan of the University of Michigan. Each facilitator summarized the discussions in their session.

MARK HECKLER

Howe and Strauss (2007) describe the Millennial Generation as those born between 1982 and sometime in the early years of the 21st century. The authors characterize members of this generation using seven "core traits," which they believe will define people born during this period. These traits include their sense that, as children, Millennials were treated as though they were *special*, and that they have been extraordinarily protected and *sheltered* from harm. Millennials exhibit a high degree of *confidence* and optimism about their future, while being fairly conformist and *conventional* in their behavior and value-systems. This generation is *team-oriented* in learning, disposed to service, and able to build strong peer networks. They have felt *pressured* to be successful in everything they do, and they have been involved in a dizzying array of activities both within and outside of school. Finally, Millennials have had to focus on *achieving* results, leading to a low tolerance for risk-taking (ibid.).

Others challenge these conclusions as generalizations and stereotypes. These critics warn against wholesale acceptance of generational characterizations focused on simple traits or overemphasizing generational differences (Carlson, 2005; Hoover, 2007). At the 2007 TIAA-CREF

Institute Conference, "Generational Shockwaves: Implications for Higher Education", presenter Donald W. Harward, Senior Fellow with the Association of American Colleges and Universities and President Emeritus of Bates College, minimized generational differences. Harward described the continuum of generations as a hemp rope, interwoven threads inextricably and imperceptibly connected in ways that provide extraordinary strength (Harward, 2007).

After spending some time getting acquainted with the latest research and commentary on generational differences, participants in the 2007 TIAA-CREF Institute adjourned to breakout rooms to discuss potential implications these differences may have for American postsecondary institutions. Discussions in each of the breakout rooms focused on three sets of questions, one set for each generation examined. For the conversation on the Millennial Generation, these questions were used as a guide:

- What strategies are advised for attracting today's students to our institutions?
- What changes in teaching and learning procedures are in order to engage and accommodate them?
- What modifications to curricula might be contemplated?
- What developments in the uses of technology for learning (or for communication or entertainment) should colleges and universities be aware of?
- What is the impact on society of gender shifts and other demographic changes in the makeup of today's college/university students?

At the conclusion of the breakout sessions, each of us (Virginia Michelich, Teresa Sullivan, and Mark Heckler) met to assemble a summary of observations that emerged for each generation as a result of the discussion as well as implications for the future of American higher education. Following are the observations and implications that emerged from breakout discussions on the Millennials.

Millennial Observations and Implications

Monolithic strategies responding to perceived generational shifts may neglect generational heterogeneity and the increasing population of non-traditional and returning students, retirees, and others who are entering higher education in increasing numbers. While it is convenient to ascribe labels to define characteristics for an entire generation of students, institutional leaders are encouraged to remember that each class that enters our higher education system is diverse—both multigenerational and multidimensional (Hoover, 2007). Institutions will be well served by developing strategies that are inclusive in responding to a wide range of student needs and experiences rather than limiting strategy to appeal to the advertised characteristics of a particular subset of the student body. The diversity of our institutions and our students are hallmarks of the American higher education system. Institutional leaders should aim to create a welcoming environment for students from multiple generations and backgrounds.

Rapidly changing demographics and generational needs of potential and actual students must be part of institutional planning Offices of institutional research and strategic planning should provide leadership with current and projected demographic information, broken out by generational identifiers. In addition, institutional researchers and planners should stay abreast of the latest research on comparative generational behaviors and higher education needs. Institutional leaders must pay attention to this research when devising strategies to accommodate the changing needs of incoming student populations.

Increasing disparities in college readiness complicate institutional strategy Because students are coming to postsecondary institutions in larger numbers, and because students who come to the majority of our institutions have widely varying levels of preparation, multiple strategies will be needed to support the full range of Millennial students who enroll. While some students will have benefited from extensive academic enrichment, advanced placement, and co-curricular learning opportunities in high school and expect a more challenging academic environment in college, many others will need remediation in writing, reading, and mathematics. Institutional leaders are advised to examine a range of indicators of college readiness from Advanced Placement courses to first-year placement examinations in order to develop educational and support strategies that engage a wide range of student preparation and experience.

Student recruitment and retention are increasingly competitive and students are becoming increasingly mobile—student mobility also complicates institutional strategy. The 20th-century notion of a typical college student is changing—that is, a student entering college as a first-year and graduating four years later from the same institution. Increasingly, students are taking six years or more to earn an undergraduate degree; many work full-time or stop out for a semester or more because of financial hardship, work demands, or dependant care. Students are more mobile than ever before, transferring from institution to institution. Their reasons may vary—lower tuition, shorter time to degree, better reputation, or more convenience. The dominant paradigm of the four-year undergraduate experience and future loyal (and generous) alumnus has been replaced by the more mobile and perhaps less loyal undergraduate student. This changing paradigm has a significant impact on future institutional strategy, from recruitment and retention to institutional advancement and alumni relations.

Tension between student/parent expectations and the faculty reward system is increasing   While student and parent expectations of faculty are increasing, both in terms of classroom teaching and student support and mentoring, the faculty reward system for tenure and promotion at many institutions focuses faculty effort on research productivity and scholarship. The emerging generation of new faculty, mirroring Millennial demands for high quality of life, greater mobility, and less institutional loyalty, appears increasingly interested in institutions that place emphasis on research and scholarship over teaching and service (The Collaborative on Academic Careers in Higher Education, 2007). As faculty focus greater time and effort on their research, tensions with students and parents are likely to increase.

Tension between Baby Boomer faculty who do not embrace new pedagogical strategies and learning technologies and student demands is increasing. Pedagogical and curricular changes are necessary to align with changing learning habits and needs of Millennials. As Millennial students are accustomed to receiving information presented in media-rich and entertaining ways, the traditional professorial approach to teaching—the sage on the stage—must adapt toward the media-rich, multi-modal learning experiences of this generation ("How the new generation of well-wired multitaskers is changing campus culture," 2007). Faculty will be hard pressed to find new pedagogical approaches that leverage the latest advances in technology and the Millennials' penchant for teamwork and social networks, while ensuring a high degree of academic rigor. As these new pedagogies emerge, the tension between Millennial demands and the traditional learning paradigm will likely increase.

Faculty will need to accommodate and respond to a broader definition of when and where learning can occur   Many Millennials routinely access information 24 hours a day, seven days a week, 365 days a year, expecting that their education experience should mirror their "on-demand" world. Faculty should consider how best to manage student expectations for 24/7 learning (and professor feedback), while taking full advantage of students' insatiable appetite for information. The concept of a 90-minute lecture delivered in a classroom every Tuesday and Thursday will likely yield to a hybrid form of learning that brings people together both physically and virtually, while permitting students to navigate through information at their own pace and at their convenience.

Social networking tools are increasingly important in the lives of students
Powerful networking websites like Facebook and MySpace and free video-conferencing tools like Skype make it easy for Millennials to make new friends and keep in touch with them around the world and around the clock. These networks may hamper efforts to build a cohesive campus community, yet may serve as extraordinary recruitment vehicles for future students. Clearly, institutional leaders should consider how best to leverage these social networks while minimizing their negative effects on learning and campus culture.

Patterns of alcohol use may be changing—some institutions see greater binge drinking, sometimes encouraged by and including parents. While overall alcohol use is dropping among Millennials (Howe and Strauss, 2007), patterns of alcohol use may be changing. This perception includes anecdotal reports of increased incidents of binge drinking and alcohol poisoning on some college campuses. Given that Millennials' values often reflect those of their parents (ibid.), reports of parental acknowledgment and tacit support of binge drinking is troubling. Campus leaders should observe these trends and consider steps for both student and parent education.

Recommendations Regarding Millennial Students

After making these observations on Millennial students and considering the implications for institutions of higher education, breakout participants next developed a set of recommendations. These recommendations are designed to assist postsecondary institutions in adapting their pedagogical approaches, educational delivery systems, student services, and student life operations to meet the needs and demands of the Millennial Generation.

Align the faculty reward system with institutional priorities and—as appropriate—with student and parent expectations Participants suggest that faculty leadership examine the faculty reward system, particularly criteria and standards for tenure and promotion, to ensure that they remain aligned with institutional priorities and needs. While student and parent demands should not erode the importance of academic freedom in teaching and research, new approaches to teaching and research, particularly research engaging faculty with students, should be considered when re-evaluating criteria and standards for promotion, tenure, and other rewards.

Evolve pedagogical approaches to embrace interdisciplinary, problem-based, and experiential learning and research opportunities for Millennials—consider alternatives to "majors" for future generations. Millennials appear to enjoy hands-on, "real world" opportunities (Carlson, 2005). Faculty members should consider how to exploit this interest through employing interdisciplinary approaches to real world problems, experiential and service learning, as well as student-faculty research projects. Might it be possible to construct a problem-based approach that would enable students to seek out and master content on their own and out of necessity rather than receiving that content in a lecture or through a Blackboard (or other course management system) module? Not all faculty members will embrace this approach to learning, but those who do should be recognized and encouraged, particularly if student learning increases as a result.

Ensure that multi-modal learning strategies, responsive to changing student learning styles, yield successful outcomes   As faculty members adapt pedagogical approaches and institutions experiment with novel educational delivery systems, clearly defined learning outcomes and rigorous learning assessment processes will be essential. As excellent oral and written communication and quantitative skills are important foundational learning outcomes for today's institutions, tomorrow's institutions may need to focus on information literacy, visual and media literacy, global competency, reading comprehension, and other foundational skills that students may need to function effectively in this future. A robust learning assessment system will be a key to determining whether or not these new pedagogies, delivery systems, and learning objectives are successful.

Exploit opportunities to encourage meaningful live, face-to-face interactions among students and faculty as education shifts increasingly toward technological solutions. Given the Millennials' comfort with interactive educational and service technology and virtual social networking, institutions should consider how to stimulate face-to-face interactions and live community-building opportunities. Institutional paradigms will shift significantly if students are recruited to a campus and left to sit in a residence hall looking at a computer monitor 24/7. Institutional leaders must be deliberate in structuring live interactive experiences for its Millennial students.

Leverage technology, including more sophisticated student portals, emergent media, and changing social networking conventions for student recruitment, retention, and learning. Use open source technology whenever possible. Media-savvy Millennials and their parents expect sophisticated and customized marketing for large-ticket items, from computers and cars to a college education. Institutions should consider how to use new media techniques, including social networking sites and viral marketing approaches, not only to bring prospective students to campus, but also to retain them once they have matriculated. Faculty leaders, particularly those who are early adopters of new technologies, should be provided opportunities and resources to experiment with emergent technologies as educational tools. Ideas developed from faculty research should be demonstrated to and widely disseminated among faculty across the institution. Given the ongoing costs and increasing commercialization of technology, open source solutions should be explored whenever possible.

Expand 24/7 student services using technology selectively and carefully
Institutions should consider how to automate selected student services to accommodate Millennials' penchant for 24/7 interactions. However, these choices should be made carefully to ensure a quality experience for students, to maintain technology security and student confidentiality, and to be financially and technologically sustainable over time. Institutional leaders are encouraged to consider any migration to a technology environment as a commitment to sustained institutional investment rather than a cost-cutting measure.

Expand articulation agreements to respond to student mobility patterns and increase the efficiency of the higher education system. Institutional leaders should examine specific student mobility patterns at their college or university. Are students transferring into or from an institution to a particular group of institutions in the state or region? Are there particular programs that evidence higher levels of mobility? After conducting this research, an institution should consider how to facilitate student transfer both into and from its programs through formal articulation agreements with sister institutions sending or receiving large numbers of students. Care should be taken to minimize non-transferable or general elective credit so that students' time to degree is not lengthened because of institutional transfer. Given increasing levels of student mobility among Millennials, institutions and students may benefit from strategic academic alliances among traditional competitors.

Explore multi-institutional consortia and collaborations to increase efficiency and respond to the contrary demands to increase services and amenities while "holding the line" on tuition. In the same way that strategic alliances among competitors may be necessary to address increased student mobility, multi-institutional consortia and other collaborative ventures may help institutions lower costs while meeting demands for increased services without significant tuition increases. Educational consortia encourage sharing courses across institutional boundaries, providing greater academic variety for smaller institutions. Other multi-institutional collaborations may increase buying power for information technology, online education, utilities, and maintenance services. Institutional leaders should explore strategic collaborations with institutions with differing roles and missions as well as with traditional competitors.

Focus new initiatives in response to changing student needs driven by changing demographics Millennial students and parents are not only placing increased demands for technology and responsiveness on institutions, they also demand greater attention to student safety and security. This may be explained in part by the degree to which Millennials have been sheltered by parents, in part because of their preoccupation with safety in this post-Columbine, post-9/11, post-Virginia Tech period in which we find ourselves. It may also be explained in part by the changing demographics of our entering students, the clear majority of whom are women.

Other regional demographic changes may drive institutional strategy—from migration to immigration patterns. Leaders should pay close attention to these institutional and regional demographic changes and develop adaptive strategies in response.

Expand faculty development programs focused on preparing Baby Boomer and Generation X faculty to respond to the needs of all generations of students. Faculty orientation and ongoing development programs provide excellent opportunities to explore generational differences among faculty as well as between faculty and students. Given that most institutions will, at any given time, have both faculty and students from all three generations inhabiting the campus, understanding generational differences and adapting work interactions and classroom approaches to account for these differences may be important to building a healthy and respectful campus culture and achieving overall student success.

Conclusion

It is important to note that, while many of these recommendations focus on institutional adaptation brought about by the influx of Millennial students, these students will become our entry-level faculty before many in senior leadership of America's colleges and universities leave their posts. The sweeping changes that many of us are experiencing, precipitating, or contemplating for students will come to institutions again within a decade, this time for employees—changes in hiring, tenure, and promotion of faculty, changes in teaching and learning, and changes in faculty–student relationships (Safer, 2007; The Collaborative on Academic Careers in Higher Education, 2007). Many of us left the 2007 TIAA-CREF Institute confident that substantial changes are already underway at many of our institutions and optimistic that the current Millennial Generation of college students and our future faculty will bring even greater positive changes to our institutions in the decade to come.

VIRGINIA MICHELICH

There have been many studies and much published about generational differences, particularly what people of different generations value and how they approach work and life. In higher education, we have tended to continue to do things "the way we were taught" or how it was when we were in college. Educational psychologists have long reported that the "sage on the stage" approach to teaching and learning does not work with the generations of students beyond the Baby Boomers (and maybe did not even work so well for them).

The purpose of the TIAA-CREF Conference on Generational Shockwaves was to explore the effect of generational differences not only on how we, in higher education, need to approach our students, but also how we need to recruit and work with newer, younger faculty. We must also consider issues with the aging, retiring Baby Boomer population that has been the bulk of our faculty and leadership in higher education.

How are our younger, newer, Generation X faculty members different than the Baby Boomers? What do they value and how does that translate to recruiting and retaining this generation of faculty in higher education?

It helps first to understand what characterizes those we refer to as Generation X. Knowing these characteristics leads to an understanding for those of us who are Baby Boomers and who see an approach to work and job expectations that differ from what we have done on the job and what we have expected.

During the conference, participants worked in breakout groups to discuss the implications of generational differences in higher education. The least amount of discussion during the breakout sessions centered around Generation X, those born between 1965 and 1980. This may have been due to the fact that most of the attendees were Baby Boomers and we all could see the differences in the Millennial Generation students we now teach. However, many of our faculty and staff are Generation Xers. They would be approximately 28–43 years old now.

We know that Gen Xers are ambitious individualists who are skeptical. To them relationships matter the most; they work to have a life rather than living to work as the Baby Boomers have done. They believe that their parents suffered from "vacation deficit disorder" and they do not want to wait until retirement to take their first vacation. The members of Generation X also embrace technology, which includes surfing the Web and buying over the Internet. How do these characteristics translate to the work environment?

Generation Xers are interested in fulfillment from challenging tasks that can be accomplished within the workday. They are not interested or willing to spend extra hours and weekends at/on work. They want flexibility, which is described as the ability to work alone with accommodating hours. They want a work environment that is challenging and fun, but does not necessarily include a secured job. Generation Xers want a job where they can have the kind of lifestyle they are seeking. In these jobs, Generation Xers require feedback frequently rather than simply through annual reviews.

The implications of these differences in characteristics between Baby Boomers and Generation Xers are extremely important factors as we think about recruiting and retaining faculty, and developing leadership in Generation X faculty members.

Generation X faculty members feel the pressure of what they consider to be unreasonable and unwanted expectations by colleges and universities. There is not enough time to "do it all" and in addition to the high expectations, there are too many demands on their time. Faculty may want to devote their time and expertise to teaching and not research, but teaching is difficult to measure, research is easier to define, and thus research productivity becomes the yardstick by which faculty performance is measured.

It is not just adjunct faculty members, but full-time faculty members who value teaching over research. They need to be rewarded.

Faculty members who are great teachers, colleagues, and advisors may never achieve "full status" as a faculty member. Why can't they be rewarded at the same level? Many institutions have differing values between tenure and non-tenure track faculty. Should there not be a different reward system developed so that each group is rewarded effectively?

Often young faculty are protected so that they can engage in productive research, however this does not result in instilling a sense of university service. They develop no loyalty toward the university. Another problem with the lack of reward/interest in developing and rewarding fine teaching faculty is that faculty who favor student values may not be respected by colleagues if they are not oriented toward research.

Thus, institutions need to determine what potential faculty members are looking for in a faculty position. The problem is that this means a shift in how long-term employees and administrators of colleges and universities have operated for years. Institutions are going to have to make changes in their culture in order to attract and retain the best faculty.

What are some changes that institutions can make? We know that a focus on a different job environment is important in attracting and retaining these faculty. Generation X faculty members are looking for the right fit in a job. They want a job that is challenging, but is fun too. They want time for family and for other pursuits outside of their job responsibilities. They additionally need help financially, for instance, with child care and paying back student loans that they have incurred to finance their undergraduate and graduate educations. Institutions need to develop a climate of collegiality. Mentoring by senior faculty members is crucial; but it must go beyond the typical "this is how I did it" advice. True care and friendship as well as opportunities to collaborate with senior faculty members are important.

Administrators need to understand and support a quality of life philosophy, meaning a balance between work and home life. Universities need to examine the nature of work and the workload expected of faculty, particularly as they are beginning in their careers. Support for research, a reasonable workload, fewer committees, and administrative work are important to allow faculty to be productive and still maintain the balance of life that they want.

Equally important is the reward system and the ability of faculty to advance in their careers. Some possibilities for institutions to consider are multiple tracks for advanced ranks. Allow faculty who are primarily interested in teaching to be rewarded for such and not be on the same track competing with research-oriented faculty. Institutions need to examine the requirements for advancement for those faculty who are interested in a research track. Research expectations for tenure, the amount of external funding expected, and the amount of time allowed to conduct research are important considerations for changing the culture. Moving away from a linear tenure and promotion process could be crucial.

Finally, how can institutions instill a sense of service in younger faculty? How can they prepare and interest younger faculty in assuming future leadership roles in academia? Leadership training at the departmental and national level are important. Even faculty who remain in faculty positions have a different understanding of administration if they have had an opportunity for leadership training.

In summary, culture and climate change in universities and colleges is essential in order to attract and retain the best academicians. Institutions need to provide equity for the different tracks faculty members may pursue. Evaluation, tenure, and promotion requirements need to be somewhat flexible and transparent. Institutions need to provide flexibility for their faculty, including both a work balance and a work and personal life balance. Faculty need to be treated as the scholars they are or they will move on to find an institution or job environment—including, possibly, some outside of the academy—that better meets their needs.

TERESA A. SULLIVAN

Baby Boomers, that large cohort of Americans born between the end of World War II and 1964, are the largest single age group in the population. They also play a major role in our institutions: now aged between their early forties and their early sixties, they are prominent in universities as administrators, faculty members, trustees, staff members, parents, alumni, and donors. As they move toward the end of their careers, the Boomers pose a series of challenges for America's colleges and universities.

To be sure, many of the Boomers have had magnificent job careers and will retire with assets and incomes exceeding anything they had anticipated. Many Boomer donors find themselves in this situation, and all of us in higher education hope that more of their largesse will be directed to their alma maters. At least some of our faculty find themselves in a similar situation of unforeseen wealth. Development officers are generally well prepared to deal with these issues.

However, what sparked the greatest conversation among conference participants in this breakout session was the implication of the Baby Boom Generation for campus workforces. The first potential repercussion comes from the *size* of this generation. The challenge is that large numbers of Boomers—including presidents, provosts, and faculty—may all retire within a short period of time, resulting in a serious loss of human capital and continuity for the institutions. Some Boomers in public colleges and universities may feel forced out by state retirement plans that reach their maximum payout at a certain age, so that some senior faculty, staff, and administrators, even if still productive, may find remaining at work to be unattractive.

The second implication is that *variations* among individuals affect how consequential the retirement decisions are for the institution. To have the most productive people retire is a disadvantage for the institution; to have the least productive people retire is a benefit. But it is difficult for the institution to encourage the former to stay or to encourage the latter to leave.

Challenges for Higher Education Institutions

The potential negative consequences of mass retirements for institutions are both programmatic and financial. Rapid turnover of faculty and staff may lead to loss of institutional memory and institutional history. People who have devoted most of their working lives to a single institution carry with them information about policies and personnel that may never have been written down. In addition, older members of institutions are likely to have relationships with alumni and donors that their younger colleagues have not yet achieved. Older faculty are often the stalwart volunteers for all sorts of events and they help carry on important college traditions. Faculty governance often relies upon the generosity and participation of experienced faculty leaders. Older faculty are also key to the successful operation of academic units. In small departments, the loss of even a few older full-time faculty may leave too few colleagues to evaluate and mentor junior faculty for tenure and promotion.

The financial consequences of mass retirements revolve around both retirement benefits and retiree health benefits. Institutions are charting rapid increases in health care for their active faculty, and are often looking at substantial costs for their retirees as well. A large number of retirements occurring at the same time will result in higher retiree benefit costs, and the replacement hires will also expect benefits. Although vested, defined-contribution plans have removed some of the financial concern about pension incomes for retirees, retirement health benefits remain a major concern for many institutions. Recent changes in accounting principles also require colleges to be explicit in the annual reporting about unfunded liabilities for retirees and dependants. These consequences are occurring at a time when parents, students, and colleges—not to mention legislators —are especially sensitive to increases in tuition and other costs of a college degree.

Opportunities for Higher Education

The upcoming retirements may also be an opportunity for colleges and universities. Retirement vacancies offer institutions a time window in which to review the curriculum and to consider hiring in new fields, especially interdisciplinary fields, rather than merely replacing the retirees with younger faculty who teach or conduct research in similarly specialized areas. Younger faculty are more likely to be at the cutting edge of their fields, to know the latest methods of their disciplines, and to be adept at information technology. Younger faculty are also likely to be up to date on curricular innovations such as service learning, collaborative learning, distance learning, and accommodating differences in learning styles.

Moreover, institutions may be able to consider broadening their usual hiring criteria to bring in more faculty with non-traditional backgrounds. Considering the demographic changes that have taken place in our country, and will likely continue in the future, experimenting with non-traditional faculty may be a practical way to prepare for a future that may be quite different from the past.

Retirement of unproductive and alienated faculty may also be an opportunity. Some older faculty are stuck in dated pedagogies; they may have entered the academy when standards were lower. Many of those born in the early Baby Boom period were hired before their dissertations were completed to help fill out the faculties seeking to accommodate the great influx of the later Baby Boomers. With their truncated professional preparation, some of them are not good teachers and they were never active researchers. And while some have become adept at using the new technologies in the classroom, others have not and have instead become increasingly remote from the interests of today's Millennial Generation students. There is concern that some of these faculty members will feel pushed to adopt technology fads and then become further alienated when the fads prove unsuccessful.

There are barriers to retirement, however, and these barriers often lead the most unproductive faculty members to hang onto their jobs even after the time they should retire. The loss of association with the institution is an important identity issue for many faculty. Others worry about their financial situation or about having adequate health insurance in retirement, even if they are eligible for Medicare. It is perhaps the worst situation for the institution if they hang on, feeling burned out and alienated, only because of their fears about their financial future. Staff members may face similar barriers, and their financial concerns may be even greater because many of them had earnings considerably lower than those of the typical faculty member through much of their careers.

Recommendations from the Conference Participants

It is valuable for all institutions to consider the typical life cycle of faculty members and provide opportunities for professional renewal in teaching and research. In tandem with these opportunities, institutions also need to develop realistic plans for succession. Recognizing that generational change is inevitable, institutions should begin to prepare for it, and consider issues such as the changing occupational mix that may characterize institutions in the future.

Institutions of higher education should consider routinely sharing best practices for phased retirement and for the recognition of emeriti faculty and retired administrators and staff members.

It may be tempting, in terms of the institution's bottom line, to consider replacing retirees from full-time employment with part-time employees (with or without benefits) or with full-time employees at a lower level of benefits. Institutions should consider carefully the implications of having two tiers of employees. Especially among faculty, there may be serious repercussions from grandfathering health care and retiree benefits for some faculty while phasing them out for others.

Providing incentives for early retirement for some employees may be an attractive idea, but institutions must be cautious about so routinizing such incentives that they lose their effectiveness. The most beneficial incentive may be providing honor and respect to retired colleagues and finding ways to maintain their beneficial association with the institution.

An idea that may help all institutions is to create flexible on- and off-ramps from employment, making part-time work attractive and honorable. Being able to rehire selectively some retirees on a part-time basis may help ease issues of succession and continuity.

In general, it is beneficial for colleges and universities to consider how they can create or enhance the portability of retirement and health plans. Risk-sharing consortia of colleges and universities would be a vehicle for strengthening academe's negotiating position for health insurance. Where laws or policies reduce flexibility, institutions are likely to be more successful in lobbying for change if they work together.

REFERENCES

Carlson, S. (2005), "The net generation goes to college: tech-savvy 'Millennials' have lots of gadgets, like to multitask, and expect to control what, when, and how they learn. Should colleges cater to them?," *The Chronicle of Higher Education*, 7 October, http://chronicle.com/weekly/v52/i07/07a03401.htm.

The Collaborative on Academic Careers in Higher Education (COACHE) (2007), http://gseacademic.harvard.edu/~coache/.

Harward, D.W. (2007), Introductory remarks, in D.W. Harward (Moderator), "The Millennials," 2007 National Higher Education Leadership Conference, Generational Shockwaves: Implications for Higher Education, TIAA-CREF Institute, New York.

Hoover, E. (2007), "At College Board meeting, researchers challenge views of 'Millennial' students," *The Chronicle of Higher Education*, 25 October, http://chronicle.com/daily/2007/10/492n.htm.

"How the new generation of well-wired multitaskers is changing campus culture" (2007), *The Chronicle of Higher Education*, 5 January, http://chronicle.com/weekly/v53/i18/18b01001.htm.

Howe, N. and W. Strauss (2007), *Millennials Go To College* (2nd edition), Great Falls, VA: LifeCourse Associates.

Safer, M. (Correspondent) (2007), "The 'Millennials' are coming" [television series episode], in K. Trextor (Producer), *60 Minutes*, 11 November, New York: CBS Interactive, Inc., http://www.cbsnews.com/stories/2007/11/08/60minutes/printable3475200.shtml.

12. Public policy reform and expanding societal expectations

F. King Alexander[1]

In November 2007 a large group of college and university officials and faculty gathered in New York to explore needed responses to changing demographic challenges facing higher education institutions. The discussions primarily focused on pedagogical innovations to accommodate evolving educational needs and learning habits of an emerging generation of students. While many ideas and fruitful avenues were explored, from a macro perspective a number of critical issues stand out on the higher education landscape that are the focus of this chapter. If higher education is to have the same success in serving current and future generations of students as it has with past generations, our society will need to address these issues.

First, is the unintended consequence of federal funding policy that has driven many public and private institutions away from addressing societal needs in order to advance institutional competition. For nearly four decades federal government policy has had a somewhat perverse effect on higher education by disproportionately aiding institutions that charge more while at the same time also providing financial incentives to states that opt out of funding of their public colleges and universities. Despite the fact that there may be no causal relationship between federal direct student aid programs and institutional tuition and fee increases (Heller, 2007), National Postsecondary Student Aid Study (NPSAS) data consistently indicate that institutions that charge more do receive disproportionately more aid while also qualifying more students for aid. This is particularly relevant in programs other than Pell Grants, which are the least cost-sensitive and primarily use family income as the primary criterion to determine awards. Unfortunately, not all federal programs use the same formula as that of Pell Grants to determine student qualification and award amounts. Tuition price sensitivity does play a role in the allocation of awards in virtually all other student aid programs and is particularly relevant when allocating federal subsidized loan and unsubsidized loan awards as well as Supplemental Educational Opportunity Grants and state student aid grant funds. This system has enabled states and institutions to rely more heavily on student tuition and fees as a revenue stream while also indirectly escalating the privatization of higher education. Furthermore, this system, which has incentivized privatization, has drawn no distinctions between institutions that maintain strong public missions and commitments to serving large numbers of lower-income students and those that have opted to pursue other less public agendas.

Second, this environment has reinforced a kind of institutional natural selection in the higher education marketplace whereby corporate self-interest stimulates rising prices and academic requirements for many institutions. Unfortunately, these trends also militate against lower-income elements of the population that have not benefited from either quality educational opportunity in the elementary and secondary educational system nor from the benefits of family income and wealth. Increasingly, this situation leaves little room for much broader policy dialogue about the expanding public needs that should be a foremost concern in our knowledge-based economies. To comprehend fully the magnitude of these developments and challenges in the current academic marketplace, it is essential to understand how the higher education landscape has changed.

Higher education in the United States is quite different than it was a few decades ago when our nation led the world in prominence and reputation. Recent data indicate that the United States no longer dominates the world in collegiate access or completion rates as was once the case. State and federal policy choices have resulted in comparatively dismal progress for the United States during the last two decades. According to the annual publication of the Organisation for Economic Co-operation and Development (OECD, 2007) *Education at a Glance 2007*, higher education graduation rates have grown rapidly in recent decades throughout all OECD countries except in Germany and the United States. The United States and Germany are the only OECD countries where the older generation has higher tertiary education completion rates than the younger generation (ibid., p. 11). This is an alarming statistic for any nation hoping to build a sustainable knowledge-based economy. Perhaps more disturbing is the fact that among young adults aged 25–34 the United States ranks seventh among OECD nations in Bachelor's degree completion rates after having been ranked first from 1970 to 1999 (Mortenson, 2007, pp. 6–10). According to Mortenson in *Postsecondary Education Opportunity*, "if this trend continues, the United States will drop to eighteenth by 2010 behind Spain and twenty-first by 2015 behind France" (p. 12). Of particular concern is the fact that all of the OECD countries have witnessed a 6 percent average improvement in college completion rates since 2000 while the United States has seen no improvement during the same period. Similar numbers are found for adults aged 25–34 in the United States who graduated from two-year institutions. In

2005 the United States tied for 12th in the two-year college completion rate category below even Russia, Ireland, and the Czech Republic (Mortenson, 2007).

Other statistics show that access to college and university education has become a rising dilemma in the United States. In 2005 the United States ranked 22nd in the percentage of young adults aged 15–19 participating in tertiary education, indicating a further drop among OECD countries from a ranking of 16th in 1995 (OECD, p. 292). Additionally, the United States ranked 16th in 2005 in the percentage of young adults aged 20–29 participating in tertiary education, another decade-long decline from 12th in 1995 (ibid.). The consistency of these declines in access and graduation rates among selected age groups clearly indicates that while the remainder of the economically advanced world has developed progressive public policies regarding tertiary and higher education the United States has been resting on its laurels that were established decades ago. The data suggest that the United States has been simply "treading water" while other developed countries have forged ahead in formulating new policies aimed at expanding education opportunities at the tertiary level.

Another substantial development of concern that has dramatically affected higher education in the United States is a troubling decline in social mobility. The growing lack of movement among economic classes in our nation is, of course, the consequence of many political, social, and economic factors. According to Krueger, "the United States has become a more polarized and static society, one in which children have become comparatively more disadvantaged" (Krueger, 2005, p. 11). This development has been fueled by societal choices and a lack of public concern to address the realities of economic and educational problems that have tended to become more difficult to remedy.

Currently, this means that our schools and educational institutions are being asked to overcome a series of obstacles that few other OECD countries are compelled to face. Of the 30 OECD nations only Mexico has a higher percentage of children living in poverty than the United States (OECD, 2007). It should come as no surprise that children from lower-income backgrounds need more public support to navigate the educational process successfully. Today the United States has over 25 percent of the public school student population living in poverty at a time when the public schools have their largest enrollment in American history, 49.1 million children. This places unprecedented burdens on our public schools and on many of the colleges and universities who remain committed to providing educational opportunity to the majority of these students.

Furthermore, according to the *Luxembourg Income Study*, it was found that the United States had the third largest income disparity between those living in the upper 10 percent income category and those living in the lowest 10 percent category. Only Russia and Mexico experienced larger decile disparity between these top and bottom economic classes (Alesina and Glaeser, 2004, pp. 16, 30–34). In fact, according to Bernasek (2006), "the top 10% of income earners in the United States now receive 42% of the total income in the nation. Not since World War II has the top 10% of income earners in the United States received such a large share of total income" (p. 4). The disparity in actual individual wealth was almost as striking as the wide disparities in income according to the same study. The results showed that the upper 1 percent of American households held 32 percent of the nation's wealth.

Why is the increasing lack of social mobility such a critical issue for our schools and other educational institutions? Public education has always been the primary force behind the vitality of social mobility in the United States. However, when the disparities become so drastic that our public schools are asked to overcome economic and societal hardships that are widening each year, then families become trapped in the same economic strata of society and mobility is stifled. This not only prevents individuals from pursuing opportunities beyond their current economic circumstances but also places a greater overburden on educational institutions founded to promote social mobility. Colleges and universities that were thought to be the principal engines of society to provide opportunity and stimulate economic mobility have, in large part failed to perform as earlier expected in the last couple of decades. However, now it appears that institutions of higher education are mirroring these same trends instead of remedying them. In today's higher education environment vast disparities in college and university wealth continue to place more onerous financial burdens on less affluent colleges and universities that tend to enroll the vast majority of financially needy students. Wealthy universities, both private and public, continue to spend unprecedented sums while poorer public institutions that are unable to privatize their operations comparably struggle to provide the necessary educational assistance to the students with the greatest needs.

To appreciate fully the magnitude of this widening gap all one has to do is compare per-student expenditures by institutional sector over the last 25 years. According to data from the Integrated Postsecondary Education Data System (IPEDS) from 1980 to 2005 institutional education and general (E & G) expenditures, when adjusted for inflation, indicate that non-research public universities (comprehensive institutions) have experienced an average per-student E & G expenditure increase from approximately $11 000 to $15 900 during the 25-year period (National Center for Education Statistics, 2008). During the same period private four-year colleges and universities (other than private research universities) saw average per-student E & G expenditure increase from approximately $12 900 to $20 600, while public research universities enhanced their average per-student E & G expenditure from approximately $19 400 to over $34 700. Private research universities, however, have seen the largest average per-student expenditure increase during this period from approximately $32 400 to $66 800. These expanding per-student expenditure differences, when coupled with the increasing endowment disparities favoring more wealthy colleges and universities, demonstrate that higher education, like society, is becoming even more bifurcated into a have and have-not system of colleges and universities. Unfortunately, the vast majority of America's neediest and poorest students, the same students needing more resource support to acquire adequate educational opportunities to enroll and complete college, attend those institutions with the lowest average per-student expenditure and endowment resources. This widening gulf between those institutions that have ample resources and those that are fiscally marginal does not project well for our future. Ultimately, this results in less educational opportunity and a corresponding grave inefficiency in the use of public resources when public policies actually drive higher education in this direction.

To exacerbate this troubling trend further, many recent state and federal higher education policies have been developed to provide disproportionate financial relief to middle-income and more affluent families instead of addressing the needs of lower-income student populations. Currently, over a dozen states have spent vast amounts of resources on merit-based scholarship programs that primarily benefit students from more affluent families. Generally, these programs have been developed in an attempt to increase voter support during election years. Unfortunately, these merit-based funding strategies tend to be among the most fiscally regressive in the history of American higher education finance, especially when the resources are generated from state lottery revenues. The federal government has followed a similar direction over the last decade by creating tuition tax credits and deductions that also disproportionately benefit middle-income and more affluent families. The cost of these federal programs currently exceeds $8 billion and will most likely increase substantially since a number of the presidential candidates have pledged to more than double the federal tax credits and deductions once they are elected to office. This policy strategy was also designed to acquire more votes instead of addressing more difficult challenges such as ensuring educational opportunity and affordability for poorer students.

The overall failure of the system has been caused, at least partially, by federal market-based policies that give financial incentives to those institutions that have higher prices rather than giving fiscal incentives to institutions that keep prices lower in order to continue enrolling the bulk of the neediest populations. In fact, there are no federal incentives for colleges and universities to attract and retain lower-income and lower middle-income students. The failure has also been caused by state legislatures that have consistently reduced their own fiscal commitment to postsecondary access. The consequence of such actions has been to increase student tuition and fees rapidly and place a greater reliance on federal direct student aid programs to provide the revenue streams necessary to finance state higher education access.

Another consequence is the apparent lack of interest on the part of institutions to serve comparatively more expensive students—those with greater educational needs—who are disproportionately from the lower-income classes. Unfortunately, federal funding has encouraged colleges and universities to pursue a free market agenda that enhances institutional prestige and prominence rather than serving the educational needs of disadvantaged students. This kind of institutional Darwinism is manifested by institutions charging ever-increasing student tuition and fees, which in turn, is stimulated by indirect federal funding programs. These federal programs, when coupled with many price-sensitive state grant aid programs, collectively work to maximize the prestige of the institutions that are more selective while indirectly allowing them to pay less attention to large-scale, needy student populations. These affluent institutions have amassed wealth never before witnessed in the history of American higher education. This structure increasingly pits those institutions that remain committed to the public good against those that are fiscally and ideologically less concerned with the public welfare. Over the last 30 years, government policy has done little to modify this tendency for wealthier institutions to serve wealthy students, expend comparatively more resources on them, and perversely, receive greater funding from federal and state aid programs. Thus, the system does little to reward the low-cost institutions that serve the masses and the neediest of students.

For the colleges and universities that remain committed to the multitude of lower-income and lower middle-income students that make up over half of the entire student population, the ability to be a primary force for providing social mobility to the neediest students has been substantially diminished. As noted earlier, since 1980 the United States has witnessed rapid expenditure escalation among the institutions serving students from the wealthiest families. During this same period, many poorer institutions, primarily public universities and community colleges, have seen a comparative and consistent decline in their primary source of support, which is state assistance. These are colleges and universities that cannot readily raise student tuition and fees to offset state fiscal reductions because of the detrimental effect that it would have on their lower-income and lower middle-income students. For these institutions, primarily state comprehensive universities and community colleges, the last 30 years have witnessed a substantial decline in fiscal competitiveness when compared with the more affluent institutions. The irony, of course, is that those institutions that serve the broader public good are increasingly placed at greater financial risk.

To attempt to change this ominous direction and focus on the new generation of students with the greatest educational need, it is imperative that we advance a new public policy agenda. First, we should revisit an idea that was initiated as part of the original Basic Educational Opportunity Grant program (later renamed the Pell Grant Program) in 1972. This program calls for the creation of "cost of education allowances" to be given directly to colleges and universities to assist with the education of lower-income students. Originally designed as a companion program that would grant additional funds to the institutions that served Pell Grant recipients, the program was premised on the well-recognized fact that it costs relatively more to educate lower-income students at all levels. The original legislation recommended that these cost of education allowances be allocated directly to institutions. Such grants should, as originally contemplated, accompany the Pell Grant recipient to his or her respective college or university. This proposal emphasized both the benefit to the individual student in the form of the Pell Grant and a supportive institution allocation for educational support by recommending that the Department of Education create "cost of attendance" allocations in the amount of $2500 per Pell Grant eligible student to be granted to those institutions serving needy students. To ensure that these funds are properly devoted to student enrichment, the proposal requires that federal funds must be used to support campus-based academic and student service programs that assist lower-income students. Such a program would also create important fiscal incentives for institutions to enroll lower-income students.

Currently, as observed above, there are no federal incentives of this kind in place. As a result, more affluent private and public institutions across the nation have not seen any measurable accommodation of lower-income students. The incentives proposed in this plan would also encourage fiscal collaboration between federal and state governments with the intent of promoting improved college access, retention, and completion rates.

Second, as part of this federal–state partnership, it is important that we create and support a "state maintenance of effort" federal legislative provision to ensure that states do not reduce their commitment to public higher education (Alexander, 2006). This would not only provide invaluable support to those institutions serving the neediest students but would better stabilize state funding. To accomplish this, the proposal requires that states maintain current levels of state support in the form of average per-student appropriations or an expected level of fiscal effort. If states do not abide by this provision and utilize these federal funds to "supplant" existing state support then the amount of the federal institutional grant could be reduced or eliminated.

Recently, the proposal to develop a "maintenance of effort" provision that would hold states more accountable has gained much traction in Washington, DC. This has resulted in an amendment to the Higher Education Act, which was passed this past summer, that includes a "maintenance of effort" provision requiring that a state must at least match its average annual funding for the previous five academic years, to public and private educational institutions or risk losing some federal funding support. Despite substantial resistance from the Council of State Governments and the National Governors Association, this amendment is the first federal higher education initiative passed which is designed to hold states more accountable by pressuring them to sustain certain levels of higher education funding.

Collectively, these two proposals have the potential to create an entirely different set of federal fiscal incentives that could actually drive colleges and universities to greater levels of interest in serving lower and lower middle-income students. Developing federal policies that pressure our states into maintaining their common commitment for financing widespread higher education access is a necessity if our nation is to reverse the international decline that we have experienced over the last decade. Creating incentives for institutions to remain committed or to recommit themselves to the public needs of society is something that also should be a high priority among all government officials. To continue on the current path without adequately addressing these issues would prove detrimental to the welfare of the entire nation. After 40 years, the time is right for a new and innovative public policy debate about the role of higher education in the United States. Until we effectively address the issues discussed in this chapter, we will not be able to sufficiently use higher education institutions as vehicles for widespread social mobility. A failure to do so will prohibit future generations of students from reaping the benefits of higher education that have accrued to more recent cohorts.

NOTE

1. This chapter is based on the transcript of a closing speech given at the TIAA-CREF Institute Conference on 2 November 2007 in New York, NY.

REFERENCES

Alesina, A. and Glaeser, E.G. (2004), *Fighting Poverty in the US and Europe: A World of Difference*, Oxford, UK: Oxford University Press.

Alexander, F.K. (2006), "The states' failure to fund higher education," *The Chronicle of Higher Education*, 30 June, B16.

Bernasek, A. (2006), "Income inequality, and its cost," *The New York Times*, 25 June, 4.

Heller, D.E. (2007), Testimony at hearing on America's workers and education for the 21st century, US House of Representatives, Committee on Appropriations, Subcommittee on Labor, Health and Human Services, Education, and Related Agencies, Washington, DC, http://www.personal.psu.edu/deh29/papers/2-07_House_testimony.pdf.

Krueger, A.B. (2005), "Inequality, too much of a good thing," in James J. Heckman and Alan B. Krueger, *Inequality in America*, Cambridge, MA: The MIT Press.

Mortenson, T. (2007), "Duh," *Postsecondary Education Opportunity*, November, No. 185.

National Center for Education Statistics (2008), *Integrated Postsecondary Education Data System*, http://nces.ed.gov/ipeds/.

Organisation for Economic Co-operation and Development (2007), *Education at a Glance 2007*, Paris: OECD.

Index